ANTHROPOLOGY AND RISK

Drawing on theory from anthropology, sociology, organisation studies and philosophy, this book addresses how the perception, communication and management of risk is shaped by culturally informed and socially embedded knowledge and experience. It provides an account of how interpretations of risk in society are conditioned by knowledge claims and cultural assumptions and by the orientation of actors based on roles, norms, expectations, identities, trust and practical rationality within a lived social world. By focusing on agency, social complexity and the production and interpretation of meaning, the book offers a comprehensive and holistic theoretical perspective on risk, based on empirical case studies and ethnographic enquiry.

As a selection of Åsa Boholm's publications throughout her career, along with a newly written introduction overviewing the field, this book provides a unified perspective on risk as a construct shaped by social and cultural contexts. This collection should be of interest to students and scholars of risk communication, risk management, environmental planning, environmental management and environmental and applied anthropology.

Åsa Boholm is a professor of social anthropology at the University of Gothenburg, Sweden, and has published on historical, cultural, organisational and institutional dimensions of risk for over 20 years.

EARTHSCAN RISK IN SOCIETY SERIES

Edited by Ragnar E. Löfstedt
King's College, London, UK

ANTHROPOLOGY AND RISK

ÅSA BOHOLM

Routledge
Taylor & Francis Group

LONDON AND NEW YORK

earthscan
from Routledge

First published 2015
by Routledge
2 Park Square, Milton Park, Abingdon, Oxon OX14 4RN

and by Routledge
711 Third Avenue, New York, NY 10017

Routledge is an imprint of the Taylor & Francis Group, an informa business

British Library Cataloguing-in-Publication Data
A catalogue record for this book is available from the British Library

Library of Congress Cataloging-in-Publication Data
Boholm, Åsa.
    Anthropology and risk / Åsa Boholm.
        pages cm
    Includes bibliographical references and index.
    1. Risk—Sociological aspects. 2. Risk perception—Sociological aspects.
    3. Ethnopsychology. I. Title.
    HM1101.B64 2015
    302'.12—dc23
                            2014041868

ISBN: 978-0-415-74561-1 (hbk)
ISBN: 978-0-415-74563-5 (pbk)
ISBN: 978-1-315-79779-3 (ebk)

Typeset in Bembo
by diacriTech, Chennai

'This book is essential to anyone concerned with the predicaments of contemporary social life – uncertainty, contingency and risk. Åsa Boholm skillfully zooms in on risk as a cultural category and situates risk perceptions and scenarios within larger frameworks of social and political change. Theoretically brilliant and thought provoking!'

Christina Garsten, Professor of Social Anthropology,
University of Stockholm, Sweden

'How individuals, groups and societies cope with contingency as part of their daily experiences is the main topic of this book. It broadens our understanding of the cultural meaning(s) of risk and uncertainty, provides a convincing middle ground between a realist and a constructivist view on risk, presents substantive evidence for the importance of cultural relationships between observer and perceived risk situations and draws valuable conclusions for informing risk policy and communication. This is a book that enlightens our understanding of risk and uncertainty.'

Ortwin Renn, Professor of Environmental Sociology and
Technology Assessment, University of Stuttgart, Germany

'Relating risk perceptions to both their social context and wider cultural values is one of the core philosophical problems of the risk field currently. This book by one of Europe's leading risk scholars examines this issue through the lens of cultural anthropology and fully deserves to be very widely read.'

Professor Nick Pidgeon, Director, Understanding Risk
Research Group, Cardiff University, United Kingdom

TABLE OF CONTENTS

LIST OF ILLUSTRATIONS

Figures

Table

ACKNOWLEDGEMENTS

This book consists of a compilation of previously published articles with an introduction that provides an overview of the research field addressing cultural and social dimensions of risk. The articles have been modified and updated so that, together, they work as parts of a coherent monograph on the topic of the anthropology of risk. These articles build on a number of externally funded research projects on risk. I therefore would like to acknowledge grants from the European Commission Nuclear Fission Safety research programme (contract No. F14PCT954016 (DG12-WSME), the Bank of Sweden Tercentenary Foundation, the Swedish Research Council, the Swedish Rescue Services Agency, the Swedish Emergency Management Agency, the Swedish Governmental Agency for Innovation Systems, the Swedish Transport and Communications Research Board, the Swedish Railway Administration, the Swedish Road Administration and the Swedish Maritime Administration.

I wish to thank a number of people who have provided valuable feedback and constructive criticism of this work: Anna Bendz, Per Binde, Anna Bohlin, Max Boholm, Hervé Corvellec, Celio Ferreira, Marcia Grimes, Sven-Ove Hansson, Annette Henning, Vicki Johansson, Marianne Karlsson, Simon Larsson, Martin Letell, Jan Lindström, Ragnar Löfstedt, Niklas Möller, Karsten Parregaard, Johannes Persson, Martin Peterson, Linda Soneryd, Lennart Sjöberg and Annelie Sjölander-Lindqvist. Finally, I am indebted to Royden Yates for invaluable editorial assistance.

I am grateful for permission to use the following previously published articles of mine in the volume:

'Risk perception and social anthropology: Critique of cultural theory', *Ethnos* 61(1–2): 64–84, 1996.
'Comparative studies of risk perception: A review of twenty years of research', *Journal of Risk Research* 1(2): 135–161, 1998.

'Visual images and risk messages: Commemorating Chernobyl', *Risk Decision and Policy* 3(2): 125–143, 1998.

'The cultural nature of risk: Can there be an anthropology of uncertainty?', *Ethnos* 68(3): 159–178, 2003.

'The public meeting as a theatre of dissent: risk and hazard in land use planning', *Journal of Risk Research* 11(1–2): 119–140, 2008.

'Speaking of risk: matters of context', *Environmental Communication: A Journal of Nature and Culture* 3(2): 335–354, 2009.

'On the organizational practice of expert-based risk management: A case of railway planning', *Risk Management. An International Journal* 12(4): 235–255, 2010.

1

INTRODUCTION

This volume aims to provide a contribution to knowledge of the cultural understanding of contingency and, particularly, of the concept of risk as one of its late modern manifestations. This task implicates several ontological and epistemological problems that are central to anthropological enquiry: how to reconcile emic and etic perspectives; how to understand core idioms of modernity; how to approach competing and alternative knowledge claims and descriptions of the world in a science-based culture; and how to investigate risk in its various manifestations in society. Addressing the culture–risk nexus through an ethnographic lens, the book explores how issues of risk are understood and engaged with by contemporary society. It answers questions about how risk is identified, understood, communicated and managed and, ultimately, how risk is embedded in social life and its variety of contexts.

This introduction begins with a discussion of the concept of contingency and provides a historical background on the meaning of risk in contemporary society. Core philosophical issues regarding the ontology and epistemology of risk are identified and discussed. A descriptive relativist approach to the significance of cultural value in the study of risk comes next. Theoretical perspectives drawing on the anthropological concepts of culture, situated cognition and practical rationality are introduced as building blocks of a comprehensive theoretical framework for the empirical investigation of risk issues as relationally constructed and of observer-dependent social phenomena.

Anthropology and the contingency of life

'Culture' has a long and convoluted trajectory as a key concept in anthropology. The classic definition, launched by Edward B. Tylor in his magnum opus, *Primitive culture* (1871: 1), characterises 'culture' as 'that complex whole which includes knowledge, belief, art, morals, law, customs, and any other capabilities and habits acquired by man as a member of society'. According to this inclusive definition, culture in principle includes everything that humans learned or established by convention. Efforts to formulate more precise and theoretically more specific analytical definitions have been a persistent endeavour throughout the history of the discipline of anthropology (Kuper 1999; Kroeber & Kluckhohn 1952; Watson 1995). Even so, anthropology provides no single answer to what culture 'is' or 'does', and questions about the characterisation of culture and how it could be studied – if at all – are controversial. Nonetheless, there are discernible theoretical alternatives (Keesing 1974). Whereas materialist approaches focus on culture as an assembly of learned behaviours and skills constituting a system for adaptation and sustainability in a natural environment (Rappaport 1996), mentalist orientations delegate culture to the domain of the mind, including ideational structures, linguistic meanings, and knowledge in the form of cognitive representations (Goodenough 1956). Post-modern approaches in turn emphasise the elusive and fragmented nature of what anthropologists have designated 'culture'. Taking a critical stance towards any homogenised view, such approaches understand 'culture' as one of the grand narratives of Western modernity; the leitmotif in the study of culture should therefore be heterodoxy, ambiguity and contestation, with a focus on the many voices through which 'culture' is articulated (Clifford & Marcus 1986).

If 'culture' is often understood in anthropology to order what is conventionally shared in a society, by steering expectations as to what is valid, customary and normal, then 'contingency' refers to the fact that events and indeed human actions are unpredictable. For better or for worse, current states of affairs may change drastically in the future. So although the world is structured, it is also intrinsically chaotic, depending on the material-social-symbolic systemic complexities involved in its constitution. Extraordinary and irregular events, hazards and disasters are always possibilities (Niehaus 2013; Oliver-Smith 1996). An awareness that a good life and well-being cannot be taken for granted is a universal condition of human life, irrespective of situation in time and space. Many hazards potentially can destroy quality of life as well as life itself. Death, illness and decay are ever-present facts (Whyte 1997). Misfortune must be reckoned with whether encountered in terms of disease, storms, earthquakes, drought, invading enemies or famine. The concept of contingency addresses potential and accidental dimensions of being (Meyer 1949–1951). Being may lack purpose; physical events can occur by unpredicted coincidence. Recognition that life is contingent paves the way for epistemic uncertainty regarding the future: what events might be expected, and what their causes and eventual consequences might be.

Many strategies to manage contingency have been identified in the social sciences. For example, anthropologists have argued that religion and ritual have universal social and psychological functions as modes to cope with contingency (Kluckhohn 1942) or 'the fragility of human life' (Keesing 1976: 387) in the face of catastrophes, crises and hazards. Religious ideas offer explanatory systems for contingency and provide practical techniques to cope with epistemic uncertainty. Religion and ritual serve to symbolically order contingency by means of explanations and interpretations founded in the transcendental realms of intentionally acting deities or supernatural beings. Anthropological research on beliefs and practices within mining communities in Africa and South America illustrates how the dangerous work of extracting underground minerals is guided by religious beliefs about malevolent mountain spirits. Believed to make mining labour more profitable and less risky, a host of ritual practices are employed, such as offerings and worship directed at the supernatural forces (Nash 1993; Taussig 1980). As shown in a study of gold miners in Benin (Grätz 2003), ritual practices may exist perfectly well in parallel with other, secular strategies.

In his classic study of Azande religion and magical practices in Sudan, the anthropologist Evans-Pritchard (1937) addressed the cultural framing of the indeterminacy of physical facts. Upon an accident – for example, a sudden collapse of a granary that kills a person sitting underneath – the Azande do not fail to accurately assess the physical cause, such as termite attack or poor construction. As Evans-Pritchard observed, the crucial question posed by the Azande concerns the coincidence of causal circumstances – the collapse and the unfortunate location of the victim – that is assumed culturally to have an underlying rationality (Ferreira & Boholm 2002). Divine or spiritual beings are assumed in many societies to have agency and power to act in ways that are able to drastically affect life, for better or for worse (Evans-Pritchard 1929, 1956; Douglas 1992; Whyte 1997). Regarding the occurrence of negative contingent events, the Azande postulate that there must be some extra-mundane force at work. They believe that 'accidents' are ultimately caused by witchcraft, which can be managed by cultural means including ritual expertise, oracles and social norms. Explanations of extraordinary negative events or misfortune couched in terms of witchcraft or sorcery are still socially powerful in many parts of the world (Niehaus 2013; Whyte 1997).

Divination is another technique to cope with the contingency of life, and the literature shows it has been used throughout history in many parts of the world. Divination is a defined and elaborate technique of interpreting specific signs and is used by divinatory experts to reveal the will of supernatural agents. For example, officially appointed divinatory experts in ancient Rome, known as 'augurs', employed elaborate formal procedures and requirements to read signs of various kinds, such as the behaviour of certain types of birds that were believed to reflect the intentions of gods. Decisions regarding actions for all sorts of private and public affairs were taken based on such augury (Smith, Wayte & Marindin 1890). Another traditional technique identified in anthropology to manage uncertainty is the practice of magic. Malinowski's documentation (1922, 1978) of the Trobrianders' practice of magic in the Kula trade or in canoe building demonstrates this point.

Anthropology has convincingly shown how cultural systems of belief offer guidance regarding the extraordinary and the irregular. Tacit knowledge intuitively tells what is and what is not potentially dangerous and harmful; it provides causal explanations for why things behave as they do; and it entails moral guidelines regarding why certain things or actions are good and right while others are bad and evil (Douglas and Wildavsky 1982; Douglas 1985, 1992; Fardon 2013). Within anthropology, culture has therefore been understood as a resource both for dealing with everyday 'normal' and taken-for-granted situations and for coping with contingencies (Niehaus 2013; Oliver-Smith 1996; Rappaport 1996).

The European concept of risk and its role in modern society

European historical ideas about contingency combine the two notions of 'fortune' and 'providence'. Whereas fortune in life was understood to be associated with random constellations of causal factors set apart from human rationality and will, providence was believed to originate from the will of God, reflecting upon the spiritual and moral qualities of a human being (Savin 2011; Walker 1999: 43–48). Contingency in the guise of 'fortune' was also differentiated according to outcome. Words such as 'luck', 'chance', 'risk' and 'hazard' all referred to potential outcomes in a future that was undetermined and dependent on stochastic variables. While 'luck' or 'good fortune' addresses the positive outcome of contingency (Rescher 1990), the word 'risk' refers to its negative manifestation.

Although human concern with the analysis and management of uncertain and unwanted events dates back to early antiquity (Covello & Mumpower 1985), the concept of risk can be traced to medieval Europe. A notion of risk appears in several socio-cultural contexts: high-stakes gambling for leisure (David 1962; Gigerenzer *et al.* 1989: 19; Kavanagh 1993); economic ventures such as long distance trade, maritime expeditions and insurance (Luhmann 1993: 9 ff); and seventeenth- and eighteenth-century mathematical efforts to explain hazard and chance (Bernstein 1996; Hacking 1990).

The word 'risk' according to the Oxford English Dictionary stems etymologically from late-medieval/post-classical Latin ('risicum'/'resicum', meaning 'cliff' or 'reef'). It was taken up in many other European languages, with the earliest sources dating to the thirteenth century, for example, French (*risqué*), Italian (*risco*), Spanish (*riesgo*), Portuguese (*risco*) and Dutch (*risico*). It has been suggested that the Latin word derives from Arabic (*rizq*), with several meanings referring to wealth, property, fortune and chance. Alternatively, *resicum* derives from a classical Latin verb *resecare* meaning 'that which cuts'. The speculation goes that a cliff or reef encountered at sea might have been seen as something that could cut a vessel into pieces (Aven 2012).

Irrespective of the precise etymology, it is clear that early historical uses of 'risk' refer to practices of maritime navigation, trade and insurance in medieval Europe. The word addressed the possibility of valuable merchandise being harmed or damaged due to the contingencies of travel, especially during long-distance sea voyages (Oxford English Dictionary, online access). In the Middle Ages and the Renaissance, long distance trade was organised by trading companies operating from commercial cities such as Venice (Lane 1973). Such ventures depended on considerable investment, including ships, crew, equipment, food and money to purchase wares as well as gifts for local entrepreneurs or brokers. Resourceful partnerships and considerable strategic planning were essential. A successful overseas trading venture could bring substantial fortune to the merchant entrepreneurs and their investors. Unsurprisingly, historical documents give witness to considerable worry among the merchant classes of Europe about potential losses due to shipwreck, piracy or other uncontrollable circumstances (Maschke 1964). An awareness of risk in a variety of identified possible circumstances was utilised by the merchants in their planning so as to minimise prospective losses. These early uses of the word 'risk' in similar fashion to modern usage therefore captures 'the realization that certain advantages are to be gained only if something is at stake' (Luhmann 1993: 11).

From the mid-seventeenth century onwards, knowledge about probability and its mathematical calculation was applied to gambling as well as to economic ventures and investments and to insurance or annuities (Bernstein 1996: 39 ff; Gigerenzer *et al.* 1989: 19). High-stakes gambling in games of chance with dice or cards (or various forms of betting) was a passionate leisure activity of the nobility during the sixteenth to eighteenth centuries in Europe. Gambling was pursued at royal courts, in noble mansions and at gambling casinos. Among the aristocracy and the gentry, gambling was associated with articulate codes of conduct, norms of appropriateness, moral obligations and cultural meanings of honour, status, prestige and self-sacrifice (Breen 1977; Kavanagh 1993: Ch. 2; Walker 1999). Gambling spread in the form of lotteries to include the broader populous (Hicks 2009), and it continues today to engage through its power to mobilise cultural symbols relating to hopes of luck, prosperity and social respect (Binde 2007, 2013).

This historical background suggests that the concept of risk invokes a human mind-set that serves to weigh evidence and to consider alternative actions and their possible outcomes by assessing probability and uncertainty with respect to costs and benefits (Luhmann 1993). In contemporary society, risk continues to have an established role in economic decision making, drawing on calculations of the probabilities of prospective utility, loss and profit (Gigerenzer *et al.* 1989: 20). More generally, the concept of risk is associated with agency and decision making (Boholm, M. 2012; Fischhoff & Kadvany 2011; Luhmann 1993). A linguistic overview of common usage in modern British and American English (Hamilton, Adolphs & Nerlich 2007: 178) shows that, both as a noun and as a verb, the word risk 'emphasized actions, agents or protagonists, and bad outcomes such as loss of a valuable asset'. The current meanings of 'risk', therefore, suggest considerable historic longevity of a persistent mentality centred upon ideas about human agency, value, gains and losses. Nevertheless, the word 'risk' has a number of everyday meanings and uses today (Hamilton, Adolphs & Nerlich 2007); the concept is multidimensional (Boholm, M. 2012; Fillmore & Atkins 1992; Jardine & Hrudey 2001).

Having its roots within the European Enlightenment, the modern concept of risk was formed as part of a secular ideology that gained currency in the mid- to late eighteenth century and emphasised liberal, rationalistic and pragmatic virtue (Bernstein 1996: 2; Reith 2004). This mentality, associated with social transformations of individualisation and secularisation, has been understood by sociologists as a characteristic of modernity (Beck 1992; Garland 2003; Giddens 1990). An understanding of contingency that acknowledges human agency and a denial of a (traditional) world view based on fatalism and pre-destination therefore is essential to the modern concept of risk. One core meaning of the concept of risk is that states of affairs vary in degree of probability; the world can in principle be different, since humans influence their fate by their own decisions.

Science-based observation and interpretation of uncertainty are central to the modern concept of risk. This perspective focuses on abstract and quantifiable dimensions of reality (Jasanoff 1999; Reddy 2006). In the modern discourse of risk, knowledge of contingency is delegated to the realm of expertise. When deploying the concept of risk, an expert approaches uncertainty as a dimension that can be analytically separated from its immediate context. An expert on risk analysis today is a scientific specialist and not a merchant, gambler or military campaigner, and such specialised expertise provides a privileged knowledge position in modern society (Giddens 1991). In the modern risk paradigm, contingency pertaining to a vast range of activities, conditions or objects can be calculated, evaluated, compared and managed in abstract terms based on statistical information about a potential negative outcome (Reith 2004). Risk is taken to be universally relevant: it is applicable to anything and everything of human concern, such as climate, nature, food, health, housing, infrastructure, consumption, landscape, family, work and leisure. It serves as a conceptual frame that enables a translation of uncertainty from an open-ended field of unpredicted possibilities to a bounded set of identified possible outcomes that can (at least in principle) be calculated and assessed, managed and controlled (Hacking 1990).

The modern and late-modern conception of risk is associated with the posing of innumerable 'what-if' questions that engage science and regulatory policy in a production of often dissonant answers and recommendations regarding how best to achieve a desired outcome in society (Corvellec 2011; Paterson 2003; Ravetz 1997, 1999). Debates flourish concerning the risks of technology, life style and the use and misuse of nature precisely because interpretations, valuations and interests often differ among members of society. Arguably, the concept of risk belongs to 'post-normal science' (Funtowics & Ravetz 1993; Ravetz 1999) that deals with solutions to societal problems that exhibit high systemic uncertainty and need high-stakes decisions. Risk therefore intertwines with policy, implicating broader relevance for government, democracy and notions of trust (Löfstedt 2005).

Quantitative risk assessment relies on statistical methods to answer questions such as: what is the probability of getting cancer if exposed to a certain chemical; what are the chances of a reactor breaking down at a nuclear plant; or what are the chances of being killed in a car accident? Framed as calculated risk, contingency is assessed and possible negative outcomes determined, measured and compared. This dimension of calculated risk is incorporated increasingly in societal risk management strategies and in government regulation and policy regarding health, environment, chemicals or food, for example, and it even becomes part of the 'biopolitics' of individual life (Rose 2001). Policy makers and regulators often take it for granted that risk is an objective product of the magnitude of an adverse outcome and its probability of occurring (Bradbury 1989).

Governmentality theory draws on the work of Michel Foucault, and regards risk as a hegemonic discourse for organizing ideas, concepts and practices referring to uncertainty and hazard (Dean 1999; Jasanoff 1999). Imposing a conceptual framework of 'calculative rationality' on events and phenomena makes the world governable with particular techniques and for particular goals (Dean 1999: 177). Organisational practices and regimes of rule and control, such as auditing, accountability and strategic planning, all belong to a mode of conceptualising social relations and public affairs in terms of risk (Power 2007). Private and public organisations must demonstrate their capacity to deal with risk in order to qualify as legitimate and responsible (Garsten & Hasselström 2003); they must answer as to how they identify, assess, manage and communicate risk issues (Power 2004, 2007). The state acts to provide 'safety' to citizens by governing risk by means of regulatory regimes (Hood, Rothstein & Baldwin 2001; Jasanoff 1999). Consequently, scholars have argued that risk is a socially, culturally and historically specific discourse about the steering and planning of human action in society, where calculation, decision making, accountability and foresight constitute core components (Dean 1999; Power 2004, 2007; Reith 2004). The concept of risk is therefore accompanied by techniques for making decisions, by modes of praxis and by organisational routines that implicate power relations between expert and layperson, decision maker and stakeholder (Boholm, Corvellec & Karlsson 2012).

Risk management today often is the responsibility of many societal actors: agencies, business corporations, interest groups, households and individuals. A plethora of authorities are responsible for risk regulation and supervision of risk management, ideally based on a comprehensive and unitary approach in terms of definitions and procedures (Löfstedt 2011). Comparative studies of 'risk regulation regimes', however, point to an absence of an overarching framework for assessing risk, costs, benefits, values at stake or what role is assigned to scientific advice in relation to political considerations (Hood, Rothstein & Baldwin 2001; Löfstedt 2011). Far from being a straightforward affair of translating scientific evidence into regulatory policy (Paterson 2003), risk discourse as a governmental idiom is manifested in contradictory approaches (Löfstedt 2011). There are a multitude of risk issues in the public domain: path dependent sectorial regulatory traditions; institutional attenuation (Rothstein 2003); fragmented or ambiguous policy frameworks (Rothstein, Huber & Gaskell 2006); precarious uncertainties regarding how to reconcile scientific evidence with legal norms (Paterson 2003); management of uncertainty in decision making (van Asselt 2005); and the ambiguous and institutionally constrained role of public participation in decision processes (Löfstedt 1999; Petts 2008; Rothstein 2013). Together these pose substantial challenges for the governance of risk (Renn 2008).

The pressure on organisations to account for how they manage risk and uncertainty promotes 'secondary' responses by organisations (Hutter & Power 2005; Power 2004, 2007; Rothstein, Huber & Gaskell 2006) that vary depending on how risk is identified, understood and made relevant. What constitutes or does not constitute risk may differ depending on organisational context and institutional setting, for example a business firm, a government regulatory body, a utility company or an academic institution (Boholm, Corvellec & Karlsson 2012; Corvellec 2009, 2010; Hutter & Power 2005). Tension between first-order societal risk and second-order institutional risk, the latter stemming from failures to manage first-order risk, triggers processes of 'spiraling regulatory logic' that yield increasingly reflexive and complex risk management (Rothstein, Huber & Gaskell 2006).

Furthermore, there are risk-versus-risk trade-offs to be accounted for in risk management policy (Graham & Wiener 1995), for example, the balancing of the public health benefits of a vaccination against swine flu versus the risk of younger vaccinated persons developing narcolepsy. Likewise, procedures to clean contaminated land so as to mitigate the risk of toxicity for local citizens might result in the toxic exposure of clean-up workers or the release of toxins into the wider natural environment. Risk-versus-risk trade-offs are ever-present in risk management policy. Due to their systemic and complex nature, they are intrinsically challenging to address and assess.

Many issues of natural, technological and social risk are transboundary, in the sense that they transgress national, regional, regulatory, governmental, scientific and cultural boundaries (Lidskog, Soneryd & Uggla 2010, 2011; Linnerooth-Bayer, Löfstedt & Sjöstedt 2000). Management of such problems requires collaboration among a multitude of private and public actors, including non-government organisations, stakeholders and the public, and these actors may not share the same goals, understandings and practices. Since decision making in the public domain calls for reflection on and deliberation about scientific risk assessment, risk communication is a growing area of interest for government administrations, industry and academia. Communication is recognised as a key component of the government of risk (Hood, Rothstein & Baldwin 2001; Renn 2008) and is relevant to a broad array of policy areas. Research on risk communication has focused on normative and descriptive questions regarding how best to communicate about risk, usually in cases where information originates from science and is then socially mediated in various ways. A key issue for risk communication has been the efficiency of communication expressed in terms of changed behaviour and/or attitude in relation to an identified problematic life style or process (Arvai & Rivers 2014; Leiss 1996; Löfstedt & 6 2008; Wardman 2008).

Information, evaluation and argumentation regarding specific risk issues derive from many sources in a plural complex society, although scientific institutions have a privileged position in this regard. The media plays a crucial role in disseminating risk information, and while some risk issues feature in highly visible alarm stories, others are passed by silently due to less narrative potential (Allan, Adam & Carter 2000; Bakir 2010; Kitzinger 1999). Anthropological studies of representations of risk have shown how media logic draws on culturally informed styles of narration (Ferreira 2004, 2006; Ferreira, Boholm & Löfstedt 2001; Mairal Buil 2003, 2008) that serve to frame news value, identify victims and malefactors and sense moral and communicative relevance (see also Corvellec 2011). Scientific information driven by the efforts of experts to calculate and predict negative events has been shown to abound with social, cultural and political idioms and analogies (Skinner 2000, 2008). Consequently, the identification and calculation of risk is hardly as pure and value free as policy makers and regulators often assume (Bradbury 1989).

Anthropology and the study of risk

Risk has been studied in anthropology in various ways over the years. Mainly, three different traditions can be distinguished: economic anthropology influenced by neoclassical theory; cultural theory; and contextual, ethnographically situated approaches. As in mainstream research, risk in economic anthropology has been understood as uncertainty regarding probability and outcomes of alternative strategies. The concept of uncertainty is linked to the possibility that basic human needs might not be fulfilled should events unfold in particular ways. Risk is understood to derive from subjective perception, that is, the beliefs and knowledge about outcomes and probabilities – not necessarily statistically accurate – that guide decisions and actions (Bartlett 1980; Cancian 1980; Cashdan 1985, 1990). The neoclassical economic theory stereotype of 'self-interested Economic Man' has played a certain, albeit disputed, role within economic anthropology (Wilks 1996), which focuses on the human propensity in non-Western 'traditional' societies for strategic action based on a calculation of the probabilities of positive and negative outcomes of alternative actions (Carrier 2009; Reddy 2006). Anthropological studies show how uncertainty is shaped by social relations, cultural conventions and ecological and biological constraints (Baksh & Johnson 1990: 226–227). Cashdan (1985), for example, demonstrates how socially obligatory reciprocity among hunters and gatherers serves as a cultural management strategy to reduce risk by sharing resources.

Risk aversion and risk sensitivity among peasants, farmers and pastoralists are topics of long-standing interest in the field of economic anthropology. An individual's propensity for economic risk taking has been shown to depend on social status and economic standing (Cancian 1972, 1980; Kuznar 2001; Henrich & McElreath 2002). Lower-status individuals are more risk-averse in making decisions than those who are better off, whereas the latter are more prone to making risky economic decisions. However, work by Henrich and McElreath (2002) indicates that this model is too simplistic. Farmers and agropastoralists rely on culturally informed beliefs and practices to make economic decisions involving risk. A search for prestige, as well as emulation of community members regarded as culturally and socially successful, informs risk taking (and risk avoidance) in economic decision making (Henrich & McElreath 2002).

Risk as a modern phenomenon pertaining to high-modern organisations of finance and business has also attracted interest from anthropologists. Studies of practices in the financial futures markets that in many ways are reminiscent of pre-modern gambling show how markets constitute cultural systems for the actors, where risk and risk taking evoke issues of morality, social stratification, competition, prestige and identity creation (Garsten & Hasselström 2003; Zaloom 2004).

The 'cultural theory of risk', developed by the British social anthropologist Mary Douglas and collaborators, is a major theoretical contribution and the basis of a research agenda for the study of hazards as culturally construed phenomena. The theory has been influential in risk research, especially in the sub-fields of risk perception and risk communication (Tansey & O'Riordan 1999). Cultural theory derives from the grid-group analyses that Douglas developed in the 1970s, aiming to explain universal 'cultural bias' by way of a general typology of group formation associated with a specific cosmology or world view. A later development is the theory of 'cultural cognition' (Kahan 2007, 2012), an amalgamation of the grid-group model and psychological theory addressing the cognitive strategies serving to protect identity and consolidate beliefs consistent with group belonging.

The third tradition in the anthropology of risk is both more ethnographic and more diverse, with a focus on how events and phenomena are voiced by 'particular informants', thus situating them in 'particular times and places' (Caplan 2000: 25). Understandings of risk have been shown to vary according to local assemblages of assumptions, conventions and practices. Risk is then context-dependent in terms of social functions and meanings. By participating in social interaction – visiting people at home and at work, talking to them and listening to their spontaneous conversations – researchers gained insights as to how people understand various kinds of risk issues and what actions they undertake to mitigate them. In this vein, ethnographic work shows how the understanding of risk relates to practical rationality and situated experience. Studies of the perception of HIV/AIDS, for example, reveal that risk is locally produced, framed by interaction, social networks and community context (Rhode *et al.* 2005) and influenced by understandings of uncertainty and choice as well as by the social and cultural dynamics relating to gender differences and sexual practices (Haram 2006), and embedded in ethical and moral considerations (Smith 2010). Shaw (2000) has studied the case of British Pakistanis and clinical screening for genetic risks and revealed the health care system as an arena for conflicting causal models of harm to human health and concomitant risk perceptions because the respective parties employ different medical idioms.

A number of studies within the ethnographic tradition explored how risk issues are embedded in local contexts, taking into account the ways in which culturally framed experience and knowledge shape how risk is understood, managed, negotiated and contested in terms of power, identity and social belonging. Fitchen (1989) and her interdisciplinary collaborators (Fowlkes & Miller 1987; Fitchen, Heath & Fessenden-Raden 1987) undertook seminal work in the community of Love Canal in upstate New York, which was severely affected by groundwater contamination in one of the biggest environmental scandals to emerge in the United States. This work demonstrated how perceptions of risk regarding water pollution and the concomitant reactions of the community were shaped by symbolic cultural notions and values pertaining to 'home', 'family' and 'homeownership', among others. These early studies point to the situated nature of risk and its contextual embedding, a theme which persists in research on facility siting, contested land use, infrastructure planning and local development (see Boholm & Löfstedt 2004). Relevant work in this area includes studies of local understandings of risk associated with huge dam projects in Spain (Mairal Buil & Bergua 1998; Mairal Buil 2004); the situated, indigenous perceptions of radiation risk (Stoffle *et al.* 1991; Stoffle & Arnold 2003) concerning the impact on Native Americans of nuclear waste storage and transportation (Stoffle & Evans 1988); disputes over environmental risks from prospective salt mining in Australia (Hobbs 2011); and narratives of pollution in an industrial urban environment (Phillimore 1998).

A number of anthropologists have studied contested paradigms of thought and understanding regarding local risk issues (Hornborg 2004; Phillimore 1998; Stoffle & Minnis 2008, Stoffle & Evans 1990; Stoffle, Zedeno, Eisenberg, Toupal & Carroll 2004; Sjölander-Lindqvist 2004). Controversies about risk in land use and in urban and environmental planning often exemplify a dissonance between space and place, where 'different worlds are occupying, or at least overlapping, the same physical space', so paving the way for conflicting interpretations of landscapes and their uses (Henning 2013: 363; see also Thomas 2001). Various risk issues therefore can be understood as constructed from specific coexisting, situated 'dwelling' perspectives (cf. Ingold 2000). Each perspective on the lived-in world depends on and actualises a practical rationality of its own, including goals, aims, concerns, strategies and planning.

In her study of La Hague, a vast nuclear industrial complex on the northwest French coast, Zonabend (1993) addressed the relationships between risk perception, collective memory and local belonging. Drawing theoretical inspiration from studies on social memory (Fentress & Wickham 1992; Halbwachs 1992; Middleton & Edwards 1990), her work focused on spontaneous narratives and emotional and intellectual ways of dealing with nuclear risk and its cultural symbolisation by inhabitants and employees at La Hague. Zonabend showed how risk perception is an active social and discursive process that constructs relevancy and meaning within the context of a social fabric. In a study of pollution risk in a German industrial city, Phillimore and Bell (2013) focused on how older citizens remembered and narrated such themes about the 1950s and 1960s. Those decades were the heyday of the local chemical industry, and the nostalgic recollections portrayed an era in which economic prosperity was juxtaposed against high attendant risks.

In different ways, these ethnographic studies illuminate how knowledge of risk is locally situated and temporally framed by cultural and social interpretations. Risk is understood and identified in local settings in terms of the knowledge, the values and the concerns that emerge from livelihood, history and collective identity. As Perin (2005) showed in her ethnographic study of risk management in the nuclear industry, decisions on risk are shaped by culturally based notions about the state of the world, what it consists of and how it works (Purcell, Clarke & Renzulli 2000).

Situated risk: towards an anthropological theory

This section outlines the fundamentals of an anthropological framework for the study of risk. First is a discussion of the distinction between objective and subjective risk. This distinction has had significant impact on risk research over the years, but it will be shown to be highly problematic. Next is a discussion of the central position of 'value' in the concept of risk, followed in turn by the characterisation of objects and relationships in terms of risk by means of conventionally established concepts and categories; the situatedness and practical rationality of human cognition; and, finally, the relative nature of risk, as being both observer-dependent and relational, in the sense that it orders – explicitly or implicitly – relationships between value and objects perceived as potentially harmful.

Subjective, objective or socially constructed risk?

Risk research abounds with meta-theoretical perspectives and positions that reflect both the disciplinary diversity of the field (Rosa, Renn & McCright 2014; Renn 1998; Strydom 2002) and some thorny, long-lasting issues in philosophy (Hansson 1999, 2007; Rescher 1983; Shrader-Frechette 1991). Philosophy explores, among other things, the relations and conditions of being (ontology) and the conditions for knowledge (epistemology). Since classical antiquity, realists and idealists have debated the relationship between the subjective and the objective and their meta-physical priority. A fundamental and much-debated issue regarding risk as a field of investigation concerns the relationship between subjective perceptions and beliefs on the one hand and, on the other, the objective, or mind-independent, external world (see Aven and Renn 2009; Pidgeon *et al.* 1992; Hansson 1999, 2007, 2010; Lupton 1999). The 'objective' and 'subjective' divide on risk reflects two assumptions about its manifestation: risk is factual and objective, residing in the mind-independent external world, and in contrast, it is subjective and experiential, a result of human thought and information processing. The notion of 'objective' or 'real' risk is used to express the risk-yielding phenomena and causality, as known by science (Hansson 1999, Hansson 2007). From this stance, risk is defined in mathematical terms as the statistical expectation of an event or outcome bringing about instances of death, injury or ill health, measured in terms of economic loss.

Psychological studies of the perception of risk have shown that the understanding of risk by laypeople deviates considerably from risk according to its scientific and 'objective' description (Lichtenstein *et al.* 1978). Numerous psychometric studies have demonstrated that risk perception is conditioned by cognitive heuristics that influence the processing of information. Such findings might suggest that risk perception inevitably presents distorted images of real-world contingencies because of the way the human mind functions and its cognitive biases. Distorted perceptions either exaggerate or underrate the 'objective' characterisation of risk (see Breakwell 2007; Slovic 2000), and psychological research helps to explain how this derives from attitudes, beliefs and cognitive models (Morgan *et al.* 2002; Slovic 2000).

That risk is socially constructed is a common-place assumption in most of the social sciences (Arnoldi 2009; Lupton 1999). Since understandings of risk are related intrinsically to value, norms, morality (Ericsson & Doyle 2003), conventions, institutions, interests, power relations, knowledge claims and the production and negotiation of meaning, it makes sense to claim that factual scientific descriptions in terms of probability, causal relationships and material properties of objects hardly exhaust the meanings of and practices related to risk in society (Clarke & Short 1993). What is considered as 'risk' (or not) in any particular societal context can therefore not just be determined from objective criteria such as statistics of fatalities or mortality, probability of cause of death or injury or scientific probabilistic models, or causal relationships. As we have seen, ideas about risk and identification of hazardous objects or activities are embedded in social institutions, local practices and experiences, and they are understood, judged and acted upon in terms of conventionally informed values and concerns (Rappaport 1996). The attribution of risk to objects and processes depends on how groups and organisations in society frame an issue, how meaning is created, how arguments are made, how action is mobilised and how social and political processes emerge and develop, driven by, among other things, scientific facts and their interpretation (Law & Mol 2008). That all humans are equipped with basically the same sensory-neural faculties does not imply that they all understand what they observe and experience in the same way (Hanson 2000). As noted earlier, the concept of 'culture' in anthropology has been used to address variation in how societies and groups perceive, characterise, categorise, represent and understand the world. As Ingold (2000: 15) points out, while not denying the possibility of knowledge of the external world, the world is variously differentiated and categorised by observers who 'process the same data of experience in terms of alternative frameworks of belief or representational schemata'.

Value is essential to the concept of risk, and this presents a fundamental philosophical argument against the notion of 'objective' risk and, consequently, any ontological divide (Hansson 2010; Rescher 1983; Rosa 1998; Shrader-Frechette 1991). If no value is at stake, there is no risk and hence, by definition, risk cannot be a mere feature of the mind-independent external world. In this vein, Rosa (1998) has argued for a realist position defining risk as being 'a situation or event where something of human value (including humans themselves) has been put at stake and where the outcome is uncertain' (Rosa 1998: 28). According to this argument, risk does not include situations in which something of value is certain to be harmed; this is a situation of fate or inevitability, rather than of risk. If no stake is involved, if there is no threat to entities valued by humans, then there can be no risk. Risk means that something of value is at stake, and uncertainty surrounding that risk can relate both to the possibility of a negative outcome and to the nature of the outcome itself. Hence, the concept of risk refers to an epistemological domain (Rosa 1998) presupposing attitudes to and representations of potential threats to valued objects (Corvellec 2009, 2010; Fischhoff & Kadvany 2011; Hansson 2010; Rescher 1983).

A lesson from the substantivist–formalist debate in economic anthropology (Carrier 2009) is that what is of value to humans is far from universal. Value has numerous, incongruous and even contradictory socio-cultural manifestations (Blim 2012), such as the ambiguity surrounding value revealed by Henning (2008) in her study of idioms of risk among Swedish home owners with regard to solar heating systems.

A viable philosophical position on the concept of risk must therefore take into account that risk is both factual and normative. It is about factual (objective) features of the world, such as natural characteristics, probability and cause and effect chains, but it is also about norms, values and subjective perceptions. Similar to concepts like temperature, weight, or colour, risk refers to natural characteristics, and similar to concepts like bad, unfair or ugly, it is about norms and ethical standards. The concept of risk is constituted dually: it refers both to properties of the natural world (as understood by science) *and* to normative properties. To characterise something as a 'risk', as Möller (2012: 74) notes, is

> typically a reason against (allowing, performing, using) it, and the larger the risk, the stronger is that reason. Risk has a negative evaluative direction. . . . But risk is also importantly different from the paradigmatic normative notions of right and good, that it is a notion with substantial descriptive content.

The concept of risk can therefore be regarded as an instance of a broader class of concepts, in philosophy denoted as 'thick concepts', which essentially combine natural and normative characteristics: 'a thick concept fills a double function: it describes a feature (world-guid*ed* function), and it evaluates it (world-guid*ing* function)' (Möller 2012: 74, italics orig.). To recognise risk as a 'thick concept' has the advantage that epistemic claims and orientations can be integrated theoretically; risk can be approached both as a factual-scientific description and as a normative, political and socially constructed entity. Theoretical acknowledgement of the dual nature of risk allows more precise analysis of how these dimensions are co-constituted and negotiated vis-à-vis each other.

A relational approach to risk

A theoretical starting point for the anthropology of risk is the observation by Rappaport (1996) that human social systems are conventionally established and are symbolic in nature. Human societies constitute 'ultra-complex' systems, since humans do not merely respond to the physical impact of the environment. Information about events and states of affairs, what is recorded and reported, in what way and by whom, is culturally mediated, socially processed and morally valued (Rappaport 1996). Adaptation, subsistence and technology therefore depend on cognition: mental operations such as ideas, thoughts, evaluations and knowledge that are embedded in practices of engaging with the environment and the social world (Hutchins 1995; Lave 1988; Lave & Wenger 1991).

Observations of the world, as we have noted, differ depending on the focus and perspective of the observer (Hanson 2000). Without the categories and distinctions provided by language and cultural representations, the world would appear as a mere undifferentiated flow of sensory impressions without meaning (Saussure 1983). Meaning requires distinctions. We know what a cat is, we know when we see a cat and not a dog and we can differentiate a cat from a kangaroo. Concepts are related and separated through associations and distinctions so that they form a representational system of the external world; we know that kangaroos and cats are both warm blooded mammals but that a cat is a eutherian, or placental, mammal while a kangaroo is a metatherial, or marsupial, species. Conceptual representations of entities – such as kangaroos or cats – are underpinned by assumptions that extend knowledge about the (analytical) definitions of concepts. Knowledge about cats in the empirical world draws on assumptions deriving from many sources: personal experience, second-hand information (what we hear or read), rumour, tradition, common sense and/or scientific exploration, to name a few possibilities. Thus, in philosophical terms there can be no absolute difference between analytic and synthetic knowledge (Quine 1951).

There is a growing literature in philosophy, anthropology, sociology, psychology and organisation studies that questions in various ways the division between subject and object, perception and reality, representation and world. This literature is vast and somewhat straggly, but nevertheless contains certain core ideas together with an overall aim to establish a relational theoretical framework focusing on thought, perception, understanding, interpretation, recognition, learning, skill and memory connected with practical rationality. From a systemic perspective on human livelihood suggested by anthropologists such as Ingold (2000), Hutchins (1995) and Rappaport (1996), 'culture' refers to intuitive, structured systems of information processing that groups of people use to organise and manage life. Such a perspective focuses on culture as a mode of practical rationality according to which information is structured and processed by means of categories and concepts and ordered in semantic networks of associations and distinctions, similarities and differences. Culture provides contexts of interpretation and action that enable mutual understanding, interaction and engagement with the surrounding world. It therefore constitutes a basic requirement for coordinated social action and collective projects, serving as a dynamic system for organising and structuring information and knowledge and for collectively producing, re-producing and contesting meanings and associations (Geertz 1973, 1983).

A focus on how risk is contextually situated and relationally established is at the heart of an anthropological approach. A substantial challenge is that the concept of risk serves both as an abstract, generic epistemic category to address contingency and as an experiential and attitudinal category focusing on concrete, contextually embedded phenomena. Risk as a cognitive schema is materialised and made present in the form of specific objectified and culturally manifested instances, such as smoking, global warming, genetically modified organisms, electromagnetic fields, vaccines, aspartame, railway tunnels, dangerous dogs or whatever. What objects in the external world become categorised as 'risks' in any specific context remains an open question to some extent (Ewald 1991). Risk issues are embedded in concrete contexts. Specific risk issues are identified and objectified by human observers who attribute value to some things as opposed to others. We relate to and manage specific potential outcomes such as falling off a bicycle, getting cancer from red meat, losing money on the stock market or whatever else we are concerned about. Hence, risk issues can be understood as contextual actualisations of 'virtual' objects, which cannot exist apart from their mode of symbolic, culturally informed representation or 'valorisation' (van Loon 2002).

Relational, contextual perspectives on risk have been suggested from such diverse disciplinary perspectives as sociology (Luhmann 1989, 1993; Garland 2003), science and technology studies (Hilgartner 1992), discourse and governmentality theory (Dean 1999; Ewald 1991; Power 2004, 2007), philosophy (Rescher 1983), theology (Gregersen 2003), social anthropology (Mairal Buil 2008, 2013) and linguistics (Fillmore & Atkins 1992). A relational position states that a risk implies a danger of something for somebody in a given social and cultural nexus of understanding and interpretation (Gregersen 2003). From a relational perspective, risk is regarded as an epistemic evaluative construct, a cognitive framework or schema that describes and categorises objects in relation to other objects depending on what is known and believed about potentially harmful interactions between them (Fillmore & Atkins 1992). To identify something as a 'risk' therefore involves a configuration of representations, by use of categories, associations, distinctions, contrasts, evaluations and arguments in order to establish the 'risky' profile of an object.

In 1992, Hilgartner proposed a theoretical approach to risk with a focus on conceptual networks of description that referred to relationally ordered objects. This approach addressed the dynamic character of risk objects, noting that such objects are socially constructed. The meanings and associations of objects, through assumed causal relationships, may change over time depending on social context and assumptions about their potentially harmful properties. Hilgartner (1992) uses the term 'risk object' to refer to the embodied, objectified source of potential harm. Å. Boholm and Corvellec (2011) developed the relational theory of risk further as an analytical model. In sum, this theory proposes that the relation (or association) between two objects – a risk object and an object at risk, the latter embodying a value at stake – derives from a hypothetical, assumed or known causal mechanism that would cause harm to the object at risk if it and the risk object should come into contact. A key element of the relational theory of risk is that the relation between the two objects, and their understood mode of association, is observer-dependent. It is an observer's knowledge and understanding of objects and their properties that frame them as either risk objects or objects at risk, or even as risk-irrelevant.

Studies of the analysis and management of risk reveal that only occasionally do people – whether specialists or the public – agree on what is (or is not) a 'risk', what the reasons for the posed risk or lack thereof are and what to do about it. Many risk issues in society are contested and actualise divergent perspectives and interpretations by various actors; the characterisations of risk objects and objects at risk may change drastically over time as new meanings are attributed to objects and as they enter into new configurations. As a conceptual schema, however, risk contains a set of stable elements that make up a semantic framing of relationships, objects and categories (Fillmore & Atkins 1992), such as harm, actor, action, valued object, victim and purpose, which are ordered into a network of associations that makes an assessment of future outcomes possible. The content of these configurations might vary considerably depending on the issue at hand, but there are certain stable (structural) elements that are characteristic of all risk issues. There always is a risk object, a source of harm, associated with a (potential) harmful influence on some value at stake and at least one observer. A relational theory of risk makes it possible to account for the complex and dynamic character of culturally framed risk association networks.

Risk association networks are dynamic, discursive and realised in communication (Boholm 2005; Corvellec & Boholm 2008; Binde & Boholm, Å. 2004; Boholm, Å. & Corvellec 2014; Boholm, M. *et al*. 2014; Maguire & Hardy 2013). A crucial implication is that a phenomenon, like a railway tunnel (Boholm, Å. 2005), an off-shore wind farm (Corvellec & Boholm 2008), boat traffic on a river (Boholm, M. 2009) or antibacterial silver in consumer products (Boholm, M. *et al*. 2014), can simultaneously be regarded as a risk object, as an object at risk or as risk-free by different observers operating under different assumptions. The strength of an anthropological approach is its capacity to address the social and cultural construction of risk from different perspectives and assumptions in a plural, complex society characterised by internal, system-bound organisational coding of the environment (Luhmann 1989). Anthropology enables a combination of inside and outside perspectives for a 'viewing of views' (Ingold 2000: 15) on risk. It enables the researching of interactions of perspectives and representations, as, for example, in planning, regulation, policy implementation and media coverage, and it facilitates in-depth, ethnographically derived contextual accounts of how risk is assessed, investigated, managed and communicated in society (Boholm, Å. & Corvellec 2014).

Outline of the book

Comparative studies show repeatedly that risk perception varies considerably due to cultural, socioeconomic and even religious dimensions (Renn & Rohrmann 2000). Chapter 2 of this book identifies and reviews comparative studies of risk perception and discusses the theoretical and methodological issues regarding the relationships between analytical concepts and socio-cultural realities. It is argued that risk perception is influenced by communication via the media, power relations, institutions and by societal dimensions of marginality, gender and ethnicity. A major conclusion is that comparative studies of risk perception need further methodological and theoretical refinement in order to account for socio-cultural dimensions of risk perception. Mainstream psychometric research on risk perception, reviewed in Chapter 2, has used culture mainly as a 'black box' of unknowns into which otherwise unaccountable 'irregularities' of risk perceptions can be referred.

Cultural theory is the topic of Chapter 3. Unfortunately, cultural theory also manifests a black box approach to culture. This theory proposes that risk is culturally defined and selected, but it lacks an account of the concept of risk and how it is understood and put into practice in context. The analytical contributions of cultural theory to risk studies and its recent modified version, 'cultural cognition' theory (Kahan 2012), are critically assessed in Chapter 3.

Chapter 4 discusses how risk can be addressed as a cultural category. It offers a framework for how risk issues in modern society can be understood and how different modes of socially situated knowledge inform the understanding of risk issues. The chapter adopts a critical stance towards simplistic ideas about risk and culture and their relationship. It is argued that the development of a robust account of the culture–risk nexus requires that risk be approached from within cognitive theory (Bloch 2012; Strauss & Quinn 1997). This chapter examines how a cognitive approach, which emphasises the shared schemata that define categories, relationships and contexts, makes it possible to process meanings and order information, and so it can contribute to an anthropological understanding of risk.

Drawing on theoretical perspectives of situated cognition and practice-based perspectives on knowledge, Chapter 5 offers an ethnographic case study of organisational risk management in railway planning. There is a growing trend evident in government and business towards the use of standardised tools and guidelines under the assumption that formal approaches will make risk management effective and successful. However, studies of organisational practice show that in fact risk and safety management is socially and experience-based. In the railway planning case study, risk identification and assessment were indeed orchestrated according to a formal risk management protocol, but the process was guided by practical reasoning based on the intuitive and situated knowledge and experience of experts. Understanding of risk and risk management work is embedded in organisational routines that are shaped by social trust among actors, by their collaborative intentions and by their experience-based knowledge. It is argued that risk management is a practice drawing on shared understandings and a sense of mutual responsibility. The conclusion is that risk management needs to be contextualised from a practical organisational perspective in which responsibility, expertise, accountability, trust, coordination and communication are essential.

Land-use and environmental planning paradigmatically involves diverse actors, such as representatives of government authorities and special-interest organisations as well as scientific experts, lawyers and concerned citizens. Chapter 6 presents a case study of local consultation meetings held about the controversial Hallandsås railway tunnel in southern Sweden. Theoretical perspectives drawing on pragmatic communication theory, Luhmann's (1993) distinction between risk and hazard, and social anthropological theory on agency and conflict generation in communication are used to analyse how an understanding of risk derives from opposing perspectives. A basic clash is that between actors in the role of decision makers and those affected by decisions, namely the local residents and, most prominent among them, farmers. This case study shows how conceptualisations of risk and hazard are imbued with meanings through dialectic interplay of victim–patient positions and their derived agency perspectives.

Photography in news media adds veracity to information and permits a projection of identification. The potential of visual images to communicate emotions and intuitive knowledge makes documentary photography an effective medium for the construction of risk messages. Chapter 7 reviews some of the literature on risk and visualisation in the media, and presents a case study of visual images in risk communication, mainly photos in European newspapers during 1996 that focused on the tenth anniversary of the Chernobyl nuclear reactor disaster. This material is analysed from a perspective of symbolic anthropology and semiotics, and it is argued that qualitative interpretative approaches can add to our understanding about the social and cultural construction of risk messages. The visual material articulates claims of veracity of knowledge because photos act as 'certified presence' and a basis for (emphatic) identification between viewers and victims. This exercise in visual anthropology (Pink 2001) highlights a growing field in the study of the perception and communication of risk, since visual images in the media and photos in particular convey forceful symbolic messages (see also Ferreira, Boholm & Löfstedt 2001).

The concluding Chapter 8 takes a theoretical and critical grip on the subject of risk communication, both as a research agenda for knowledge production and as a practical agenda relevant to decision making and policy work. The risk communication field is dominated by the practical and normative, socio-technical aim of improving communication on risk, especially from the viewpoint of regulatory agencies and government administrations. Despite some change of scope and orientation over the years, two theoretical ideas have persisted: the subjective–objective risk dichotomy and the transmission (also known as code) model of communication. This theoretical legacy in risk communication puts context in a blind spot. It is argued that the study of the communication of risk themes must consider (a) the socially constructed nature of risk and (b) the fact that communication is a situated social practice of information sharing. Results of research on public participation in the highly publicised and troubled Hallandsås railway tunnel project point to the crucial contextual dimensions of communication on risk. It is argued that the variable ontology of risk, the constitutive nature of power relationships and the practical rationality of actors must all be taken into account in research on the social communication of risk.

References

Allan, S., Adam, B. & Carter, C. (eds.). 2000. *Environmental risks and the media.* London: UK, Routledge.

Arnoldi, J. 2009. *Risk: An introduction.* Cambridge, UK: Polity Press.

Arvai, J. & Rivers, L. (eds.). 2014. *Effective risk communication.* London, UK: Earthscan.

Aven, T. 2012. The risk concept – historical and recent development trends. *Reliability Engineering and System Safety* 22: 33–44.

Aven, T. & Renn, O. 2009. On risk defined as an event where the outcome is uncertain. *Journal of Risk Research* 12(1): 1–12.

Bakir, V. 2010. Media and risk: Old and new directions. *Journal of Risk Research* 13(1): 5–18.

Baksh, M. & Johnson, A. 1990. Insurance policies among the Machiguenga. In *Risk and uncertainty in tribal and peasant economies*. Cashdan, E. (ed.), pp. 193–227. Boulder, CO: Westview Press.

Bartlett, P. 1980. *Agricultural decision making*. San Diego, CA: Academic Press.

Beck, U. 1992 [1986]. *Risk society: Towards a new modernity*. London, UK: SAGE.

Bernstein, P.L. 1996. *Against the gods: The remarkable story of risk*. New York, NY: John Wiley & Sons, Inc.

Binde, P. 2007. The good, the bad and the unhappy: The cultural meanings of newspaper reporting on jackpot winners. *International Gambling Studies* 7(2): 213–232.

Binde, P. 2013. Why people gamble: A model with five motivational dimensions. *International Gambling Studies* 13(1): 81–97.

Binde, P. & Boholm, Å. 2004. Schismogenesis in a Swedish case of railway planning. In *Facility siting: Risk, power and identity in land-use planning*. Boholm, Å. & Löfstedt, R. (eds.), pp. 160–176. London, UK: Earthscan.

Blim, M. 2012. Culture and economy. In *A handbook of economic anthropology*, 2nd edition. Carrier, J. (ed.), pp. 344–369. Cheltenham, UK: Edward Elgar.

Bloch, M. 2012. *Anthropology and the cognitive challenge*. Cambridge, UK: Cambridge University Press.

Boholm, Å. 2003. The cultural nature of risk: Can there be an anthropology of uncertainty? *Ethnos* 68(3): 159–178.

Boholm, Å. & Löfstedt, R. (eds.). 2004. *Facility siting: Risk, power and identity in land use planning*. London, UK: Earthscan.

Boholm, Å. & Corvellec H. 2011. A relational theory of risk. *Journal of Risk Research* 14(2): 175–190.

Boholm, Å. & Corvellec, H. 2014. A relational theory of risk: Lessons for risk communication. In *Effective risk communication*. Arvai, J. & Rivers, L. (eds.), pp. 6–22. London, UK: Earthscan.

Boholm, Å., Corvellec, H. & Karlsson, M. 2012. The practice of risk governance: Lessons from the field. *Journal of Risk Research* 15(1): 1–20.

Boholm, M. 2009. Risk and causality in newspaper reporting. *Risk Analysis* 29(11): 1566–1577.

Boholm, M. 2012. The semantic distinction between 'risk' and 'danger': A linguistic analysis. *Risk Analysis* 32(2): 281–293.

Boholm, M., Arvidsson, R., Boholm, Å., Corvellec, H. & Molander, S. 2014. Dis-Ag-reement: The construction and negotiation of risk in the Swedish controversy over antibacterial silver. *Journal of Risk Research*, dx.doi.org /10.1080/13669877.2013.879492.

Bradbury, J. 1989. The policy implications of differing concepts of risk. *Science, Technology and Human Values* 14(4): 380–399.

Breakwell, G.M. 2007. *The psychology of risk*. Cambridge, UK: Cambridge University Press.

Breen, T.H. 1977. Horses and gentlemen: The cultural significance of gambling among the gentry of Virginia. *The William and Mary Quarterly* 34(2): 239–257.

Cancian, F. 1972. *Change and uncertainty in a peasant economy: The Maya corn farmers of Zinacantan*. Stanford, CA: Stanford University Press.

Cancian, F. 1980. Risk and uncertainty in agricultural decision making. In *Agricultural decision making: Anthropological contributions to rural development*. Bartlett, P.F. (ed.), pp. 171–176. Orlando, FL: Academic Press.

Caplan, P. 2000. Introduction. In *Risk revisited*. Caplan, P. (ed.), pp. 1–28. London, UK: Pluto Press.

Carrier, J. 2009. Simplicity in economic anthropology: Persuasion, form, and substance. In *Studies in rhetoric and culture: Economic persuasions*. Gudeman, S. (ed.), pp. 15–30. New York, NY: Berghahn Books.

Cashdan, E. (ed.). 1990. *Risk and uncertainty in tribal and peasant economies*. Boulder, CO: Westview Press.

Cashdan, E.A. 1985. Coping with risk: reciprocity among the Basarwa of northern Botswana. *Man*, n.s. 20(3): 454–474.

Clarke, L. & Short, J.F. 1993. Social organizations and risk: some current controversies. *Annual Review of Sociology* 19: 375–399.

Clifford, J. & Marcus, G. (eds.). 1986. *Writing culture: The poetics and politics of ethnography*. Berkeley & Los Angeles, CA: University of California Press.

Covello, V. & Mumpower, J. 1985. Risk analysis and risk management: An historical perspective. *Risk Analysis* 5(2): 103–120.

Corvellec, H. 2009. The practice of risk management: Silence is not absence. *Risk Management* 11(3–4): 285–304.

Corvellec, H. 2010. Organizational risk as it derives from what managers value: A practice-based approach to risk assessment. *Journal of Contingencies and Crisis Management* 18: 145–154.

Corvellec, H. 2011. The narrative structure of risk accounts. *Risk Management* 13: 101–121.

Corvellec, H. & Boholm, Å. 2008. The risk/no-risk rhetoric of environmental impact assessments (EIA): The case of off-shore wind farms in Sweden. *Local Environment* 13(7): 627–640.

David, F.N. 1962. *Games, gods and gambling: The origins and history of probability and statistical ideas from the earliest times to the Newtonian era*. London, UK: Griffin.

Dean, M. 1999. *Governmentality: Power and rule in modern society*. London, UK: SAGE.

Douglas, M. 1985. *Risk acceptability according to the social sciences*. New York, NY: Russell Sage Foundation.

Douglas, M. 1992. *Risk and blame: Essays in cultural theory*. London, UK: Routledge.

Douglas, M. & Wildavsky A. 1982. *Risk and culture: An essay on the selection of technological and environmental dangers*. Berkeley, CA: University of California Press.

Ericson, R. & Doyle, A. (eds.). 2003. *Risk and morality*. Toronto, Canada: University of Toronto Press.

Evans-Pritchard, E.E. 1929. Witchcraft (mangu) amongst the Azande. *Sudan Notes and Records* 12: 29–37.

Evans-Pritchard, E.E. 1937. *Witchcraft, oracles and magic among the Azande*. Oxford, UK: Clarendon Press.

Evans-Pritchard, E.E. 1956. *Nuer religion*. Oxford, UK: Oxford University Press.

Ewald, F. 1991. Insurance and risk. In *The Foucault effect: Studies in governmentality*. Burchell, B., Gordon, C. & Miller, P. (eds.), pp. 197–210. Chicago, IL: University of Chicago Press.

Fardon, R. (ed.). 2013. *Mary Douglas – culture and crises: Understanding risk and resolution*. London, UK: SAGE.

Fentress, J. & Wickham, C. (eds.). 1992. *Social memory*. Oxford, UK: Blackwell.

Ferreira, C. 2004. Risk, transparency and cover up: Media narratives and cultural resonance. *Journal of Risk Research* 7(2): 199–211.

Ferreira, C. 2006. Food information environments: Risk communication and advertising imagery. *Journal of Risk Research* 9(8): 851–868.

Ferreira, C. & Boholm, Å. 2002. Kulturell riskhantering. In *Osäkerhetens Horisonter*. Boholm, Å., Hansson S.-O., Persson, J. & Peterson, M. (eds.), pp. 85–109. Nora, Sweden: Nya Doxa.

Ferreira, C., Boholm, Å. & Löfstedt, R. 2001. From vision to catastrophe: A risk event in search of images. In *Risk, media and stigma*. Flynn, J., Slovic, P. & Kunreuther, H. (eds.), pp. 283–299. London: Earthscan.

Fillmore, C. & Atkins, B.T. 1992. Toward a frame-based lexicon: The semantics of RISK and its neighbors. In *Frames, fields, and cognition: New essays in semantics and lexical organization*. Lehrer, A. & Feder Kittay, E. (eds.), pp. 75–102. Hillsdale, NJ, Hove & London, UK: Lawrence Erlbaum Associates.

Fischhoff, B. & Kadvany, J. 2011. *Risk: A very short introduction*. Oxford, UK: Oxford University Press.

Fitchen, J.M. 1989. When toxic chemicals pollute residential environments: The cultural meanings of home and homeownership. *Human Organization* 48: 313–324.

Fitchen, J.M., Heath, S.S. & Fessenden-Raden, J. 1987. Risk perception in community context: A case study. In *The social and cultural construction of risk*. Johnson, B.B. & Covello, V.T. (eds.), pp. 31–54. Dordrecht, the Netherlands & Boston, MA: D. Reidel Publishing Company.

Fowlkes, M.R. & Miller, P.Y. 1987. Chemicals and community at Love Canal. In *The social and cultural construction of risk*. Johnson, B.B. & Covello, V.T. (eds.), pp. 55–78. Dordrecht, the Netherlands & Boston, MA: D. Reidel Publishing Company.

Funtowicz, S. & Ravetz, J. 1993. Science for the post-normal age. *Futures* 25(7): 735–755.

Introduction **23**

Garland, D. 2003. The rise of risk. In *Risk and morality*. Ericson, R. V. & Doyle, A. (eds.), pp. 48–86. Toronto, Canada: University of Toronto Press.

Garsten, C. & Hasselström, A. 2003. Risky business: Discourses on risk and (ir)responsibility in globalizing markets. *Ethnos* 68(2): 249–270.

Geertz, C. 1973. *The interpretation of cultures*. New York, NY: Basic Books.

Geertz, C. 1983. *Local knowledge*. New York, NY: Basic Books.

Giddens, A. 1990. *The consequences of modernity*. Cambridge, UK: Polity Press.

Giddens, A, 1991. *Modernity and self-identity*. Stanford, CA: Stanford University Press.

Gigerenzer, G., Swijtink, Z., Porter, T., Daston, L.J., Beatty, J. & Krueger, L. 1989. *The empire of chance: How probability changed science and everyday life*. Cambridge, UK: Cambridge University Press.

Goodenough, W.H. 1956. Componential analysis and the study of meaning. *Language* 32(1): 195–216.

Graham, J.D. & Wiener, J.B. (eds.). 1995. *Risk vs. risk: Trade-offs in protecting health and the environment*. Cambridge, MA: Harvard University Press.

Grätz, T. 2003. Gold-mining and risk management: A case study from northern Benin. *Ethnos* 68(2): 192–208.

Gregersen, N. H. 2003. Risk and religion: Toward a theology of risk taking. *Zygon* 38(2): 355–376.

Hacking, I. 1990. *The taming of chance*. Cambridge, UK: Cambridge University Press.

Halbwachs, M. 1992 [1941]. *On collective memory*. Chicago, IL: Chicago University Press.

Hamilton, C., Adolphs, S. & Nerlich, B. 2007. The meaning of 'risk': A view from corpus linguistics. *Discourse and Society* 18(2): 163–181.

Hanson, N.R. 2000. Observation. In *Readings in the philosophy of science: From positivism to postmodernism*. Schick, T. (ed.), pp. 175–182. Mountain View, CA: Mayfield.

Hansson, S.O. 1999. A philosophical perspective on risk. *Ambio* 28: 539–542.

Hansson, S.O. 2007. Risk. In *Stanford encyclopedia of philosophy (winter 2003 edition)*. Zalta, E.N. (ed.). Available online at plato.stanford.edu/entries/risk (accessed 1 November 2008).

Hansson, S.O. 2010. Risk: Objective or subjective, facts or values. *Journal of Risk Research* 13(2): 231–238.

Haram, L. 2006. AIDS and risk: The handling of uncertainty in northern Tanzania. *Culture, Health and Sexuality* 7(1): 1–11.

Henning, A. 2008. The illusion of economic objectivity: Linking local risks of credibility to global risks of climate change. *Journal of Risk Research* 11(1–2): 223–235.

Henning, A. 2013. Solar collectors for historic homes: Linking consumption to perceptions of space. In *Making sense of consumption: Selections from the 2nd Nordic Conference on Consumer Research 2012*. Hansson, L., Holmberg, U. & Brembech, H. (eds.), pp. 349–366. Gothenburg, Sweden: Centre for Consumer Science, University of Gothenburg.

Henrich, J. & McElreath, R. 2002. Are peasants risk-averse decision makers? *Current Anthropology* 43(1): 172–181.

Hicks, G. 2009. *Fate's bookie: How the lottery shaped the world.* Stroud, UK: The History Press.

Hilgartner, S. 1992. The social construction of risk objects: Or, how to pry open networks of risk. In *Organizations, uncertainties and risk.* Short, J.F. & Clarke, L. (eds.), pp. 39–53. Boulder, CO: Westview Press.

Hobbs, E. 2011. Performing wilderness, performing difference: Schismogenesis in a mining dispute. *Ethnos* 76(1): 109–129.

Hood, C., Rothstein, H. & Baldwin, R. 2001. *The government of risk: Understanding risk regulation regimes.* Oxford, UK: Oxford University Press.

Hornborg, A. 2004. Environmentalism, ethnicity and sacred places: Reflections on modernity, discourse and power. *Canadian Review of Sociology* 31(3): 245–267.

Hutchins, E. 1995. *Cognition in the wild.* Cambridge, MA: MIT Press.

Hutter, B. & Power, M. (eds.). 2005. *Organizational encounters with risk.* Cambridge, UK: Cambridge University Press.

Ingold, T. 2000. *The perception of the environment: Essays in livelihood, dwelling and skills.* London, UK & New York, NY: Routledge.

Jardine, C. & Hrudey, S.E. 1997. Mixed messages in risk communication. *Risk Analysis* 17(4): 489–498.

Jasanoff, S. 1999. The songlines of risk. *Environmental Values* 8: 135–152.

Kahan, D.M. 2012. Cultural cognition as a conception of the cultural theory of risk. In *Handbook of risk theory.* Roeser, S., Hillebrand, R., Sandin, P. & Peterson, M. (eds.), pp. 726–759. Berlin & Heidelberg, Germany: Springer.

Kahan, D.M., Braman, D., Gastil, J., Slovic, P. & Mertz, C.K. 2007. Culture and identity-protective cognition: Explaining the white male effect in risk perception. *Journal of Empirical Legal Studies* 4(3): 465–505.

Kavanagh, T.M. 1993. *Enlightenment and the shadows of chance: The novel and the culture of gambling in eighteenth-century France.* Baltimore, MD & London, UK: The Johns Hopkins University Press.

Keesing, R.M. 1974. Theories of culture. *Annual Review of Anthropology* 3: 73–97.

Keesing, R.M. 1976. *Cultural anthropology: A contemporary perspective.* New York, NY: Holt Rinehart & Winston.

Kitzinger, J. 1999. Researching risk and the media. *Health, Risk & Society* 1(1): 55–69.

Kluckhohn, C. 1942. Myths and rituals: A general theory. *Harvard Theological Review* 35: 45–79.

Kroeber, A. & Kluckhohn, C. 1952. *Culture: A critical review of concepts and definitions.* Peabody Museum Papers 47(1). Cambridge, MA: Harvard University Press.

Kuper, A. 1999. *Culture: The anthropologists' account.* Cambridge, MA: Harvard University Press.

Kuznar, L.A. 2001. Risk sensitivity and value among Andean pastoralists: Measures, models, and empirical tests. *Current Anthropology* 42(3): 432–440.

Lane, F.C. 1973. *Venice: A maritime republic.* Baltimore, MD & London, UK: The Johns Hopkins University Press.

Lave, J. 1988. *Cognition in practice.* Cambridge, UK: Cambridge University Press.

Lave, J. & Wenger, E. 1991. *Situated learning: Legitimate peripheral participation.* Cambridge, UK: Cambridge University Press.

Law, J. & Mol, A. 2008. The actor-enacted: Cumbrian sheep in 2001. In *Material agency.* Knappett, C. & Malafouris, L. (eds.), pp. 57–77. Berlin & Heidelberg, Germany: Springer.

Leiss, W. 1996. Three phases in the evolution of risk communication practice. *Annals of the American Academy of Political and Social Science* 545: 85–94.

Lichtenstein, S., Slovic, P., Fischhoff, B., Layman, M. & Combs, B. 1978. Judged frequency of lethal events. *Journal of Experimental Psychology* 4: 551–578.

Lidskog, R., Soneryd, L. & Uggla, Y. 2010. *Transboundary risk governance.* London, UK: Earthscan.

Lidskog, R., Soneryd, L. & Uggla, Y. 2011. Making transboundary risk governable. *Ambio* 40: 111–120.

Linnerooth-Bayer, J., Löfstedt, R. & Sjöstedt, G. 2001. *Transboundary risk management.* London, UK: Earthscan.

Löfstedt R.E. 1999. The role of trust in the North Blackforest: An evaluation of a citizen panel project. *Risk: Health, Safety and Environment* 10: 10–30.

Löfstedt, R. 2005. *Risk management in post-trust societies.* New York, NY: Palgrave Macmillan.

Löftstedt, R. 2011. Risk versus hazard – how to regulate in the 21st century. *European Journal of Risk Regulation* 2: 149–168.

Löfstedt, R.E. & 6, P. 2008. What environmental and technological risk communication research and health risk research can learn from each other. *Journal of Risk Research* 11(1–2): 141–167.

Luhmann, N. 1989. *Ecological communication.* Chicago, IL: The University of Chicago Press.

Luhmann, N. 1993. *Risk: A sociological theory.* New York, NY: Aldine de Gruyter.

Lupton, D. 1999. *Risk.* London, UK & New York, NY: Routledge.

Maguire, S. & Hardy, C. 2013. Organizing processes and the construction of risk: A discursive approach. *Academy of Management Journal* 56(1). 231–255.

Mairal Buil, G. 2003. A risk shadow in Spain. *Ethnos* 68(3): 179–191.

Mairal Buil, G. 2004. The invention of a minority. In *Facility siting: Risk, power and identity in land use planning.* Boholm, Å. & Löfstedt, R. (eds.), pp. 144–159. London, UK: Earthscan.

Mairal Buil, G. 2008. Narratives of risk. *Journal of Risk Research* 11(1–2): 41–54.

Mairal Buil, G. 2013. *La década del riesgo: Situaciones y narrativas de riesgo en España a comienzos del siglo XXI.* Madrid, Spain: Catarata.

Mairal Buil, G. & Bergua, J.A. 1998. From economism to culturalism: the social and cultural construction of risk in the River Ésera (Spain). In *Anthropological perspectives on local development: Knowledge and sentiments in conflict.* Abram, S. & Walden, J. (eds.), pp. 75–95. London, UK: Routledge

Malinowski, B. 1922. *Argonauts of the Western Pacific.* London, UK: Routledge & Kegan Paul.

Malinowski, B. 1978 [1935]. *Coral gardens and their magic: A study of the methods of tilling the soil and of agricultural rites in the Trobriand Islands.* New York, NY: Dover Books.

Maschke, E. 1964. Das Berufsbewusstsein des mittelalterlichen Fernkaufmanns. In *Beiträge zum Berufsbewusstsein des mittelalterlichen Menschen.* Wilpert, P. & Eckert, W.P. (eds.), pp. 306–335, Berlin, Germany: Walter de Gruyter & Co.

Meyer, J. 1949–1951. Contingency. *Synthese* 8(1): 73–90.

Middleton, D. & Edwards, D. (eds.). 1990. *Collective remembering.* London, UK: SAGE.

Möller, N. 2012. The concepts of risk and safety. In *Handbook of risk theory.* Roeser, S., Hillerbrand, R., Sandin, P. & Peterson, M. (eds.), pp. 56–85. Berlin & Heidelberg, Germany: Springer.

Morgan, G.M., Fischhoff, B., Bostrom, A. & Altman, C.J. 2002. *Risk communication: A mental models approach.* Cambridge, UK: Cambridge University Press.

Nash, J. 1993. *We eat the mines and the mines eat us: Dependency and exploitation in Bolivian tin mines.* New York, NY: Columbia University Press.

Niehaus, I. 2013. Confronting uncertainty: Anthropology and zones of the extraordinary. *American Ethnologist* 40(4): 651–660.

Oxford English Dictionary. 2014. risk, n. *OED Online.* September 2014. Oxford, UK: Oxford University Press. Available at www.oed.com.ezproxy.ub.gu.se/view/Entry/166306?rskey=LXUSik&result=1 (accessed 29 September 2014).

Oliver-Smith, A. 1996. Anthropological research on hazards and disaster. *Annual Review of Anthropology* 25: 303–328.

Paterson, J. 2003. Trans-science, trans-law and proceduralization. *Social & Legal Studies* 12(4): 525–545.

Perin, C. 2005. *Shouldering risk. The culture of control in the nuclear power industry.* Princeton, NJ: Princeton University Press.

Petts, J. 2008. Public engagement to build trust: False hopes? *Journal of Risk Research* 11(6): 821–835.

Phillimore, P. 1998. Uncertainty, reassurance and pollution: The politics of epidemiology in Teeside. *Health and Place* 4(3): 203–212.

Phillimore, P. & Bell, P. 2013. Manufacturing loss: Nostalgia and risk in Ludwigshafen. *Focaal – Journal of Global and Historical Anthropology* 67: 107–120.

Pidgeon, N., Hood, C., Jones, D., Turner, B. & Gibson, R. 1992. Risk perception. In *Risk: analysis, perception and management.* Royal Society Study Group (eds.), pp. 89–134. London, UK: The Royal Society.

Pink, S. 2001. *Doing ethnography: Images, media and representation in research.* London, UK: SAGE.

Power, M. 2004. *The risk management of everything.* London, UK: Demos.

Power, M. 2007. *Organized uncertainty: Designing a world of risk management.* Oxford, UK: Oxford University Press.

Purcell, K. Clarke, L. & Renzulli, L. 2000. Menus of choice: The social embeddedness of decisions. In *Risk in the modern age: Social theory, science and environmental decision making.* Cohen, M.J. (ed.), pp. 62–79. London, UK: Macmillan Press.

Quine, W.V. 1951. Main trends in recent philosophy: Two dogmas of empiricism. *The Philosophical Review* 60(1): 20–43.

Rappaport, R.A. 1996. Risk and the human environment. *Annals of the American Academy of Political and Social Science* 545 (May): 64–74.

Ravetz, J.R. 1997. The science of 'what if'? *Futures* 29(6): 533–539.

Ravetz, J.R. 1999. What is post-normal science? *Futures* 31: 647–653.

Reddy, S.G. 2006. Claims to expert knowledge and the subversion of democracy: The triumph of risk over uncertainty. *Economy and Society* 25(2): 222–254.

Reith, G. 2004. Uncertain times: The notion of 'risk' and the development of modernity. *Time & Society* 13(2–3): 382–402.

Renn, O. 1998. Three decades of risk research: Accomplishments and new challenges. *Journal of Risk Research* 1(1): 49–71.

Renn, O. 2008. *Risk governance: Coping with uncertainty in a complex world.* London, UK: Earthscan.

Rescher, N. 1983. *Risk: A philosophical introduction to the theory of risk evaluation and management.* Washington, DC: University Press of America.

Rescher, N. 1990. Luck. *Proceedings and Addresses of the American Philological Association* 64(3): 5–19.

Rhode, T., Singer, M., Bourgois, P., Friedman, S. & Strathdee, A. 2005. The social structural production of HIV risk among injection drug users. *Social Science & Medicine* 61: 1026–1044.

Rosa, E.A. 1998. Metatheoretical foundations for post-normal risk. *Journal of Risk Research* 1(1): 14–44.

Rosa, E., Renn, O. & McCright, A.M. 2014. *The risk society revisited: Social theory and governance.* Philadelphia, PA: Temple University Press.

Rose, N. 2001. The politics of life itself. *Theory, Culture, Society* 18(6): 1–30.

Rothstein, H. 2003. Neglected risk regulation: The institutional attenuation phenomenon. *Health, Risk and Society* 5(1): 85–103.

Rothstein, H. 2013. Domesticating participation: Participation and the institutional rationalities of science-based policymaking in the UK food standards agency. *Journal of Risk Research* 16(6): 771–790.

Rothstein, H., Huber, M. & Gaskell, G. 2006. A theory of risk colonization: The spiralling regulatory logics of societal and institutional risk. *Economy and Society* 35 (1): 91–112.

Saussure, F. de. 1983 [1916]. *Course in general linguistics.* Chicago, IL: Open Court Publishing.

Savin, K. 2011. *Fortunas klädnader: Lycka, olycka och risk i det tidigmoderna Sverige.* Lund: Sekel Bokförlag.

Shaw, A. 2000. Conflicting models of risk: Clinical genetics and British Pakistanis. In *Risk revisited.* Caplan, P. (ed.), pp. 85–107. London, UK: Pluto Press.

Shrader-Frechette, K.S. 1991. *Risk and rationality: Philosophical foundations for populist reforms.* Berkeley, CA: University of California Press.

Sjölander-Lindqvist, A. 2004. *Local environment at stake: The Hallandsås railway tunnel in a social and cultural context.* Lund: Lund Dissertations in Human Ecology 2, Lund University.

Skinner, J. 2000. The eruption of Chances Peak, Monteserrat, and the narrative containment of risk. In *Risk revisited*. Caplan, P. (ed.), pp. 156–183. London, UK: Pluto Press.

Skinner, J. 2008. The text and the tale: Differences between scientific reports and scientists' reportings on the eruption of Mount Chance, Monteserrat. *Journal of Risk Research* 11(1–2): 255–267.

Slovic, P. 2000. *The perception of risk*. London, UK: Earthscan.

Smith, D.J. 2010. Imagining HIV/AIDS: Morality and perceptions of personal risk in Nigeria. *Medical Anthropology* 22: 343–372.

Smith, W., Wayte, W. & Marindin, G.E. 1890. Augur. In *A dictionary of Greek and Roman antiquities*. London, UK: John Murray Ltd. Available at www.perseus.tufts.edu/hopper/text?doc=Perseus:text:1999.04.0063:entry=augur-cn (accessed 17 January 2014).

Stoffle, R.W. & Evans, M.J. 1988. American Indians and nuclear waste storage: The debate at Yucca Mountain, Nevada. *Policy Studies Journal.* 16(4): 751–767.

Stoffle, R.W. & Evans, M.J. 1990. Holistic conservation and cultural triage: American Indian perspectives on cultural resources. *Human Organization* 49(2): 41–49.

Stoffle, R.W. & Arnold, R. 2003. Confronting the angry rock: American Indians' situated risk from radioactivity. *Ethnos* 68(3): 230–248.

Stoffle, R.W. & Minnis, J. 2008. Resilience at risk: Epistemological and social construction barriers to risk communication. *Journal of Risk Research* 11(1–2): 55–68.

Stoffle, R.W., Traugott, M.W., Stone, J., Mcintyre, P.D., Jensen, F.V. & Davidson, C.C. 1991. Risk perception mapping: Using ethnography to define the locally affected population for a low-level radioactive waste storage facility in Michigan. *American Anthropologist* 93(3): 611–635.

Stoffle, R., Zedeño, M.N., Eisenberg, A., Toupal, R. & Carroll, A. 2004. Shifting risks: Hoover dam bridge impacts on American Indians sacred landcape. In *Facility siting: Risk, power and identity in land use planning*. Boholm, Å. & Löfstedt, R. (eds.), pp. 127–143, London, UK: Earthscan.

Strauss, C. & Quinn, N. 1997. *A cognitive theory of cultural meaning*. Cambridge, UK: Cambridge University Press.

Strydom, P. 2002. *Risk, environment and society: Ongoing debates, current issues and future prospects*. Buckingham, UK: Open University Press.

Tansey, J. & O'Riordan, T. 1999. Cultural theory and risk: A review. *Health, Risk & Society* 1(1): 71–90.

Taussig, M.T. 1980. *The devil and commodity fetishism in South America*. Chapel Hill, NC: University of North Carolina Press.

Thomas, J. 2001. Comments on part I: intersecting landscapes. In *Contested landscapes: Movement, exile and place*. Bender, B. & Winer, M. (eds.), pp. 181–188. Oxford & New York: Berg Publishers.

Tylor, E.B. 1871. *Primitive culture: Researches into the development of mythology, philosophy, religion, art and custom*. London, UK: John Murray Ltd.

van Asselt, M. 2005. The complex significance of uncertainty in a risk era: Logics, manners and strategies in use. *International Journal of Risk Assessment and Management* 5 (2/3/4): 125–158.

van Loon, J. 2002. *Risk and technological culture*. London, UK: Routledge.

Walker, J. 1999. Gambling and Venetian noblemen c. 1500–1700. *Past & Present* 162: 28–69.

Wardman, J. 2008. The constitution of risk communication in advanced liberal societies. *Risk Analysis* 28(6): 1619–1637.

Watson, P.J. 1995. Archaeology, anthropology, and the culture concept. *American Anthropologist* 97(4): 683–694.

Whyte, S.R. 1997. *Questioning misfortune: The pragmatics of uncertainty in eastern Uganda*. Cambridge, UK: Cambridge University Press.

Wilks, R.R. 1996. *Economics and cultures: Foundations of economic anthropology*. Boulder, CO: Westview Press.

Zaloom, C. 2004. The productive life of risk. *Cultural Anthropology* 19(3): 365–391.

Zonabend, F. 1993. *The nuclear peninsula*. Cambridge, UK: Cambridge University Press.

2

COMPARATIVE STUDIES OF RISK PERCEPTION

Lessons and challenges

Comparative, cross-national or cross-cultural research in the social sciences may be undertaken for several interrelated reasons (for overviews of the research field in social psychology and psychology, see for example Berry *et al.*1992; Hantrais & Mangen 1996; Kohn 1989a, 1989b; Kagitcibasi & Berry 1989; Miller-Loessi 1995; Schooler 1996; Triandis & Berry 1980). A key argument in this literature is that the investigation of systematic variation is a crucial element in theoretical development. By replicating earlier studies on new samples, the generality of the findings can be examined, and such re-examinations are taken to be instrumental in refining and substantiating theories. But comparisons across national or cultural boundaries are not without complications. If cross-national similarities are indeed encountered, how might one tell whether they result from common processes and structures or from specific historical, sociological or psychological circumstances? There are similarities in conduct, ideas and institutions between societies, but that does not signify that the meanings, or the processes which order them, are the same. Quite to the contrary, a mass of ethnographic evidence from all kinds of societies shows that human social life is culturally highly variable.

As is the case with other experiential phenomena, the actions and understandings regarding risk issues are informed by socially and culturally structured conceptions and evaluations about the world – what it looks like, what it should be or should not be. Perceptions of events and phenomena are conditioned by values that vary according to local assumptions, conventions and practices. Human societies constitute 'ultra-complex' systems, in that humans do not merely respond to the physical impact of measurable and quantifiable components of events. Information about events, what is recorded and reported, in what way and by whom, is crucial to human life as is the way that information is processed socially and valued morally (Rappaport 1996).

It follows from the specificity and variability of human social life that one should not presume that scores and ratings in response to a questionnaire will have the same meanings as those offered in a different context. There are considerable methodological problems in answering questions of whether or not, and if so to what degree, social and psychological phenomena are comparable and equivalent across nations and cultures (Berry 1980):

> To compare two phenomena, they must share some features in common; and to compare them to some advantage, they should usually differ on some feature. That is, it must be possible to place two phenomena on a single dimension in order to judge them validly in relation to each other; and for the comparative judgment to be of value they should not be identical in all respects (Berry 1980: 8).

Berry's words of warning that far more is required than just the collection and comparison of data from two countries remind us of the imperative that the methodology must be sound if cross-national research is to be successful. Otherwise, methodological inconsistencies may bring about divergent results which stem from the design, rather than being valid indicators of processes or structures intrinsic to the study area. That a study initially needs to be designed as comparative in order to allow comparisons might appear to be a truism, but a failure to meet this requirement is a common problem encountered in the replication of earlier studies. If the collection of data is not accomplished under equivalent circumstances or through the use of equivalent measures, the comparative value of the results will be seriously compromised. Theoretical concepts and definitions must also be equivalent between one national study and another, as of course must be the scales adopted for measurement and for comparison (Berry *et al.* 1992: 237–238).

Assuming that these pre-conditions for sound comparative research have been met, the next challenge will be the interpretation of the results. If valid cross-national differences and similarities are demonstrated, how might such results be understood? From among myriad national differences, how do we select those that should be adopted as the pertinent analytical variables (Kohn 1989b)?

Even if cross-national research is costly in terms of time and money, and raises these serious methodological and interpretative problems, there are strong arguments in its favour (see Kohn 1989a). By taking into account inconsistencies and differences that are inconspicuous in a study of a single nation but which become more noticeable in a comparative exercise, cross-national research can oblige a discipline or research field to revise earlier assumptions about relationships (Kohn 1989b; Schooler 1996).

Recognition of the value of cross-national and cross-cultural studies of risk perception has increased (Renn & Rohrmann 2000; Rohrmann & Chen 1999;

Rosa *et al.* 1995). Comparative studies of risk perception have been guided by diverse explorative as well as more theoretical aims, such as the following:

1. To learn more about the way people in specific social categories perceive risks: for instance, women as opposed to men; experts rather than laypeople; various occupational categories; people with different educational backgrounds; and ethnic minorities (see for example Bastide *et al.* 1989; Flynn, Slovic & Mertz 1994; Nyland 1993; Sjöberg *et al.* 1996).
2. To use the psychometric paradigm to test the generality of results regarding the qualitative dimensions of risk perception (Englander, Farago & Slovic 1986; Teigen, Brun & Slovic 1988; Goszczynska, Tyszka & Slovic 1991; Keown 1989; Kleinhesselink & Rosa 1991, 1994).
3. To evaluate the proposition emerging from cultural theory that risk is culturally construed, such that what people fear and why is determined by broader values (Rohrmann 1994; Kahan *et al.* 2007).

This chapter will examine a broad range of comparative studies of risk perception that, in various ways, probe the national, social and cultural variables of risk perception. More specifically, it will look at studies that replicate existing research designs on new samples; aim to identify explanatory background variables in terms of gender, occupation and ethnicity; focus on local (geographical) contexts; and address specific risk issues. A complete inventory of all such studies is not the aim here; rather, it is to disclose themes of research, theoretical foci and methods and results that identify some state-of-the-art findings regarding general and specific dimensions of risk perception. Selected studies are confined to published articles and reports, and the selection was made by a 'snowballing' strategy: references in the relevant literature were examined to identify pertinent articles, further searches then were made from these new sources and so on. Searches utilised Google Scholar and databases in sociology and psychology.

Psychometric research on risk perception and the efforts to replicate the early American studies provide a starting point for the discussion, which then will move on to purposively comparative cross-national studies. Studies on the influences of gender, ethnicity and social marginality on risk perception and the role of the media then will be reviewed and discussed, followed by consideration of the role played by broader cultural values. The final section of the chapter reviews studies that compare specific risk issues across countries, or across specific local populations or communities within a country.

The psychometric paradigm – the background

Research by cognitive psychologists has demonstrated that when laypersons make estimates of risk they do not merely calculate the bad outcome in accordance with statistical (probabilistic) information. Other considerations also affect judgments about uncertain events; under experimental conditions, people tend to construe the world in terms of causal or rule-governed schemata rather than by means of probabilistic calculations. They resort to heuristic cognitive devices – mental guidelines that make knowledge about risk readily accessible – and these schemata do not fully explore information concerning alternative steps that might be taken to reduce or eliminate risk (Tversky & Kahnemann 1973). As defined by cognitive psychologists, the 'availability heuristic' relates to what people *remember*, and not to what actually has taken place. It is a cognitive schema for processing information, and not an imprint of the material world upon the mind. People may or may not recall what they experience directly or indirectly through channels of communication and the transmission of information.

In the 1970s, research centres emerged in Europe and the United States with the goal of investigating the psychological and cognitive dimensions of the estimation of risk. The Decision Research Group in Oregon (United States) initiated research to explore how laypersons rate and perceive risk. When subjects were asked to estimate the number of deaths due to a range of hazards, including natural disasters, diseases, crime and road traffic, they tended to overestimate fatalities due to unusual and spectacular cases such as botulism, tornadoes and floods, and underestimate deaths caused by common afflictions such as cancer, stroke and heart disease (Lichtenstein *et al.* 1978). These findings were interpreted in the light of what cognitive psychologists had discovered about the role of heuristic schemes in decision-making: dramatic and spectacular hazards may be more easily remembered than common ones and this greater cognitive 'availability' may explain the tendency for subjects to overrate the risk that they pose (Lichtenstein *et al.* 1978).

An early assumption of psychometric research was that the way in which risks are semantically construed (the mental models used to structure information) and how the probabilities of those risks are estimated constitute interdependent cognitive activities. Interest in various qualitative attributes such as the immediacy of an adverse effect; the available choices of mitigation; and the knowledge of, familiarity with and control of a hazard gave rise to further research questions about risk perception (Lowrance 1976; von Winterfeldt & Edwards 1984). In a study by Fischhoff *et al.* (1978), subjects were asked to rate 30 hazards on a scale indicating nine qualitative characteristics of risk: whether it was voluntary, chronic, catastrophic, common, fatal, immediate, ascertainable, controllable or novel. Factor analysis of these ratings identified two major factors. A 'dread' factor corresponded with characteristics such as uncontrollable, potentially catastrophic, dangerous to future generations and involuntary. A 'knowledge' factor was related to the elements chronic, unknown to those exposed, delayed and new.

Slovic, Fischhoff and Lichtenstein (1980) extended this study with a questionnaire listing 90 activities, substances and technologies. A broad variety of risk issues were included, for example, trampolines, hand guns, nuclear reactors, chemical substances, smoking, aviation, traffic, drugs and home appliances. College student subjects (*n* = 175) were asked to rate the 'risk' of each item for 'society at large' on a scale between 0 (not risky) and 100 (extremely risky). Risk was operationalised as 'risk of dying' from exposure to the hazard. In addition, four other samples of respondents consisting of (a) members of the League of Women Voters, (b) college students, (c) business people and (d) experts on risk assessment were asked to rate a subset of 30 hazards on the scale of nine qualitative characteristics of risk (Slovic, Fischhoff & Lichtenstein 1980). Judgments of many of the qualitative dimensions were strongly correlated, and the same two major factors were identified that had emerged in the earlier study. In addition, a third significant factor was identified, relating to 'magnitude', or the number of people affected by the risk. Hazards considered to be 'voluntary' were also highly likely to be understood as 'controllable' and 'well known'. Another result was that the risk characteristics could be grouped into two higher-order dimensions: Factor 1, labelled Unknown Risk, was determined primarily by whether the risk was 'unknown' to those exposed and to science and to a lesser extent by 'unfamiliarity', 'involuntariness' and the 'delay of effects'. Factor 2, labelled Dread Risk, tended to be most strongly determined by 'severity of consequences', 'dread' and 'catastrophic potential'. Broadly speaking, nuclear issues occupied a position at one extreme of the factor axes: this technology was perceived to be highly unknown, dreaded, uncontrollable, catastrophic and having delayed adverse effects on future generations (Slovic, Fischhoff & Lichtenstein 1980).

Research by the Oregon group and others (for example, by Vlek & Stallen 1980, 1981; Otway & von Winterfeldt 1982) provided evidence that risk perception is influenced by qualitative understandings – meanings – associated with hazards that do not derive from the computation of fatality statistics. However, the acceptability of new technologies to the general public cannot be reduced to cognitive dimensions (von Winterfeldt & Edwards 1984). Technology is socially and politically embedded so that attitudes towards it are influenced by both the vested interests of social actors and public debate regarding risks and benefits. Values and moral considerations as well as political, social and ideological concerns must be taken into account when explaining controversies about the risks of technology. These points were taken further by advocates of cultural theory (see Dake 1991; Douglas 1992; Douglas & Wildavsky 1982; Rayner & Cantor 1987; Thompson, Ellis & Wildavsky 1990; Wildavsky & Dake 1990) as well as by others pursuing constructionist approaches to risk perception (Clarke & Short 1993; Short & Clarke 1992).

Replications of psychometric studies of risk perception

Several replications of the original study by Slovic, Fischhoff and Lichtenstein (1980) have been made in other countries, because little was known about how risk was understood by the public in countries other than the United States. What guided these comparative attempts was a mixture of ambitions: first, to test general theory and second, to generate an exploratory body of new knowledge about public opinion in different countries. Self-evidently, these two aims do not necessarily overlap. The original list of 90 hazards was modified in most of these replicating studies so as to match a 'hazard profile' relevant to the country in question. Sampling strategies also diverged from the original study, although in most cases small, conveniently assembled samples of college or university students were used. The scales for measuring the various qualitative criteria have also varied among the studies. This lack of consistency must be kept in mind when comparing the results of psychometric studies in different countries (see Royal Society Study Group 1992). Moreover, even if similar ratings of perceived risk are demonstrated across samples, the underlying reasons should not be assumed to be the same. As an example, radiation therapy might be judged as risky by both artists and scientists, yet for different precise reasons, as the former most likely would be poorly informed about the physics of the negative side-effects of such treatment, whereas that would not be true for the latter (Karpowicz-Lazreg & Mullet 1993).

In 1983 the first of a series of comparative studies of risk perception was carried out in Hungary (Englander, Farago & Slovic 1986) with the goal of comparing the structure of risk perception and the ratings of perceived risk in Hungary with earlier results from the United States (Fischoff *et al.* 1978; Slovic, Fischhoff & Lichtenstein 1980). Hungarian college students were given two questionnaires. The first questionnaire listed the 90 activities, substances and technologies formulated earlier by Slovic, Fischhoff and Lichtenstein (1980), whilst the second was the subset of 30 hazards to be rated on the nine qualitative dimensions previously used by Fischhoff *et al.* (1978). Results of the factor analysis of the Hungarian data were found to be very similar to those of the American sample. Two dominant factors closely resembled the American factors Unknown Risk and Dread Risk. In the Hungarian case, however, the attribute 'certain to be fatal' was most closely associated with 'known' risk. Comparison between the specific locations of hazards within the factor space revealed further differences between respondents in Hungary and those in America. For example, nuclear power was rated highly as a Dread Risk in the Hungarian set but not as extreme in terms of Unknown Risk. The most striking difference between the two countries was that the mean of the judgments of risk posed by the 90 hazards was almost twice as high for the Americans as it was among Hungarians.

The specific concerns about hazards were also to some extent different between the two countries. While Americans in general were relatively more concerned about technological risk issues resulting from radiation and chemicals (herbicides, pesticides and medically prescribed drugs), the Hungarians gave higher ratings to common, everyday risks associated with traffic and transport (cars, bicycles, trains and boats), hazards at home and at work (electricity and gas furnaces) and health conditions related to pregnancy and childbirth. The conclusion was that Hungarians seemed to be most sensitive to risk associated with 'the failure of machines and the people who operate them' (Englander *et al.* 1986: 64), while Americans tended to be more concerned about the delayed negative effects of substances caused by failing societal risk management.

Another replication was made in Norway a few years after the Hungarian study (Teigen, Brun & Slovic 1988). This project again used samples of students and focused on the structure of risk perception and the ratings of perceived risk. Two surveys were conducted, the first during the winter of 1985/86 and the second in

November 1986, with the catastrophic accident at the Chernobyl nuclear plant in Ukraine in April 1986 fortuitously falling in between. With regard to the qualitative dimensions of risk, the Norwegian students seemed to have more confidence in science than did those in the American sample. Risk issues were understood as 'older' and with less immediate consequences. There was an almost identical ordering of scales in the American and Norwegian samples, but there were some conspicuous differences in the way in which the scales were clustered. Unknown Risk and Delayed Risk had diverged from the dimension Involuntary/Control towards an association with the dimension Not Necessarily Fatal. Norwegian scores on the magnitude of risk, apart from a handful of items, fell below the American ratings but were higher than the corresponding mean ratings from Hungary. More specifically, Norwegians had a risk profile closer to that of the Americans, in that they tended to be more concerned with drugs and narcotics than were the Hungarians.

A third replication was made in Poland (Goszczynska, Tyszka & Slovic 1991), with data being obtained on this occasion from respondents with professional occupations. These subjects were selected from two regions in Poland, one highly industrialised and the other moderately so. On the criterion of occupation, each of the two regional groups was divided into a 'technical' subgroup, including engineers and technicians, and a 'social' subgroup, comprising teachers, journalists and physicians. Correlations among the 15 qualitative risk dimensions produced the same two main factors as seen in the American and Hungarian studies: a Dread Risk factor and an Unknown Risk factor. In comparison with previous results, the mean ratings of the estimates of perceived risk in Poland were closest to those from America. The Polish ratings with regard to the magnitude of risk for the 27 hazards common to the questionnaires used in all four countries were somewhat lower than the American scores, somewhat higher than the Norwegian and considerably above the mean ratings in Hungary. Risk associated with warfare, nuclear weapons, alcoholic beverages and railways were ranked higher in Poland than in the other countries. In this study, economic and social hazards – risks that had not been included in the questionnaires used in the other countries – were rated higher than those from industries characteristic of Poland such as coal mines, steel mills and petrochemical plants. The sub-sample of respondents who lived in a more industrialised area gave higher ratings of perceived risk than did respondents from the less industrialised region. However, this difference was only for the 'social' professions, as the technical professions did not vary in relation to the area of residence.

A replication in France by Karpowicz-Lazreg and Mullet (1993) also aimed to investigate the effects of gender and education on the perception of risk. Student respondents were divided into four groups differentiated by gender and a fine arts or a science educational orientation. Women gave higher mean ratings than men with regard to the magnitude of risk. The mean ratings for the French sample were very close to the mean ratings in the American study (Slovic, Fischhoff & Lichtenstein 1980). Compared to the results in Hungary and Norway, the mean ratings of the French respondents were considerably higher. Specific differences between the Norwegian and French samples related to risk associated with violence, advanced technology and chemical substances, all of which were considered more risky in France. There were major differences in comparison with the Hungarian sample, the French ratings being higher in each instance. In France, women gave higher ratings of perceived risk than did men, regardless of background. Students of science feared certain medical techniques and toxic substances more than did the arts-educated. The American results and the French ones reported by Karpowicz-Lazreg and Mullet (1993) showed marked similarities. To a large extent the American and French subjects seemed to share the same preoccupations. French concerns regarding the nuclear industry were similar to those expressed by Americans. Another cross-national study of risk perception in France and the United States reached similar conclusions (Poumadere *et al.* 1995). Perceptions of risk showed many similarities between the two countries, although the French were much more trustful of the competence and efficiency of experts and authorities.

Up to this point, cross-national research covering European countries has been the focus, and the results have been comparable to those from earlier American studies. There are other studies based on samples of Asian subjects. The first of these was by Keown (1989), who found that the mean ratings of the perceptions of the magnitude of risk among Hong Kong students were not significantly higher than corresponding American ratings. However, the ratings of risks of specific hazards differed a great deal. In the Hong Kong sample, some items – such as food colouring, heroin, caffeine, space exploration, crime, non-nuclear electrical power, commercial aviation, food preservatives, railways and bicycles – were rated considerably higher. Others, for example, risk associated with DDT, research into DNA, pesticides and alcoholic beverages, were rated much lower. Factor scores for the subset of 15 hazards revealed the same two factors present in the American study: Unknown Risk and Dread Risk. Keown postulated that perception of risk was likely to vary depending on a wide array of factors: what the media reports, what is on the agenda of citizens, what cultural norms are predominant and what technical and legal opportunities exist for the control and regulation of risk.

There are certain limitations to the survey methods used in the replication of studies examining risk perception. For one, the samples were not strictly equivalent: there were no systematic controls for such variables as age, gender, education, income and occupation. There was also a considerable time lag between studies, such that Slovic, Fischhoff and Lichtenstein's American study (1980) served as a point of comparative reference for studies in other countries made decades later.

An additional methodological problem is one of variable meaning. The questionnaires included quite different sets of risk issues, and the definitions of risk were not consistent. It is far from clear how respondents understood the standard instruction that they should focus on risk to society 'as a whole' or 'in general'. How do people in Norway, Hungary, the United States or Hong Kong conceive of 'society as a whole'? It is wrong simply to assume that the construct 'society in general', even if defined as a national arena, is understood uniformly in every context of sampling and is not conditioned by specific cultural perceptions.

Potential variation in meaning also is at issue with regard to the characterisation of the bad outcome of a risk issue as human death. Should dying be considered a direct or an indirect consequence of a particular risk? The risk embodied by a hand gun might not be understood primarily as due to the weapon itself, but to the intentions of the person holding it. Should risk, as an estimation of probability of harm, be understood to derive from a material cause or an intended cause of death? Furthermore, although 'death' might seem to be a clear-cut and uncontroversial concept, matters concerning death – its morality, exegesis and ontology – take us into a field of human existence that is highly determined by cultural conventions, practices and values (see Bloch & Parry 1982; Huntington & Metcalf 1979). Reservations noted here about the equivalence of samples, the time gap between surveys and variations in meaning mean that the validity of the comparisons between nations is an open question.

Psychometric cross-national studies with comparative design

Some psychometric cross-national studies of the perception of risk were designed methodologically to be comparative at the outset (Hinman *et al.* 1993; Kleinhesselink & Rosa 1991, 1994). The means for collecting data were similar between studies, the samples used had equivalent characteristics, the same measurements were used and the studies were conducted at roughly the same juncture in time. Kleinhesselink and Rosa (1991) aimed to evaluate and test two alternative hypotheses on risk perception: (1) the psychometric paradigm, which claims that there are cognitive patterns that are stable across cultures; and (2) the anthropological suggestion that perceptions of risk are determined by culture and therefore are highly variable. They focused on Japan and the United States, two nations with similar levels of industrialisation but with divergent cultural traditions. To provide some control with respect to other social characteristics, so as to allow cultural background to act as a variable influencing the outcome of the responses, the American and Japanese subjects chosen were all students residing in the United States; if culture does indeed influence the perception of risk, then the responses from each of the two samples of students would be expected to differ considerably.

Kleinhesselink and Rosa's (1991) questionnaire on risk derived from the one originally used by Slovic, Fischhoff, and Lichtenstein (1980). The list of hazards was modified so as to better accommodate the Japanese respondents, and it came to include 70 items that were rated on nine qualitative dimensions. No ratings were made regarding the perceived magnitude of risk. Additional questions referred to self-efficacy, general political efficacy and perceived general vulnerability to risk. The American sample of college students rated higher when it came to political efficacy, efficacy of response and self-efficacy. However, the factor scores for the qualitative dimensions of risk were rather similar between the samples. The two higher-order characteristics for structuring risk perception appeared to be the Dread Risk and the Unknown Risk factors. The most dreaded activity in both samples was nuclear war. All seven nuclear issues were closely clustered together and regarded with dread. A notable difference between the two samples was that risk issues were differently construed along the dimension relating to the factors 'known-unknown'. For the Japanese students, nuclear risk was regarded as 'well-known' by both individual and society, whereas the Americans saw this issue as being more 'unknown'. Crime was much more dreaded by the American students, while the Japanese rated a number of items related to safety of foods, drugs and transport as more dreaded and catastrophic.

A follow-up of this study was made using the same questionnaire on a larger sample of Japanese students, this time resident in Japan (Kleinhesselink & Rosa 1994). Again, nuclear risk was viewed as 'well known' by Japanese subjects and as moderately 'unknown' by Americans. The seven nuclear risk issues were regarded as being some of the most 'well known' and 'older' to the Japanese, both individually and as a society. All nuclear items were more dreaded by the Japanese respondents, although nuclear risk was highly dreaded in both samples. The nuclear risk issues were viewed as being highly uncontrollable, highly involuntary and highly catastrophic by both Americans and Japanese. The most dreaded risk issue in both samples was nuclear weapons (war). Kleinhesselink and Rosa (1994) point to the dropping of atom bombs on Hiroshima and Nagasaki in 1945 as a plausible explanation for the tendency among the Japanese respondents to regard the nuclear risk as being more 'well-known'. Rather than reflecting some cultural difference in the structuring of risk perception, Kleinhesselink and Rosa (1994) therefore suggest that the divergent understandings of nuclear risk in America and in Japan derive from historical experiences.

A study by Rohrmann and Chen (1999) using a psychometric framework compared risk perception among samples of Chinese and Australian students with differing professional orientations (geography, psychology and engineering). Although there was no difference between the countries with regard to magnitude of perceived risk, the study revealed that the Chinese respondents were less willing to 'accept' risk.

A modified psychometric model was used to cross-nationally study risk perception and the coverage of risk by the media in France, the United Kingdom, Spain, Sweden and Norway (Sjöberg 1999). A key finding was that risk perception varied greatly between two clusters of similarly responding countries: French and Spanish respondents generally had a very high level of perceived risk, whereas perceived risk was lower in the United Kingdom, Norway and Sweden. This study made a distinction between perceived risk to oneself ('personal risk') and perceived risk to others ('general risk'). For many risk issues there was a considerable difference in how respondents rated these two kinds of risk (Sjöberg 2003). This cross-national study also focused on trust as an explanatory variable for risk perception. Trust was found to be 'a necessary, but not a sufficient condition of a low level of perceived risk' (Sjöberg 1999: 547). The influence of trust on perceived risk varied among countries and between different types of risk issues, nuclear risk being the most sensitive to trust (Viklund 2003). Viklund (2003) concluded that trust does explain risk perception, but that the influence depends on the type of risk issue and the type of trust, whether general trust or more specific trust in particular institutions.

One lesson from cross-national research is that the prominence of specific risk issues might vary from one country to another. Whereas students in Hungary were concerned about risk associated with smoking, alcohol, crime and motor vehicles (Englander *et al.* 1986), those in France (Poumadere *et al.* 1995) and Norway (Teigen, Brun & Slovic 1988) expressed concern about hidden chemicals (herbicides and pesticides) in the environment and in food, drugs and narcotics. The big risk issues in Brazil were dynamite, fireworks and fires in skyscrapers (Nyland 1993), whereas heroin, crime and chemical substances in food and the hazards of bicycles and trains preoccupied respondents in Hong Kong (Keown 1989). Another cross-national finding was that the mean ratings regarding the magnitude of risk varied considerably. American respondents tended to give high mean ratings, as did Bulgarian, Japanese, Hong Kongese, French, Brazilian and Polish subjects. Low ratings were evident among Russian, Hungarian, Romanian and Swedish respondents. Despite such variation in perception of the magnitude of risk, the correlations between the rank orders of hazards tended to be quite strong across national samples: similar rank orders were obtained in comparisons of Brazil and Sweden (Nyland 1993); of Bulgaria, Romania and Sweden (Sjöberg *et al.* 1996); of Norway and the United States; and of the United States and Poland, Poland and Norway and Poland and Hungary (Goszczynska *et al.* 1991).

Despite the variations in level of perceived risk displayed between countries, psychometric studies show that the qualitative risk characteristics are rated much the same; hazards in general are grouped together along common factors relating to 'dread' and 'knowledge'. Results such as this are proffered as evidence that the cognitive structuring of risk is similar across nations, irrespective of cultural background. However, the conclusion that the cognitive structuring of risk should be regarded as universal seems a step too far, since the psychometric scales – adopted by reason of their use in earlier studies – do not exhaust all possible meanings of risk.

Perceived risk and media reporting

Comparative research has led to the recognition that media reporting on risk perception is a significant explanatory parameter (af Wåhlberg & Sjöberg 1997; Sjöberg 1999). For many everyday hazards, information builds on personal and interpersonally shared experience to a large extent, but some hazards are encountered only indirectly through statements made by experts and risk management institutions, public agencies, companies or non-governmental organizations (NGOs) and reported largely only in the news media. The expectation is that messages about risk in the media will influence public attitudes and responses, whether risk is accepted and tolerated or not. If the availability heuristic is to be taken seriously as a theoretical framework for understanding risk perception, attention should be directed towards how various hazards are socially represented in the media (Stallings 1990). The theory of the social amplification of risk addresses how available information often exaggerates or underrates risk, for example, when it is presented in the media (Kasperson *et al.* 1988; Renn *et al.* 1992). It should be noted that this model presupposes a distinction between real (objective) and perceived (subjective) risk. Risk is taken for granted as a given, factual entity, and information on risk is understood to be distorted when information is transmitted through societal channels. The social amplification of risk framework builds on a transmission model of communication, derived from engineering. This model will be discussed with more detail in Chapter 8 in relation to the topic of risk communication, and an interpretive approach will be suggested that accommodates interacting viewpoints including expert opinion, official statistics, personal experience and common sense practical rationality (Clarke & Short 1993).

Several studies suggest that media reporting on risk varies among countries. A cross-national study of the United Kingdom, Germany, France, Italy and Portugal (Lévy-Leboyer et al. 1996) analysed the content of three leading daily newspapers in each country. This revealed substantial national differences in coverage. Nuclear pollution received almost the same amount of attention in all countries except Italy, where it lacked mention. In the United Kingdom, 20 per cent of all media reporting on environmental issues dealt with the status of the fauna. In the other countries, neither flora nor fauna conservation was given particular attention. The German press was most concerned with environmental pollution of all kinds, while in Portugal degradation of natural sites was given high priority. Little interest in degradation was expressed by the French press, which was more preoccupied with natural events and natural disasters. In Italy, the press most often dealt with the degradation of landscapes and buildings.

Englander *et al.* (1986) suggest that the significantly lower level of perceived risk in Hungary as compared to the United States was due to the then-Communist government stifling reports in the news media about domestic hazards for political reasons. A tentative estimate of media content in the two countries revealed that American newspapers to a larger extent reported about domestic risk and causes of premature human death of all possible kinds, whereas the Hungarian press, traffic accidents excepted, mostly reported about deaths occurring outside the country. In the terminology of the social amplification of risk framework (Kasperson *et al.* 1988; Renn *et al.* 1992), the Hungarian media attenuated risk, while the American press amplified it.

Seeking explanations of cross-national variation in mean ratings of risk magnitude, Teigen, Brun and Slovic (1988) discussed the effects the size of a country had in combination with media impact. Members of a 'large' society might feel more exposed to and unprotected from risk, since there would be a large number of media reports about a broad variety of risk issues as well as more divergent opinions about what is and is not hazardous. A larger flow of messages would give room for ambiguous or conflicting information that might amplify estimations of risk. This argument presupposes a direct relationship between the total national output of the news media and the matters that interest individuals in their daily lives. However, the actual interests of a consumer of the media cannot be deduced simply from the overall supply of information, since the audience takes an active part in the process of interpretation, is socially and culturally constituted and participates actively in the interpretation and construction of meaning (Alasuutari 1999; Fiske 1987). Furthermore, there is considerable cross-national variation with respect to what groups in society engage with news media, as well as where, when and how often this happens (Gustafsson & Weibull 1996).

A study by Sjöberg *et al.* (1996) in Romania and Bulgaria included an analysis of daily newspapers published during 1985 and 1993, respectively. Reporting on risk was greater in the latter year than it was in the former in both countries, but the increase was considerably larger in Bulgaria, as was the mean rating of risk magnitude. This media coverage was analysed in detail, and correlations were sought with the scores for mean perceived risk and with the rank order of specific hazards obtained for the respective countries. No measurable correspondence emerged, and this result did not support the idea that media coverage influences risk perception, at least not directly.

Relationships between media and risk perception can be expected to be complex. The role of the media in society as well as its institutional logic must be accounted for, and it must not be assumed that the media represent risk in an invariant way from one country to the next (af Wåhlberg & Sjöberg 1997; Sjöberg *et al.* 1996: 67–68). Far from being monolithic, the media comprises a broad spectrum of information technologies, business models, organisational rationalities and political orientations. Various forms of media can be expected to have different interests, both national and traditional, and modes of operating that influence choices of what is newsworthy and how the selected material is presented and evaluated.

Risk perception and social background factors: marginality, poverty and occupation

A French study by Bastide *et al.* (1989) explored connections between risk perception and sociological and psychological factors. Comparisons of the respondents' estimates of the frequency of mortality resulting from 30 diseases and accidents and the actual statistics of causes of death showed that the most overestimated causes of death were motor vehicle accidents, industrial injuries, homicides, AIDS, leukaemia and drowning. Conversely, asthma and bronchitis, pneumonia, cerebrovascular diseases and accidental falls were the most underestimated. Crucially, this study demonstrated that respondents displaying a tendency to systematically overestimate the frequency of causes of mortality shared certain sociodemographic characteristics. They were more likely than not to be divorced, to be unemployed or to have a low income and to be a resident in a medium-sized town. Respondents who tended to underestimate the frequency of mortality causes were more likely to have a higher education, to have a better income and to be a resident of a big city or, if a farmer, to live in a village. In this study, age, gender and size of family did not significantly differentiate respondents with respect to their tendency to over- or underestimate mortality rates.

Some circumstances that cross-cut the socio-demographic divide did predispose respondents to overestimate mortality: respondents who were depressed or had been subject to a serious physical accident (or had a relative so involved), or declared personal discomfort with everyday pollution all tended to overestimate causes of death in the study by Bastide *et al.* (1989). This study also found that respondents who overestimated or underestimated fatality causes would tend to do the same when estimating risk associated with a number of activities, substances and technologies. Furthermore, women were more sensitive to the risks of technology than men. Factor analysis of the ratings of 'hazards' due to technology disclosed a qualitative distinction between two kinds: one category consisted of risks considered voluntary and 'worth their benefit', for example, vaccines, railroads and blood transfusions; the other included risks perceived to lack benefits, including handguns, drugs, smoking and alcohol. The factor scores were taken to indicate a contrast between 'legitimacy' and 'illegitimacy' with regard to the perceived risk, a result regarded as consistent with those of psychometric studies of risk perception in other countries. Legitimacy of activities and technologies, as well as their ideological and ethical dimensions, do influence individuals' risk perception (see Sjöberg & Winroth 1986).

The conclusion drawn from the French study was that risk perception is related not only to the activity, substance or technology of concern, but also to a more general 'feeling of security' that 'a society as a whole procures to its members' (Bastide *et al.* 1989). This idea draws on Emile Durkheim's (1951) classic theory of suicide as a social fact, which posits that a lack of social control and rules of conduct in a society make individuals disoriented and poorly integrated. According to Bastide *et al.* (1989), individuals in a state of anomie due to a vulnerable and insecure social position – which might be triggered by divorce, poverty, illness or unemployment – can experience a sense of hopelessness which creates a tendency to overestimate risk. In cases where risk perception studies have included respondents with marginal social status, their ratings of perceived risk indeed have tended to be very high (Nyland 1993; Sjöberg *et al.* 1996). Poverty might therefore be considered as a determinant of a higher risk perception as it correlates with struggling for survival and the experience of a range of threats on an everyday basis (Nyland 1993: 90).

American studies of risk perception among ethnic minority groups also point in a similar direction. Reviewing this field of research, Vaughan and Nordenstam (1991) concluded that for many environmental risk issues there are significant differences in risk perception associated with ethnicity, gender, socioeconomic status and education. Concerning technological risk, the literature reported significantly higher concern among ethnic minorities about nuclear power and nuclear waste. In the United States, a vast majority of ethnic minorities have been unsupportive of this technology, and, compared to whites, a greater proportion of them wants to phase out the operation of existing plants (Gallup 1979, 1986). A Swedish study by Olofsson and Rashid (2011) similarly showed higher levels of perceived risk among respondents of ethnically 'foreign backgrounds' than occurred among the locally born population.

Results indicating higher levels of perceived risk by ethnic minorities should take into account the physical conditions of the neighbourhoods in which they live. To a greater extent than the majority population, ethnic minorities in the United States live in urban environments characterised by air and solid waste pollution. Poverty is the primary demographic variable associated with high perceived risk, and this relationship was independent of the actual levels of pollution present in a community (Cutter 1981).

Economic and educational status tend to confound attempts to examine the role of ethnicity: ethnic minorities tend to have lower education, lower income and lower socioeconomic status. Poor economy, bad housing conditions and neighbourhood instability have more power than does ethnicity in explaining the variability of risk perception between social groups. In Swedish society a foreign background is associated with being underprivileged and having an inferior social status, and those circumstances likely conditioned the attitudes of respondents to risks. In the United States, low-income minority groups live in older, poorly built houses and closer to hazardous chemical or toxic waste sites. Ethnic minorities often are more at risk at work as well, in industry, agriculture and mining with poor working conditions and higher exposure to dust and toxic materials. All these circumstances likely contribute to an increased perceived risk (Vaughan & Nordenstam 1991). Underprivileged people of colour are also more exposed to drugs and violence and have higher mortality rates than the more well-to-do white part of the population (see also Flynn, Slovic & Mertz 1994).

Aside from these misgivings, theoretical and methodological doubts have been raised about ethnicity being a determinant of risk perception (see Vaughan and Nordenstam 1991: 53–54). Members of ethnic minorities often are grouped together as a single category, and there is need for a much more differentiated approach. Equally, the heterogeneity evident within ethnic groups should also be accounted for (varying levels of education, income, etc.). Such factors often are not controlled, and it is therefore far from proven that 'ethnicity' actually explains variation in risk perception between Anglo Americans and minorities.

Studies that have employed respondents differentiated by occupational groups have come to the conclusion that occupation partly determines risk perception (Goszczynska et al. 1991; Nyland 1993; Sjöberg et al. 1996). In two studies, one comparing Brazil and Sweden (Nyland 1993) and the other comparing Romania and Bulgaria (Sjöberg et al. 1996), samples of nurses all gave high ratings of perceived risk, whereas all ratings by engineers and 'manual workers' were low. Aiming to account for socio-cultural dimensions to the understanding of risk, a comparative study of perceptions of the risks from pollution in a rural industrial town in China specifically looked at professional groups (Tilt 2006). Three occupational groups were compared: industrial workers, commercial and service sector workers and farmers. Perceptions of seven risk 'themes', or values at stake, were investigated: human health, agriculture, landscape, animal health, economy, food chain and longevity. All groups gave quite high risk ratings to each of the themes, but industrial workers consistently provided lower ratings than did the other two groups.

The suggested explanation is that 'denial' of risk constituted an adaptive strategy for industrial workers, as they depended upon the comparatively high incomes received whilst working in polluted factory environments, and had few opportunities for other means of livelihood.

Gender and risk perception

A recurrent finding of research is that women exhibit a different sensitivity to risk than do men (Bastide *et al.* 1989; Flynn *et al.* 1994; Gustafson 1998; Kleinhesselink & Rosa 1991, 1994; Karpowicz-Lazreg & Mullet 1993; Olofsson & Rashid 2011; Teigen, Brun & Slovic 1988; Sjöberg *et al.* 1996; Royal Society Study Group 1992: 109). An overview of American research concluded that women tend to express greater concern for risk associated with technology and the environment. This tendency was particularly strong for nuclear technologies, environmental pollution and health risk deriving from local facilities (Davidson & Freudenburg 1996). This gender effect has been noticed both with regard to ratings of risk magnitude and specific hazard items and also with respect to the ordering of hazards on qualitative dimensions.

An American study (Flynn *et al.* 1994) explored the effects of ethnicity and gender on perceptions of environmental health risks. An intriguing finding was the 'white male effect': the mean ratings of white men were considerably lower than the means of the other three groups: non-white men, white women and non-white women. Non-white men and all women showed only one statistically significant difference: on the personal risk perception questionnaire, men gave lower ratings to the item 'stress'. When the low-scoring white men were treated as a special sub-sample and were examined with respect to societal characteristics, it emerged that these respondents generally were better educated, had higher income, were politically more conservative and were also more likely to express stronger trust in government, authority and industry than the other categories of respondents. A cross-national study of risk perception in Bulgaria and Romania by Sjöberg *et al.* (1996) to some extent provided similar results: women were more sensitive to risks than (some) men. In the Bulgarian sample the difference between men and women was small – both men and women experienced their environment as highly insecure. However, in Romania there was a substantial difference between men and women and, generally, women rated risk as greater than did men. For both samples, the three variables gender, country and group interacted. Olofsson and Rashid's (2011) study of risk perception in Sweden did not find a white male effect, attributing this result to the relatively high gender equality in Swedish society in terms of general ideology, parental social benefits and labour legislation. Taken together, the results of these studies suggest that gender effects vary cross-nationally.

The study by Kleinhesselink and Rosa (1994) reported significant gender differences in the perception of technological risk. Women in both the American and the Japanese student samples perceived a higher number of risk issues as 'dreaded' and 'catastrophic', while men perceived more risk issues as 'uncontrollable', 'newer', and 'lacking scientific knowledge'. American women dreaded social (crime and guns) and medical hazards more than men did. Japanese men were more likely to perceive some risks as 'involuntary', but for Americans the pattern was reversed, with women being more likely to perceive risk as 'involuntary'. In this respect Japanese women and men were more like their American gender opposites. Both Japanese men and American women were less likely to think that individuals have knowledge about risk. Japanese men focused on lack of knowledge concerning medical risk and some non-nuclear technologies (dams and fossil-fuel electrical power), while American women thought that individuals lacked knowledge about environmental risk and nuclear technology. Irrespective of nationality, men were more likely than women to perceive risk as being more novel. There were no gender differences with respect to self-efficacy. A significant gender-by-culture interaction was noted: Japanese men had significantly higher risk vulnerability than Japanese women, and this finding was reversed in the American sample. For the involuntary dimension, a puzzling gender reversal appeared: Japanese men and American women viewed more risk issues as 'involuntary'. According to Kleinhesselink and Rosa (1994), a higher sense of risk vulnerability combined with political fatalism may contribute to a perception of risk as 'involuntary'. They suggest that these results point to intriguing 'cross-cultural, cross-gender reversal': gender effects on risk perception reflect a subtle interaction between factors that relate to culturally and socially construed agency.

Why should women generally perceive higher risk? A biological explanation, refuted by Flynn et al. (1994), suggests that since women bear children and tend to have the main responsibility for raising them, they will be more concerned about health and safety. Such biological factors should apply uniformly across social, ethnic and national boundaries. This is not the case. Explanations of gendered risk perception instead point to social factors, such as power relations, inequality, institutional trust, social roles and norms, gendered practices and ideology (Davidson & Freudenberg 1996; Gustafson 1998). In American society, for example, women, in general, have less familiarity with science and might therefore distrust technology, which they may perceive as somewhat alien and male dominated (Davidson & Freudenburg 1996). In the study by Flynn et al. (1994), it was not the responses of women that stood out as peculiar but that of white men with power, good income and education and who gave very low ratings of perceived risk. An interpretation of this result is that because white men primarily control, manage and benefit from the world, they also see it as less risky. A major conclusion of this study, therefore, was that gendered risk perception must be explored from perspectives emphasising 'the role of power, status, alienation, trust, and other sociopolitical factors' (Flynn et al. 1994: 1107).

Kahan et al. (2007) undertook another study of the 'white male effect' on perceived risk in a sample of American respondents. Three sets of risk issues formed the focus: 'environmental risk' (sub-divided further into nuclear power, global warming and environmental pollution), firearms and abortion. Overall, a white male effect was evident; white males rated risk significantly lower than white females and than African American respondents of both sexes. A key finding was that risk perception for the three sets of risk issues varied according to four types of 'cultural world views': hierarchic, egalitarian, individualist and communitarian. The next section pursues the role of world view and values in general as explanatory variables for perceived risk and in the cultural theory of risk.

World views and general values

According to the cultural theory of risk, perceived risk is a cultural construal shaped by the general orientations or world views of the observers. People have different risk perceptions not primarily because they belong to separate nationalities but because they have separate world views, including general orientations on the role of the individual in society and on the constitution of the relationship between the social group and its members (Adams 1995; Dake 1991; Douglas 1992; Douglas & Wildavsky 1982; Rayner & Cantor 1987; Tansey & O'Riordan 1999; Thompson et al. 1990; Wildavsky & Dake 1990). Cultural theory has been both well received and criticised as a theoretical contribution to research on risk perception. It has contributed to a broadening of the research field of risk perception to include not only individual psychological factors but also the influence of social and cultural parameters. Critique of cultural theory, however, argues that the theory is able to explain risk perception only to a limited extent (Marris, Langford & O'Riordan 1998; Sjöberg 1996, 1997; also see next chapter). A study in the United Kingdom by Marris et al. (1998) to test the cultural theory and the psychometric theory of risk perception found that the cultural biases predicted by the theory – hierarchy, individualism, egalitarianism and fatalism – did not form homogeneous group-like clusters. Using 13 risk issues referring to various technologies, products and activities, the study also found very low correlations between risk perception and cultural bias.

Cultural theory has not been employed to any great extent in cross-national studies of risk perception. A reason for this lack of application presumably is that cultural theory defines 'culture' as cultural bias – a set of given mental and cognitive orientations – which as an explanatory variable does not coincide with nation-state or other geographical-political boundaries. Cultural theory partly informed a complex study by Rohrmann (1994) of risk perception that combined cross-national comparisons with comparisons of sub-groups within each country. This study focused on differences between four 'societal groups/cultural orientations' designated as 'technological', 'ecological', 'monetarian' and 'feminist' in Germany, New Zealand and Australia. The structure of risk judgments of a number of hazards based on a wide range of evaluative criteria was analysed by means of statistical modelling of the causal relationships between cognitive elements and group characteristics. Risk acceptance was found to be determined by consid-erations of the perceived risk's 'magnitude' and the 'benefit' associated with the identified risk. Concern about 'health impacts' was greater than that about the 'probability of dying'. Attitudes such as environmental concern, negative evalu-ations of technology and 'post-materialist' value orientations appeared to have considerable influences on risk perception. Cross-national comparisons revealed differences between the Australian and German respondents: Australians were more accepting of sport-related risk and 'unhealthy' private behaviours, and gave lower risk ratings to 'conventional' technologies. Risk-exposed occupations, environmental pollution and large-scale technology such as nuclear energy were given more negative evaluations in Australia. The results from Australia and New Zealand were quite similar apart from slight discrepancies regarding earthquakes, a hazard much more familiar to the New Zealanders. Rohrmann's (1994) findings give support to the idea that societal groups affiliated with particular professional, cultural and political orientations differ considerably in their identification and evaluation of risk and that this also is true across national boundaries.

A cross-national study was conducted in Australia, England, France, Germany and the Netherlands in 1986–87 (Eiser *et al.* 1990) to examine perceptions of nuclear power in the immediate aftermath of the Chernobyl accident using the theory of cognitive dissonance, which states that people will strive to reduce inconsistencies between contradictory cognitions (Festinger 1957). In all five countries the rated seriousness of the accident covaried with attitudes on other topics pertaining to nuclear matters. Furthermore, there was a strong relationship between more pronuclear attitudes and more right-wing political preferences. These results suggest that attitudes to nuclear issues form part of much broader value systems and ideologies. Similar results regarding the risk perception of nuclear power are reported from the United States. A study by Whitfield *et al.* (2009) based on national survey data shows that attitudes to nuclear power are explained by several factors, such as perceived risk and trust in science and the nuclear industry, and that 'traditional' values were associated with more positive attitudes to nuclear power.

Risk issue comparison – cross-nationally and across local settings

Interest in broad, comparative cross-national studies of risk perception based on the psychometric paradigm has dwindled today. A development towards more contextual approaches focusing on public perception of a limited set of risk issues now is evident. Lorenzoni *et al.*'s 2007 study of how citizens in the United Kingdom and the United States respectively understand the issue of global warming/climate change is a good example of contemporary cross-national research. The study explores understandings of this risk issue using a more open-ended qualitative analysis of national surveys. Respondents in both countries understood this risk issue as personally distant; it was conceived as a threat without immediate personal relevance. It also was associated with other atmospheric problems, such as the ozone hole. But there were also cross-national differences: unlike the British, Americans did not associate global warming with human health.

Using longitudinal survey data, a study by Poortinga, Ayoagi and Pidgeon (2013) compared public perceptions of climate change and future energy sources in Britain and Japan, both before and after the Fukushima nuclear disaster in March 2011. Even before the accident, the Japanese respondents were less accepting of nuclear power than the British, and afterwards they had almost completely lost trust in risk regulation by authorities. Attitudes in Britain towards nuclear power and trust in regulation of the industry were shown to be more positive overall and also more stable over time.

In a comparative ethnographic case study of understandings of risk, governmental trust and risk regulation in a German and a UK industrial town, Phillimore *et al.* (2007) identified different traditions and modes of public engagement with environmental risk within each locality. Risk regulation in the German town was found to be elitist and technocratic, historically rooted in strong local bonds of trust and loyalty between trade unions, industry and local politicians. Room for public engagement was limited there, and industrial pollution was framed as a normal state requiring adaptation rather than drastic measures to reduce risk. Matters were different in the United Kingdom, where industrial pollution was seen as a risk issue and was highly contested politically. Public concern was outspoken, and several initiatives were made by regulators to engage in public dialogue, although the citizens were highly distrusting of government and regulators.

Comparative studies of risk perception have shown a growing interest in the local context of specific, and often highly contested, risk issues. Combining questionnaires and focus groups, Poortinga *et al.* (2004) undertook a comparative study of local risk perception and attitudes to risk management in the aftermath of the foot and mouth disease (FMD) crisis in the United Kingdom. The study examined two towns that had different exposure to FMD. In both cases, respondents expressed a high level of concern over FMD as a risk to health, the welfare of animals, the rural economy and the psychological well-being of humans. Regarding causes of FMD, blame was put mainly on the European Union, the British government, food retailers and consumers who wanted 'cheap' food. Regardless of their residence, respondents were highly critical of the ways in which authorities had handled the disease outbreak. Just minor differences in attitudes and perceptions between respondents of the two towns were found, even though the inhabitants of one had much more direct contact with the agricultural sector and, presumably, the effects of the crisis.

Focusing on indoor radon and overhead power line radiation, Poortinga, Cox and Pidgeon (2008) used questionnaire data in another UK study to explore how physical proximity and exposure to a risk issue influences risk perception, trust and attitudes to acceptance of risk. The results showed that risk perception varied in relation to exposure in terms of the proximity of the respondent to the risk source. The suggested explanation is that the salience of a risk issue derives from how relevant it is as a matter of local concern. Another conclusion was that people living in areas with high indoor radon levels not only were the most concerned about this risk, but also believed that the risk was acceptable. This group also had a greater degree of trust in the regulatory authorities.

Similarly, Signorino (2012), focusing on two petrochemical sites in Sicily, Italy, found that risk perception correlated positively with proximity to a source of industrial pollution. Parkhill *et al.* (2010) also explored the effects of local proximity to a risk issue in a qualitative interview study of two communities living close to a nuclear plant. Respondents here framed the nuclear risk in a way that emphasised its normality and familiarity – it was part of everyday life. This meta-narrative of nuclear power was not, however, absolutely stable, as scenarios such as major accidents, terrorist attacks or unexpected events at the plant or in its vicinity were brought up in the interviews as instances that could disrupt normality and create moments of worry and anxiety about risk.

Discussion

Apart from the psychometric paradigm, comparative studies of risk perception form a heterogeneous field of research that displays little agreement on basic theoretical issues and a low consensus about research problems or methodology. This is not surprising considering that we are dealing with a research field that has attracted scholars from diverse disciplines and attendant academic traditions. A general finding of comparative studies is that perception of risk is uniform in some respects and variable in others; cross-national results contain 'mixed bags' of similarities and differences (Kleinhesselink & Rosa 1991: 22). Although humans live in a multifaceted world, they share similar concerns to some extent, since modernisation and current information systems ensure the rapid, global dissemination of new technological achievements, lifestyles, modes of thinking and perception. Depending on a complex interplay of factors – such as organised safety systems, technological infrastructure, living and housing conditions, public health, levels of pollution and the quality of government and other institutions in combination with natural, climatic and geographic conditions – people in various parts of the world will be exposed to diverse hazards of different magnitudes. It is plausible to accept that road traffic is considered relatively more dangerous in Brazil, Hong Kong and Hungary than it is in the United States and Sweden, because traffic conditions are not the same. Road traffic indeed is more aggressive and crowded and is conducted at higher speed with less regulation; in older, less-safe cars; with poorer driver education; and on more dangerous roads in some countries than in others. Such factual features of the local environment may well be reflected in risk perception and so contribute to cross-national variation for reasons other than cultural considerations (Kleinhesselink & Rosa 1991, 1994).

One perhaps disconcerting lesson is that it is far from easy to accomplish cross-national comparisons of risk perception. Collecting data in two or more countries, comparing the results and proffering plausible explanations may present no particular problem, but such interpretations still tend to be problematic overall. There is a repeated emphasis in the literature that in all societies there are real hazards implying real risk. It is assumed that people are realists and so are aware of such factual circumstances and that this awareness is reflected in the ratings offered in response to questionnaires. As elaborated below, such common-sense scholarly interpretations will be of limited value since they are proffered as *post hoc* explanations of results and are uninformed by a theory of risk as a social and cultural construct.

As anthropology has demonstrated, the environment is socially produced and re-produced over generations (Ingold 2000). We should ask, why are vehicles and roads of poorer standard and traffic more dangerous in some countries than in others? This question will lead to other questions about allocation of resources, power relations, authority, morality, equity, rights and duties, justice and honour, questions about meanings of symbols and values that sustain and promote one kind of world rather than another. Researchers in the field of risk perception therefore need to problematise findings from comparative studies in the light of contextual information, taking into account the relative, observer-dependent construction of risk. For example, to discover that Hong Kongese perceive it to be highly risky to ride a bicycle in city traffic and to explain that finding in terms of the objective characteristics of traffic in that city (Keown 1989) does not tell us much about risk perception. Returning to a cornerstone of anthropological theory about human society, namely the idea that human societies constitute 'ultra-complex' systems, dependent on higher-order, intuitive and conventional systems for processing information (Rappaport 1996), we should not merely pose questions about the factual and metric properties of the environment and its specific, instrumental aspects.

Comparative cross-national and cross-cultural risk perception studies need to address questions about how risk is embedded in the social fabric and take into account 'conceptions of morality, equity, justice, and honour; religious doctrine; ideas concerning sovereignty, property, and rights and duties; and aesthetic values and what constitutes quality in life' (Rappaport 1996: 65). In order to avoid producing new empirical results accompanied by trivial explanations just for the sake of it – a fallacy of unrestrained empiricism (Faucheaux 1976) – comparative exploration of risk perception should be guided by relevant front-line research in behavioural and social disciplines and strive to formulate theoretically well-founded designs that allow more profound interpretations. Hence, as Mangen (1999) has suggested, qualitative case studies are a valuable methodological asset in the development of contrastive insights into how public perceptions of risk are sensitive to social context (see for example Vari, Kemp & Mumpower 1991; Parkhill *et al.* 2010; Phillimore *et al.* 2007; Poortinga *et al.* 2004, 2008, 2013).

References

Adams, J. 1995. *Risk*. London, UK: UCL Press.

Alasuutari, P. (ed.). 1999. *Rethinking the media audience*. London, UK: SAGE.

Bastide, S., Moatti, J.-P., Pages, J.-P. & Fagnanai, F. 1989. Risk perception and the social acceptability of technologies: the French case. *Risk Analysis* 9: 215–223.

Berry, J.W. 1980. Introduction to methodology. In *Handbook of cross-cultural psychology: Volume 2, Methodology*. Triandis, H.C. & Berry, J.W. (eds.), pp. 1–28. Boston, MA & London, UK: Allyn & Bacon, Inc.

Berry, J.W., Poortinga, Y.H., Segall, M.H. & Dasen, P.R. 1992. *Cross-cultural psychology: Research and applications*. Cambridge, UK: Cambridge University Press.

Bloch, M. & Parry, J. (eds.). 1982. *Death and the regeneration of life*. Cambridge, UK: Cambridge University Press.

Clarke, L. & Short, J.F. 1993. Social organizations and risk: Some current controversies. *Annual Review of Sociology* 19: 375–399.

Cutter, S. 1981. Community concern for pollution: Social and environmental influences. *Journal of Environmental Psychology* 13: 105–124.

Dake, K. 1991. Orientating dispositions in the perceptions of risk: An analysis of contemporary worldviews and cultural biases. *Journal of Cross-Cultural Psychology* 22(1): 61–82.

Davidson, D.J. & Freudenburg, W.R. 1996. Gender and environmental risk concerns: A review and analysis of available research. *Environment and Behavior* 28: 302–339.

Douglas, M. 1992. *Risk and blame: Essays in cultural theory*. London, UK: Routledge.

Douglas, M. & Wildavsky A. 1982. *Risk and culture: An essay on the selection of technological and environmental dangers*. Berkeley, CA: University of California Press.

Durkheim, E. 1951 [1897]. *Suicide*. New York, NY: Free Press.

Eiser, J.R., Hannover, B., Mann, L., Morin, M., van der Pligt, J. & Webley, P. 1990. Nuclear attitudes after Chernobyl: A cross-national study. *Journal of Environmental Psychology* 10: 101–110.

Englander, T., Farago, K. & Slovic, P.A. 1986. Comparative analysis of risk perception in Hungary and the United States. *Social Behaviour* 1: 55–66.

Faucheaux, C. 1976. Cross-cultural research in experimental social psychology. *European Journal of Social Psychology* 6: 269–322.

Festinger, L. 1957. *A theory of cognitive dissonance*. Evanston, IL: Row, Peterson.

Fischhoff, B., Slovic, P., Lichtenstein, S., Read, S. & Combs, B. 1978. How safe is safe enough? A psychometric study of attitudes towards technological risks and benefits. *Policy Sciences* 9: 127–152.

Fiske, J. 1987. *Television culture*. London, UK: Methuen.

Flynn, J., Slovic, P. & Mertz C.-K. 1994. Gender, race and environmental health risks. *Risk Analysis* 14: 1101–1108.

Gallup Organization. 1979. Nuclear power plants. *Gallup Report* 167: 8–12.

Gallup Organization. 1986. Nuclear power plants. *Gallup Report* 250: 16–19.

Goszczynska, M., Tyszka, T. & Slovic, P. 1991. Risk perception in Poland: A comparison with three other countries. *Journal of Behavioural Decision Making* 4: 179–193.

Gustafson, P.E. 1998. Gender differences in risk perception: Theoretical and methodological perspectives. *Risk Analysis* 18(6): 805–811.

Gustafsson, K.E. & Weibull, L. 1996. European newspaper readership – an overview. In *Europeans Read Newspapers*. Brussels: European Newspaper Publishers Association.

Hantrais, L. & Mangen, S. (eds). 1996. *Cross-national research methods in the social sciences*. London, UK & New York, NY: Pinter.

Hinman, G.W., Rosa, E.A., Kleinhesselink, R.R. & Lowinger, T.C. 1993. Perceptions of nuclear and other risks in Japan and the United States. *Risk Analysis* 13: 449–455.

Huntington, R. & Metcalf, P. 1979. *Celebrations of death: The anthropology of mortuary ritual.* Cambridge, UK: Cambridge University Press.

Ingold, T. 2000. *The perception of the environment: Essays on livelihood, dwelling and skill.* London, UK & New York, NY: Routledge.

Kagitcibasi, C. & Berry, J.W. 1989. Cross-cultural psychology: current research and trends. *Annual Review of Psychology* 40: 493–531.

Kahan, D.M., Braman, D., Gastil, J., Slovic, P. & Mertz, C.K. 2007. Culture and identity-protective cognition: Explaining the white male effect in risk perception. *Journal of Empirical Legal Studies* 4(3): 465–505.

Karpowicz-Lazreg, C. & Mullet, E. 1993. Societal risk as seen by the French public. *Risk Analysis* 13: 253–258.

Kasperson, R.E., Renn, O., Slovic, P., Brown, H.S., Emel, J., Goble, R., Kasperson, J.X. & Ratick, S. 1988. The social amplification of risk: A conceptual framework. *Risk Analysis* 8: 177–188.

Keown, C.F. 1989. Risk perceptions of Hong Kongese vs. Americans. *Risk Analysis* 9: 401–405.

Kleinhesselink, R.R. & Rosa, E. 1991. Cognitive representations of risk perceptions: A comparison of Japan and the United States. *Journal of Cross-Cultural Psychology* 22: 11–28.

Kleinhesselink, R.R. & Rosa, E.R. 1994. Nuclear trees in a forest of hazards: A comparison of risk perceptions between American and Japanese university students. In *Nuclear power at the crossroads: Challenges and prospects for the twenty-first century.* Lowinger, T.C. & Hinman, G.W. (eds.), pp. 101–119. Boulder, CO: International Research Center for Energy and Economic Development.

Kohn, M.L. (ed.). 1989a. *Cross-national research methods in sociology.* London, UK: SAGE.

Kohn, M.L. 1989b. Cross-national research as an analytic strategy. In *Cross-national research methods in sociology.* Kohn, M.L. (ed.), pp. 77–102. London, UK: SAGE.

Lévy-Leboyer, C., Bonnes, M., Chase, J., Ferreira-Marques, J. & Pawlik, K. 1996. Determinants of pro-environmental behaviors: a five-countries comparison. *European Psychologist* 1: 123–129.

Lichtenstein, S., Slovic, P., Fischhoff, B., Layman, M. & Combs, B. 1978. Judged frequency of lethal events. *Journal of Experimental Psychology* 4: 551–578.

Lorenzoni, I., Leiserowitz, A., de Franca Doria, M., Poortinga, W. & Pidgeon, N. 2007. Cross-national comparisons of image associations with 'global warming' and 'climate change' among laypeople in the United States of America and Great Britain. *Journal of Risk Research* 9(3): 265–281.

Lowrance, W.W. 1976. *Of acceptable risk: Science and the determination of safety.* Los Altos, CA: W. Kaufman.

Mangen, S. 1999. Qualitative research methods in cross-national settings. *International Journal of Social Research Methodology* 2(2): 109–124.

Marris, C., Langford, I.H. & O'Riordan, T. 1998. A quantitative test of the cultural theory of risk perceptions: comparison with the psychometric paradigm. *Risk Analysis* 18(5): 635–647.

Miller-Loessi, K. 1995. Comparative social psychology. Cross-cultural and cross-national. In *Sociological perspectives of social psychology*. Cook, K.S., Fine, G.A. & House, J.S. (eds.), pp. 397–420. Boston, MA: Allyn & Bacon, Inc.

Nyland, L.G. 1993. *Risk perception in Brazil and Sweden*, Rhizikon: Risk Research Report, 15. Stockholm, Sweden: Center for Risk Research, Stockholm School of Economics.

Olofsson, A. & Rashid, S. 2011. The white (male) effect and risk perception: Can equality make a difference? *Risk Analysis* 31(6): 1016–1032.

Otway, H.J. & von Winterfeldt, D. 1982. Beyond acceptable risk: On the social acceptabilities of technologies. *Policy Sciences* 14: 247–256.

Parkhill, K.A., Pidgeon, N., Henwood, K.L., Simmons, P. & Venables, D. 2010. From the familiar to the extraordinary: Local residents' perceptions of risk when living with nuclear power in the UK. *Transactions of the Institute of British Geographers, NS*, 35: 39–58.

Phillimore, P., Schlüter, A., Pless-Mulloli, T. & Bell, P. 2007. Residents, regulators, and risk in two industrial towns. *Environment and Planning C: Government and Policy* 25: 73–89.

Poortinga, W., Bickerstaff, K., Langford, I., Niewöhner, J. & Pidgeon, N. 2004. The British Foot and Mouth crisis: A comparative study of risk perception, trust and beliefs about government policy in two communities. *Journal of Risk Research* 7(1): 73–90.

Poortinga, W., Cox, P. & Pidgeon, N. 2008. The perceived risks of indoor radon gas and overhead powerlines: A comparative multilevel approach. *Risk Analysis* 28(1): 235–248.

Poortinga, W., Ayoagi, M. & Pidgeon, N. 2013. Public conceptions of climate change and energy futures before and after the Fukushima accident: A comparison between Britain and Japan. *Energy Policy* 62: 1204–1211.

Poumadere, M., Mays, C., Slovic, P., Flynn, J. & Johnson, S. 1995. What lies behind public acceptance? Comparison of US and French perceptions of the nuclear power option. In *The Nuclear Power Option*. Vienna: Proceedings of an international conference on the nuclear power option organized by the International Atomic Energy Agency, Vienna, Austria, September 1994.

Rappaport, R.A. 1996. Risk and the human environment. *Annals of the American Academy of Political and Social Science* 545 (May): 64–74.

Rayner, S. & Cantor, R. 1987. How fair is safe enough? The cultural approach to societal technology choice. *Risk Analysis* 7: 3–9.

Renn, O. & Rohrmann, B. (eds.). 2000. *Cross-cultural risk perception: A survey of empirical studies*. Dordrecht, the Netherlands: Kluwer Academic Publishers.

Renn, O., Burns, W.J., Kasperson, J.X., Kasperson, R.E. & Slovic, P. 1992. The social amplification of risk: Theoretical foundations and empirical applications. *Journal of Social Science Issues* 48: 137–160.

Rohrmann, B. 1994. Risk perception of different societal groups: Australian findings and crossnational comparison. *Australian Journal of Psychology* 46(3): 150–163.

Rohrmann, B. & Chen, H. 1999. Risk perception in China and Australia: An exploratory cross-cultural study. *Journal of Risk Research* 2(3): 219–241.

Rosa, G., Renn, O., Jaeger, C. & Webler, T. 1995. Risk as a challenge to cross-cultural dialogue. Paper presented at the XXXII Congress of the International Institute of Sociology, 'Dialogues Between Cultures and Changes in Europe and the World', Trieste, Italy, 3–7 July.

Royal Society Study Group (eds.). 1992. *Risk: Analysis, perception and management. Report of a Royal Society Study Group*. London, UK: The Royal Society.

Schooler, C. 1996. Cultural and social-structural explanations of cross-national psychological differences. *Annual Review of Sociology* 22: 323–349.

Short, J.F. Jr. & Clarke, L. (eds.). 1992. *Organizations, uncertainties and risk*. Boulder, CO: Westview Press.

Signorino, G. 2012. Proximity and risk perception. Comparing risk perception 'profiles' in two petrochemical areas of Sicily (Augusta and Milazzo). *Journal of Risk Research* 15(10): 1223–1243.

Sjöberg, L. 1996. A discussion of the limitations of the psychometric and cultural theory approaches to risk perception. *Radiation Protection Dosimetry* 68: 219–225.

Sjöberg, L. 1997. Explaining risk perception: an empirical evaluation of cultural theory. *Risk Decision and Policy* 2(2): 113–130.

Sjöberg, L. 1999. Risk perception in Western Europe. *Ambio* XXVIII (6): 543–549.

Sjöberg, L. 2003. The different dynamics of personal and general risk. *Risk Management* 5(3): 19–34.

Sjöberg, L. & Winroth, E. 1986. Risk, moral value of actions, and mood. *Scandinavian Journal of Psychology* 27: 191–208.

Sjöberg, L., Kolarova, D., Rucai, A.-A., Bernström, M.-L. & Flygelholm, H. 1996. *Risk perception and media reports in Bulgaria and Romania*. Stockholm, Sweden: Center for Risk Research, Stockholm School of Economics.

Slovic, P., Fischhoff, B. & Lichtenstein, S. 1980. Facts and fears: Understanding perceived risk. In *Social risk assessment: How safe is safe enough?* Schwing, R.C. & Alberts, W.A. Jr. (eds.), pp. 181–216. New York, NY: Plenum Press.

Stallings, R.A. 1990. Media discourse and the social construction of risk. *Social Problems* 37: 80–95.

Tansey, J. & O'Riordan, T. 1999. Cultural theory and risk: a review. *Health, Risk & Society* 1(1): 71–90.

Teigen, K.H., Brun, W. & Slovic, P. 1988. Societal risks as seen by the Norwegian public. *Journal of Behavioural Decision Making* 1: 111–130.

Thompson, M., Ellis, R. & Wildavsky, A. 1990. *Cultural theory*. Boulder, CO & San Francisco, CA: Westview Press.

Tilt, B. 2006. Perceptions of risk from industrial pollution in China: A comparison of occupational groups. *Human Organization* 65(2): 115–127.

Triandis, H.C. & Berry, J.W. 1980. *Handbook of cross-cultural psychology: Volume 2, Methodology*. Boston, MA & London, UK: Allyn & Bacon, Inc.

Tversky, A. & Kahnemann, D. 1973. Availability: A heuristic for judging frequency and probability. *Cognitive Psychology* 4: 207–232.

Vari, A., Kemp, R. & Mumpower, J.L. 1991. Public concerns about LLRW facility siting: A comparative study. *Journal of Cross-Cultural Psychology* 22: 83–102.

Vaughan, E. & Nordenstam, B. 1991. The perception of environmental risks among ethnically diverse groups. *Journal of Cross-Cultural Psychology* 22: 29–60.

Viklund, M.J. 2003. Trust and risk perception in Western Europe: A cross-national study. *Risk Analysis* 23(4): 727–738.

Vlek, C.J.H. & Stallen, P.J.M. 1980. Rational and personal aspects of risk. *Acta Psychologica* 45: 273–300.

Vlek, C.J.H. & Stallen, P.J.M. 1981. Judging risks and benefits in the small and in the large. *Organizational Behaviour and Human Performance* 28: 235–271.

af Wåhlberg, A. & Sjöberg, L. 1997. Risk perception and the media. A review of research on media influence on public risk perception. *Journal of Risk Research* 3(1): 31–50.

von Winterfeldt, D. & Edwards, W. 1984. Patterns of conflict about risky technology. *Risk Analysis* 4: 55–68.

Whitfield, S.C., Rosa, E.A., Dan, A. & Dietz, T. 2009. The future of nuclear power: Value orientations and risk perception. *Risk Analysis* 29(3): 425–437.

Wildavsky, A. & Dake, K. 1990. Theories of risk perception: Who fears what and why? *Daedalus* 112: 41–60.

3

RISK PERCEPTION AND SOCIAL ANTHROPOLOGY

The contribution from cultural theory

In his book *Risk society: Towards a new modernity*, the German sociologist Ulrich Beck outlined a theory of post-modern society (Beck 1992). Adopting a historical and sociological meta-perspective, Beck saw a transition from modern industrialised society, constituted by social classes, to a new form of society, still industrialised but in which solidarity based on class interest had lost much of its old significance. In this new era of highly individualised 'reflexive modernity', the main issue was not the distribution of wealth between social classes as of old but the distribution among individuals of the hazards and dangers produced by society. In terms of technology, economic development and management, unwanted side effects and trustworthiness, modernity itself becomes a focal topic of concern, resulting in a constant preoccupation with the various risk scenarios and possible dangers associated with modern life. Following Beck, the members of 'risk society' – scientists as well as ordinary citizens – will be engaged actively in the production of political and moral discourse on technological dangers and human-induced threats to nature and the human body.

As shown in Chapter 1, a growing number of social scientists from various disciplines have argued that perception of risk cannot be studied in isolation from the society at large. The works of social anthropologist Mary Douglas, explicitly addressing the topic of risk across cultures, have had a major impact on the formulation of problems of risk in relation to culture and society. Based on Douglas' grid-group theory of society, the 'cultural theory of risk' formulated by her and collaborators, such as political scientist Aaron Wildavsky, social anthropologists Michael Thompson and Steve Rayner and social psychologist Karl Dake, has been used in a program to 'predict and explain what kinds of people will perceive which potential hazards to be how dangerous' (Wildavsky and Dake 1990: 42). Cultural theory argues that how people understand and react to various kinds of risk issues can be explained neither by traits of personality nor because human beings in general act according to any given hierarchy of psycho-physiological needs and preferences;

instead, risk is seen as culturally 'biased' and perception of risk as being conditioned by socially embedded values and beliefs. Hence, choices of risk taking and avoidance are understood to be made selectively on the basis of 'way of life' or world view.

Since the early 1980s, cultural theory has produced a considerable amount of literature addressing the topic of risk (Tansey & O'Riordan 1999). Cultural theory was outlined by Michael Thompson, Richard Ellis and Aron Wildavsky (1990) in the book *Cultural theory*. It has also been explored in a number of other works by, among others, Adams (1995); Dake (1991, 1992); Douglas (1985, 1992, 1996); Douglas and Wildavsky (1982); Fardon (2013); Kahan (2012); Rayner (1992, 1987); Rayner and Cantor (1987); Schwartz and Thompson (1990); and Wildavsky and Dake (1990). However, as noted by Rayner (1992: 84), despite cultural theory's grand aspirations, its empirical results tend to be rather meagre:

> Cultural theorists have made few systematic empirical studies of risk perception and management. The studies that do exist tend to be scholarly analysis of past debates and decision making about technology rather than contributions to the solutions of current problems. It appears that while the principles of cultural theory have been enormously influential, its practical applications have been very limited (Rayner 1992: 84).

Why should this be the case? If a theory is influential in a field, one should expect the production of a substantial body of high-quality research, yielding new insights and increasing knowledge. Apparently, for cultural theory this was not so, with empirical results failing to match the claims and attempts to empirically test its hypotheses being largely unsuccessful (Marris, Langford & O'Riordan 1998; Sjöberg 1997). This lack of empirical substantiation of the theory has raised concern about the validity of the measurement scales used and, more broadly, about whether or not cultural theory can actually be tested at all on individuals rather than on the group (Rippi 2002).

Defining 'way of life': cultural bias and social relations

Cultural theory is a general sociological theory about the structural relationship between individuals and society, constructed by way of deduction from a limited number of basic axioms. The theory provides a basic distinction between on the one hand, 'cultural bias', defined as 'shared values and beliefs', and, on the other, 'social relations', defined as relationships between individuals. The crucial explanatory concept 'way of life' is defined as a 'combination of social relations and cultural bias' (Thompson, Ellis & Wildavsky 1990: 1). The relationship between cultural bias and social relations is described thus in the book *Cultural theory*:

> Causal priority, in our conception of ways of life, is given neither to cultural bias nor to social relations. Rather each is essential to the other. Relations and biases are *reciprocal, interacting*, and *mutually reinforcing*. Adherence to a certain pattern of social relationships *generates* a distinctive way of looking at the

world; adherence to a certain worldview *legitimizes* a corresponding type of social relations (Thompson, Ellis & Wildavsky 1990: 1 [italics added]).

However, the picture presented is confusing conceptually, since the characterisations imply contradictory positions. Cultural bias (defined as shared values and beliefs) and social relations (defined as patterns of interpersonal relationships) are stated to be closely interrelated, yet they also are analytically distinct. Words such as 'reciprocity', 'interaction' and 'mutual reinforcement' suggest an organic-like interdependency within a systemic whole. Multi-causal links operate in both directions: cultural bias and social relations reinforce and condition each other. But it is also stated that social relationships generate 'a distinctive way of looking at the world', i.e., a particular cultural bias, which in turn is stated to 'legitimate' a particular set of social relations. In the last chapter of *Cultural Theory*, when discussing the grounds by which the theory might be empirically refuted, it is suggested that a piece of counter-evidence would be if it could be proved that values are little 'constrained' by 'institutional' relationships (Thompson, Ellis & Wildavsky 1990: 273). So, in addition to the list of possible relationships among values and beliefs and social relations, we should therefore add 'constraint'.

Furthermore, Thompson, Ellis and Wildavsky argue that since they must be compatible, the possible combinations of cultural biases and social relationships are constrained:

> A change in the way an individual perceives physical or human nature, for instance, changes the range of behavior an individual can justify engaging in and hence the type of social relations an individual can justify living in. Shared values and beliefs are thus not free to come together in any which way; they are always closely tied to the social relations they help legitimate (Thompson, Ellis & Wildavsky 1990: 2).

A way of life is understood as a predetermined combination of cultural bias (shared values and beliefs) and specific types of social relationships. Changes in shared values and beliefs will necessarily lead to changes in social relationships, and vice versa. However, the characterisation of the link between the two dimensions of social life is somewhat confusing. A link that is said to be 'reciprocal', 'interactive' and 'reinforcing' suggests a two-directional connection, but if values and beliefs are 'generated' or 'constrained' by social relations, this suggests a connection that goes one way.

It appears, then, that cultural theory harbours two diverging theoretical conceptions of way of life. An interactive model of way of life, suggestive of a Weberian conceptualisation of society, states that people organise their social relations in accordance with their values at the same time as their values are also influenced by those same social relations. This is well in line with fairly conventional sociological theory, postulating that people live in a social world, where they have organised themselves in a certain manner, interact with their fellows and think and feel in accordance with the organisations they have created, and that their beliefs and values are part of this system and consequently influence how they act and interact within it. On the other hand, the view that social relations 'constrain' the values and beliefs people have, so that certain values and beliefs are not possible given certain types of social relations, indicates a more deterministic, Marxist-like functionalist conception. Values and beliefs are also said to be 'generated' by social relationships, the former being causally produced by the latter. The argument that values and beliefs legitimate social relations by conserving and maintaining them paraphrases the classical Marxist view of the relationship between the economic base (the relations of production) and the superstructure (the ideological system).

It can be argued that determinism finds little support in human history. It is possible for systems of values and beliefs to change social relations and generate new social structures. One famous example is Max Weber's (1958) classic study of the influence of the Calvinist ethic of work on the growth of industrial capitalism. Contrary to the belief that social relations automatically constrain or determine ideational systems, social anthropologists have shown that it is quite possible to have systems of ideas and beliefs with little or no correspondence with forms of social organisation. To paraphrase Claude Lévi-Strauss, certain ideas might just be good to think. They exist in their own right as elements in symbolic structures that are self-explaining and have their own validity irrespective of social and economic structures (see for instance the discussion on ideal marriage rules in relation to social practice in Morocco [Bourdieu 1990 (1980); Lévi-Strauss & Didier 1991 (1988)]).

A typology of cultural bias

Douglas (1978, 1992) addressed the problem of cross-cultural comparison and has developed the grid–group theory model to compare societies irrespective of their place in time and space. Gross and Rayner (1985) have discussed the methodological dimensions and implications of the grid–group model when it comes to the study of perceptions of technological risk. The dimensions 'grid' and 'group' are taken to be universal in human society. Cultural theory conceptualises these dimensions as gradual coordinates that measure 'possible social structures' (Douglas 1978: 7). Douglas offers the following characterisation of the term 'group':

> The group itself is defined in terms of the claims it makes over its constituent members, the boundary it draws around them, the rights it confers on them to use its name and other protections, and the levies and constraints it applies. Group is one obvious environmental setting, but we seem unable to conceive of the individual's environment if it is not a group of some kind (1978: 8).

Analysis of social structure, of how people are interconnected to form various aggregates, has been a long-standing theoretical problem in social anthropology. Despite this, Douglas characterises a social group as an 'obvious' setting. One lesson from the literature preoccupied with social structure, however, is that social categories should be distinguished from social groups (Keesing 1976: 231). People who belong to a common category – for example, vegetarians – share certain characteristic features that distinguish them from other people – in this case, not eating meat – and in particular contexts, they might be considered as a special category of people. 'Groups' refers to bounded, conventionally recognised and collectively represented social units to which people belong due to some kind of activity or belief which they exercise together with other group members (such as a vegetarian dinner collective). It is characteristic of groups that they are not reducible to individual members. Individuals are replaced, but the group persists as an institutionalised, ongoing social order. A social network, in contrast, is made up of interpersonal relationships; as individuals come and go, so the relationships, and thus the network, change. It needs noting that well-established conceptual distinctions among 'categories', 'groups' and 'networks' are taken lightly indeed by cultural theorists.

Reconsidering the classical issue of methodological individualism vs. collectivism, the conventional sociological concept of a 'group' has been critically revised in various ways (Verdon 1981, 1980). Far from being obvious entities, human groups tend to be evasive, ambiguous and complex, the analysis of which often is marred by theoretical confusion. Dimensions pertaining to the behaviours of individuals, to the aggregation of people into groups and to the norms of complex systemic units are not analysed sufficiently. Contradictory definitions and presuppositions might be used interchangeably or in an inconsistent manner. A critique has been raised that most definitions of groups are reductionist, falling back on interpersonal behaviour and invoking norms, values, beliefs or ideologies as active powers (Verdon 1981, 1980). Consequently, as pointed out by Verdon, social cohesion – a feature of the aggregate level of a social group – needs to be analysed in its own right and not as a feature deriving from individuals' mental representations.

Douglas explains the other dimension of grid-group theory, 'grid', as follows:

> The term grid suggests the cross-hatch of rules to which individuals are subject in the course of their interaction. As a dimension it shows a progressive change in the mode of control. At the strong end there are visible rules about space and time related to social roles; at the other end, near zero, the formal classifications fade, and finally vanish. At the strong end of grid, individuals do not, as such, freely transact with one another. An explicit set of institutionalized classifications keep them apart and regulates their interactions, restricting their options (1978: 8).

If the extreme poles of the grid and group scales are combined with each other so that they form a diagram, four universal 'cosmological types' (also denoted 'ways of life' in other texts) emerge, from which decisive cultural orientations can be deduced. According to Douglas, these orientations will include notions that concern fundamental and ever-present human issues such as nature, foreign people and places, animals, death, medicine, cookery, moral judgment, taste, aesthetics, justice and retribution. It should be noted that although grid and group each are presented as if they were gradual scales, when combined to form a typology, they function as binary pairs. Grid-group theory identifies a set of 'cosmological types', all of which, in principle at least, are taken to coexist in every society (see Figure 3.1).

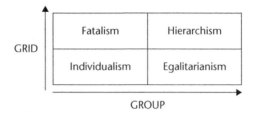

Figure 3.1 The four cosmological types according to grid-group theory

It is argued that each cosmological type implies a characteristic stance towards the environment, other people and the self and, since they offer different solutions to problems encountered in life, that each makes its own 'bid for space, time and resources for a particular social organization' (Douglas 1996: 175). The cosmological types will also contest each other (see also Douglas 1996: 83–85). A fifth possibility that is considered occasionally is the autonomous state of hermit-hood, which holds a position detached from the grid-group classification. In Thompson, Ellis and Wildavsky (1990: 3) these 'cosmologies' are termed 'ways of life' and there are 'five and only five ways of life – hierarchy, egalitarianism, fatalism, individualism and autonomy'.

The individual's cultural bias

Individual preferences are of focal interest for cultural theory even though it rejects psychological variables. Individuals are conceptualised as socially constrained: 'ways of life channel the thought and behaviour of individuals' (Thompson, Ellis and Wildavsky 1990: 2). Advocates of cultural theory often appear to imply that there is a one-to-one correspondence between an individual and a particular way of life, at least in principle. The individual struggles to support and maintain a way of life through appropriate actions and beliefs. People therefore will be one of four, or even five, kinds: egalitarians, hierarchists, individualists, fatalists and autonomists. Within society individuals' tastes, moral preferences, consumer habits and attitudes towards government as well as their ideas about surrounding nature are moulded by the common way of life, so that they share with their fellows a standardised mode of living (Douglas 1996). Cultural theory states that each way of life in this way constitutes a bounded rationality, a self-explanatory system of mutually reinforcing beliefs, values and social relationships (Rayner & Cantor 1987: 4). Each world view implies distinct ways of coping with contingency by way of adopting conventionalised interpretative schemes. Misfortune, it is argued, is not only imbued with meaning but actually strengthens the world view; the efficacy of the world view is restated through the presence of potential bad outcomes. Casting blame; ideas about pollution, purity and danger; and actions undertaken to counteract various instances of threat and defilement therefore serve to support and sustain a way of life (Douglas 1966).

Each way of life, furthermore, corresponds to one of four (or even five) basic 'myths of nature' (Thompson, Ellis & Wildavsky 1990: 26–29; Dake 1992;

Douglas 1996: 85–90). Egalitarians are afraid of technology and hold that it has little benefit; they think that nature is ephemeral, fragile and vulnerable. Individualists claim that nature is benign, affluent and full of promise ('cornucopian'). Hierarchists are afraid of social deviance; they regard nature as being 'perverse/tolerant', bound by certain rules: it will be benign if treated properly or dangerous if the rules are violated. Fatalists regard nature as 'capricious' and unpredictable. Autonomists, being asocial, do not care.

However, a circularity of evidence mars this typology and its claims to explanatory power. For example, Dake formulates the following hypotheses: 'hierarchists should express great concern about behaviors such as demonstrations and civil disobedience because they see these acts as disrespectful to the authority'; 'egalitarians . . . are predicted to abhor the role differentiation characteristic of hierarchy because ranked stations signify inequality'; and 'individualists . . . support self-regulation, especially the freedom of bid and bargain' (Dake 1991: 66). Since the conclusions are already contained in the premises, these predictions can hardly be considered as proper hypotheses. To predict that 'a greedy person strives to appropriate wealth belonging to others' cannot qualify as a research hypothesis, since the predicted behaviour 'greediness' is already semantically entailed in the agent's being 'a greedy person'. Dake's explanations regarding the egalitarian's abhorrence of 'role differentiation', the hierarchical person's concern for law and order and the individualism of the individualist are trapped in the very definitions of these ways of life.

A recent development in cultural theory (Kahan *et al.* 2007; Kahan 2012) offers a modified model of risk perception, which adds an element of 'cultural cognition'. Cultural cognition is a social psychological theory stating that an individual's group membership affects how they process information (Kahan *et al.* 2007). It is argued that group membership creates a sense of well-being and that if beliefs held by a group are challenged, individual members will experience a threat to their identity. Using an identity-protecting mechanism, individuals will therefore process information (on risk or any other matter) in a biased manner. Empirical findings about how American individuals perceive various risk issues, such as climate change, nanotechnology, guns, vaccines and abortion, arguably demonstrate that 'cultural world views' explain risk perception (Kahan *et al.* 2007, 2009; Kahan 2012).

A problem with these studies, similar to that exhibited by the work by Dake (1991), is a circularity of reasoning and measurement. Cultural cognition studies focus empirically on risk issues that in American society are all strongly contested. Attitudes towards these issues reflect well-defined and strongly polarised political ideologies regarding the standing of the individual vis-à-vis the collective, the citizen vis-à-vis the state and freedom versus restrictions. It is hardly surprising, therefore, that the characterisation of world view by cultural theory co-varies with particular perceptions of risk regarding the selected issues. Based on the same parameters that are used to characterise individual perception, political ideology can be expected to structure the social discourse regarding abortion or guns (at least in the United States).

Another problem with the cultural cognition studies is the black box approach taken to the risk issues investigated. The risk of guns does not mean the same thing for an advocate of the right to bear arms as it does for someone who does not believe in gun ownership. Guns constitute an ambiguous risk issue: the right to carry a gun might be conceptualised as either a value at stake or a risk object depending on the perspective of the observer. Likewise, in the case of abortion rights, what constitutes the value at stake (the rights of the mother, the rights of the foetus, or the principle of life) depends very much on the observer. Therefore, it is not very clear what conclusions actually can be made from comparison of risk perception between different sub-populations (Kahan *et al.* 2007).

In contrast to other social sciences, cultural theory purports to explain 'why people want what they want' (Dake 1991: 63–65), but the explanations that are offered, to be blunt, merely reduce to 'people strive for things that they want'. This reasoning implies a circular use of culture as an explanatory concept. It has been a common fault in anthropology to regard culture as an all-inclusive category serving in a circular manner as an explanatory concept both for observable events, actions and artefacts produced by human beings and for the ideational systems of shared knowledge, beliefs and meanings understood to structure conduct (Schneider 1973: 119). Used in this multi-purpose way, the concept of culture offers merely tauto-logical explanations: people of culture A habitually do X because they share this particular culture A that prescribes them to do X.

Cultural theory echoes the grand culture and personality project of the 1940s and 1950s in American anthropology (Bock 1988) when it presupposes a one-to-one correspondence between way of life and individual orientation, although it does refrain from using 'personality' as an explanatory device when discussing risk perception. Motivated by the Second World War and then the Cold War, the US government urgently wanted to detect what kind of personality was attracted to 'democracy', or to 'totalitarianism', or what personality profile characterised enemy nations, like Japan (Benedict 1946). Anthropologists like Margaret Mead, Ruth Benedict and others argued that personality constituted a microcosm of culture, and that culture was to be understood as a macroscopic projection of personality. Benedict's (1934) classic comparative study of personality and culture had used clinical and psychoanalytical models to diagnose four basic cultural personality types: the Apollonian, exemplified by the Pueblo Indians, who were 'moderate'; the Dionysian, exemplified by the Plains Indians, who were 'excessive' and 'sensory'; the Paranoiac, exemplified by the Dobuans, who were suspicious and full of fear; and finally the Megalomaniac, exemplified by the Kwakiutl Indians, who were aggres-sively competitive and destructive.

Culture was understood within the culture and personality school to correlate with personality stereotypes. Various attempts to assess and measure such types were made by using concepts such as 'national character' or 'modal personality', which refer to the most frequent personality characteristics in a particular group. Anthropologists and psychologists combined fieldwork with batteries of projective tests in their efforts to discern the relationship between culture and personality. In the light of modern insights, both in cross-cultural psychology and in anthropology, this entire project has many shortcomings, circularity of reasoning being the most glaring:

> one inferred a society's basic 'personality type' by observing culturally stan-dardized ways of behaving, and then 'discovered' that this was a culture which people with that personality would fit in nicely (Keesing 1976: 204).

One underlying assumption of cultural theory is a 'configurationalist' assump-tion that there is a neat correspondence between culture and individual orienta-tion, the latter taken to be a microscopic version of the former (Berry *et al.* 1992: 180–181). A major problem with this kind of theory is that it assumes the existence of detached world views, conceptualised as bounded, consistent, self-supporting and self-explaining yet mutually incompatible perspectives that leave no room for new information or change of orientation. As envisaged by cultural theory, a soci-ety is crowded with people adhering to disparate ways of life, the presuppositions of which having nothing in common. Consequently, since people simultaneously live in 'worlds apart' in their own society, they are unable to communicate or under-stand each other. Individualists, hierarchists, egalitarians, fatalists and autonomists all have completely different perspectives on life.

A critique has been raised that a typology comprising a limited number of stereo-types will run into difficulties should it attempt to account for complex social real-ity, inhabited not by imagined constructs but by real people. Johnson (1987) raised this point early on in his discussion of American environmental movements and the difficulties of fitting them into the scheme of grid-group classification. Discussing various criticisms of cultural theory, Rayner (1992: 102) dismisses Johnson's argu-ment as a pointless 'gut-level objection' against using categorisation in social theory. But why assume that the only alternative to the cultural theory stereotypes is to refrain from analytical distinctions altogether? There is a vast difference between research that explores cultural categories as these are articulated in society and research that imposes pre-conceived and arbitrary constructs. Two approaches are often distinguished in discussions about cultural comparison (Harris 1976). The *etic* approach, which adopts an external perspective, uses an apparatus of descriptive and explanatory devices – typologies, categories, and concepts – achieved by means of comparison and generalised reasoning. The *emic* approach, which analyses culture in terms of indigenous distinctions and categories, assumes an internal perspective. The crucial point is that these two approaches, far from being incompatible, need to be combined in the various stages of the research process (see Bourdieu 1977). For cultural theory, however, cultural relativism is accepted only within a pre-defined conceptual framework; etic considerations rule decisively over emic ones.

How to account for social dynamics?

Recognising the dilemma that social life is processual and dynamic and that individ-uals as well as social institutions change, a 'ghost' that makes 'the machine' move must be introduced. For cultural theory, that ghost is individual choice and the principle of self-interested maximisation. So, in order to circumvent the static picture of a society of the mutually alienated – individualists, fatalists, hierarchists, egalitarians and auton-omists – each clinging to their own 'way of life' and unable to understand the others', it is argued that people indeed are well aware of and understand other world views. The reason for this lies with the idea that they have rationally chosen their world view and that they could therefore at any moment opt for an alternative. In what is char-acterisable as an alternative version of cultural theory, ways of life are understood to take form in relation to one another; they constitute alternatives, and each way of life therefore suggests its opposing way of life (Thompson, Ellis & Wildavsky 1990: 13).

Douglas presents a similar argument regarding cultural bias and grid-group anal-ysis that is said to account for the 'cumulative effect of individual choices' (1978: 13). Cultural theory proclaims that ways of life are competitive, soliciting adherents, and that if people recognise that a cherished cosmology is no longer sensible or viable, they may abandon it for another, more viable one. Such shifts from one way of life to another might occur if an individual is confronted by a cumulative mass of 'surprise'. This experience is defined as 'the discrepancy between the expected and the actual' and is taken to be of 'central importance in dislodging individuals from their way of life' (Thompson, Ellis & Wildavsky 1990: 3):

> Both theories and ways of life are resistant to change; anomalies are explained away, pigeonholed, ignored, or just not seen. . . . But ways of life, like theo-ries, cannot exclude reality altogether. As evidence builds up against theories, or as ways of life do not pay off for adherents, doubts build up, followed by defections. A persistent pattern of surprise forces individuals to cast around for alternative ways of life (or theories) that can provide a more satisfying fit with the world as it is (Thompson, Ellis & Wildavsky 1990: 69).

If in the long run, values, beliefs and social relations no longer match 'reality' in the way expected, allegiances might strategically reorient towards another way of life or towards an alliance with a competing alternative (Thompson, Ellis & Wildavsky 1990: 86–87). It is notable that reality here is an external factor of change; people are assumed capable of perceiving 'reality' as it 'is' and appropriately manipulating their actions in response. It must be kept in mind that the social construction of perception – cultural bias – is a base-line argu-ment for cultural theory. A new term, 'constrained relativism' (Thompson, Ellis & Wildavsky 1990: 69), was introduced to cope with the coexistence of both possibilities – perception being ultimately constrained by social forms as well as by 'reality' as it 'is' – but this hardly solves the problem of theoretically recon-ciling two such contrary positions. Also, 'surprises' might be sorted into a nice typology. If the 'myths of nature' are combined with the 'ways of life', what will constitute surprise within each cosmology might be predictable (Thompson, Ellis & Wildavsky 1990: 71–75): An individualist would be surprised by the col-lapse of the market, an egalitarian by his own success, a fatalist by consistency and a hierarchist by the success of the incompetent and disobedient. Once again, these predictions are contained in the premises.

How does one sustain cultural theory's 'rationality postulate', that is, 'rational people support their way of life' (Thompson, Ellis & Wildavsky 1990: 96), if people in fact can choose between alternatives? Choices between ways of life presuppose a meta-rationality that transcends the bounded rationality of each cultural bias. Drawing an analogy between cultural biases and scientific theories, Thompson, Ellis and Wildavsky (1990: 69) suggest that culture-free, self-interested maximisation governs the social interaction of human beings who choose between alternative opportunities. It is assumed that people have a meta-awareness of cultural premises; not only are they aware of what they think and do, but also they distance themselves from their own way of thinking. A critical scrutiny of their world view could quite possibly lead to a deliberate abandonment of their prevailing 'thought style'. If cultural theory is believed, people would ask, depending on their 'level of cultural consciousness' (Thompson, Ellis & Wildavsky 1990: 2–3), questions like: which way of life matches 'reality' the best; which one makes me prosper; and which one explains the world in the most satisfying manner?

Evaluating this proposal requires a consideration that 'way of life' refers to an integrated system including a complete cosmology, an ontological system that structures the world and concerns basic topics of human life such as belonging, continuity, dominance, death, morality, aesthetics, taste, time, space and food, as well as concomitant social arrangements. There is very little, if any, evidence supporting the idea that individuals deliberately select their cosmology as well as the institutional settings they are embedded in. Such ideas are more in line with those of ethnomethodologists like Garfinkel (1967) or the dramaturgical perspective of Goffman (1969). Yes, people are pragmatic, and it is true that they manipulate and strategically operate their social environment, and break normative rules, but decades of research in anthropology and sociology provide evidence for the persistent and stable character of conventional cultural forms and social structures. Research into the history of mentalities and focusing on the stubborn and deep-rooted continuity of perceptions over long spans of time points in much the same direction.

Discussion so far has concerned two distinct versions of cultural theory, which both share the assumption that there is a one-to-one correspondence between an individual's orientation and way of life. These two versions differ in their views on the long-term stability of this bond. If individuals are understood to be determined by their way of life, the bond will be stable and static. But if, on the other hand, individuals themselves determine their way of life, actively choosing the most rewarding one, the bond will be construed as fragile and shifting. The modes for construing the relationship between individuals and ways of life are, however, not exhausted by these two possibilities. Yet another version of cultural theory claims that the correspondence is not between individuals and ways of life but between 'organisational contexts' and ways of life (Rayner 1987; Rayner & Cantor 1987). And even Thompson, Ellis and Wildavsky (1990: 265) propose that despite a certain 'strain to consistency', individuals may very well encompass more than one 'way of life'. Ways of life correspond in a one-to-one relationship not to individuals, but to 'social contexts'. Consequently, a person may very well be a hierarchist at work, an egalitarian at home and a fatalist in their spare time (Thompson, Ellis & Wildavsky 1990: 265). Individuals are then portrayed as mosaics of ways of life, each enacted in its proper context. The self is understood as 'compartmentalised' so that individuals are able to cope with 'multiple' social contexts that make different demands of them (Thompson, Ellis & Wildavsky 1990: 266). This version also invokes the principle of self-interested maximisation: an individual may find it beneficial to pursue different ways of life in different realms. In this version of cultural theory, society is presented as fragmented – a poorly integrated assemblage of incompatible, rival social contexts. Integration in such a society is accomplished by individuals who are knowledgeable of and competent in enacting each way of life in its proper surrounding and who are able to translate between diverging contexts, transforming and adapting to them. In this extreme, anti-Durkheimian view of society, social integration derives from individuals and their actions.

It is worth noting that Rayner (1992: 106–108), preferring the more 'dynamic', alternative version of cultural theory, admits that there is indeed a difference among cultural theorists in their beliefs of just how strongly individuals are 'locked' into a particular world view:

> Some, including Douglas, subscribe to the *stability hypothesis.* This states that individuals will seek to homogenize their experience of social structure in different areas of their lives. According to this view, individuals from hierarchical families will seek hierarchical jobs and join hierarchical organizations. . . . According to the *stability hypothesis*, it is possible to argue that individuals will tend actually to think exclusively in terms constrained by one of the four possible cultural types. An alternative view, the *mobility hypothesis*, posits that cultural theory is limited only to predicting how things can be said in a particular context. . . . Appeals to the common good are unlikely to carry much weight in the competitive marketplace, but arguments about opportunities for individual advancement might do well. According to this view, individuals may flit like butterflies from context to context, changing the nature of their arguments as they do (Rayner 1992: 107–108).

Where does this welter of ideas leave studies of risk perception? Can cultural theory predict anything useful for risk perception? Can it contribute to explorations of risk as a social phenomenon? When questioned about 'risk', in what mode will people answer? Do subjects respond in a hierarchist or an individualist, etc., mode, or perhaps in a hierarchist mode on the way to becoming an individualist mode? The alternatives are many, as is indicated by the typology of twelve types of 'microchange' reflecting one way of life changing into another (Thompson 1990: 75–78). To put it starkly, perhaps subjects will change their way of life during the course of an interview or while filling out a questionnaire. Equally, if way of life is tied to social contexts rather than individuals, why address individuals at all on the topic of risk (see Rippi 2002)? If way of life corresponds to social context, cultural theory would predict the answers to such questions to be entirely context-dependent. Questionnaires would be pointless, unless the methodology presupposed some sort of context-free research mode into which subjects entered when filling out forms or answering questions posed by social scientists.

In Dake's 1991 study, subjects were confronted with a list of propositions that should reveal their views on 'risk taking in society', among other things. They were asked to disagree or agree on a seven-point scale to propositions such as 'American society is becoming overly sensitive to risk; we now expect to be sheltered from all dangers' or 'Every citizen should become more informed about the great risks we are taking with our technological developments' (Dake 1991: 68). But if risk perception is determined by way of life and way of life corresponds to social context, and if individuals are assumed to be moving freely around, passing in and out of social contexts and their corresponding world views, how can these general and context-free questions and their concomitant answers be construed at all? If the responses proffered derive from the respondent's way of life, which in turn is dependent on social context, it would be necessary to clarify the response in relation to its context in order to assess it; how is that to be done?

Another problem is that the type of questions posed by Dake makes no distinction between verbally expressed normative standards and actual behaviour. First-year students of social anthropology or sociology are supposed to learn that there is considerable discrepancy between discourses on ideal, normative notions of social organisation and behaviour and what humans actually do. Verbal accounts of values and interactions cannot be taken as accurate descriptions of actual social life, perceptions and states of consciousness. In examining social interaction as well as in the constitution of individual persons, it is the verbal accounts that people produce and exchange that should be studied as formative and constructive forces in their own right:

> We need to see mental life as a dynamic activity, engaged in by people, who are located in a range of interacting discourses and at certain positions in those discourses and who, from the possibilities they make available, attempt to fashion relatively integrated and coherent subjectivities for themselves (Harré & Gillet 1994: 180).

Returning to cultural theory, it may be asked further, what is its analytical target? Advocates often state that it concerns individuals, although 'socially construed'; individual belief and action are the *explananda*. Cultural theory, however, seeks to move beyond explaining how mental characteristics of individuals influence their actions. It claims that dynamics at the institutional and organisational level of society – the market, the political establishment and corporate organisations – can be explained by the same biases that apply to individuals (Thompson & Wildavsky 1986; Wildavsky 1987). This means that occupational categories, political movements, corporate organisations and economic enterprises are characterised in exactly the same terms and with the same individual-focused conceptual apparatus. This creates a certain amount of confusion since individuals appear equated with institutions and organisations, which are equated with nations. Dealing with nations encounters the same confusion with shifting from rigid stereotypes to amorphism. For example, when assessing work by the political scientists Almond and Verba (1963), Thompson, Ellis and Wildavsky (1990: 248) state that 'in grid-group terms Italy is characterised by a fatalistic way of life, in which group involvement is low and social prescriptions are high'. However, when re-examining the notion of 'political culture' they *strongly reject* the tendency to homogenise national 'political' culture into fixed stereotypes, because the variation between political attitudes and values within a country often is larger than that between countries (Thompson, Ellis & Wildavsky 1990: 219). What is to be believed?

Discussion

Cultural theory suffers from the maladies characteristic of a functionalist paradigm. A long-published critique on the role of functionalist explanations in social anthropology offered the following verdict:

> A theory makes a satisfactory explanation when it is not circular, not ad hoc, and it is testable independently of the facts it is intended to explain. But a functional theory does not go beyond the facts it intends to explain; therefore a certain tinge of circularity, or of ad hoc-ness, is an inevitable consequence. To be told that the function of church-going is to express and reinforce social solidarity and that the main test of the desire to express and reinforce social solidarity is church-going is to get into a circle which cannot be broken in favor of a 'deeper' explanation. Circular, or ad hoc, or non-independently testable explanations do not tell us anything new; they are methodologically unsatisfactory (Jarvie 1968: 199).

This criticism could apply just as well to explanations forwarded by exponents of cultural theory today. This chapter presents the argument that cultural theory encompasses disparate and contradictory theoretical stances. Depending on empirical data at hand, cultural theory can therefore change from rigidity to flexibility, from methodological collectivism to methodological individualism. It is marred by the common faults of functionalist explanation: circular reasoning and inbuilt *ad hoc* causal mechanisms that refer to hidden parameters such as 'surprise', 'reality', 'maximisation', and 'rational choice'. If cultural bias governs perception, how can external factors like surprise, maximisation and meta-rational choice – unaccounted for by theory – be credited with crucial causal impact? By introducing such new terms, serving as *deus ex machina*, a static functionalist theory appears rejuvenated as a device capable of accounting for dynamic processes.

If cultural theory is profoundly lacking, in what other ways could social anthropology contribute to risk perception studies? What are the cultural dimensions of 'risk', and how could they be problematised and empirically investigated? In assuming that perception of risk depends on certain decisive factors that are generally classifiable, cultural theory aspires to be a general theory of risk. However, when discussing the meaning elements of risk – for example, the probability of an adverse event and the magnitude of its consequences – Rayner and Cantor (1987:4) conclude that 'risk', even when considered abstractly, is a 'polythetic' concept 'lacking any single essential feature'.

The observation that the various meanings of 'risk' merely share family resemblances ought to cast doubt on the value of a unified general theory of risk perception. What is the use of cultural theory if there is no discernible phenomenon that the theory can be applied to? To return to Beck's (1992) ideas, the debates produced by 'risk society' concern tangible or putatively concrete activities and objects that are perceived to be dangerous or potentially harmful, and new issues of worry emerge every day. Many diverse things get subsumed as a risk, for example, cigarette smoking, alcohol, automobile traffic, nuclear power, air and water pollution, greenhouse gases and climate change, allergenic substances, unhealthy food and catastrophic diseases. In this discourse, 'risk objects' are construed as culturally defined, conceptual 'things' understood to be characteristically 'risky' in some way or another. Putative harm is attributed to risk objects to form associative links (see Hilgartner 1992). The symbolic representation of risk objects in verbal discourse, as well as in non-verbal images and in ritual-like forms of expression, poses challenging research problems. Cultural theory's assumption that there are four or five given types of attitudes and relationships towards risk is a problem, because it takes the cultural construction of risk objects very much for granted.

The cultural meanings of risk objects could well be revealed by using the tenets of symbolic anthropology and focusing on the rich symbolism imbuing various kinds of risk objects in their various contexts. There needs to be further sustained study of the role of technology and its cultural construction in post-modern society. This chapter has presented arguments about some fundamental theoretical inconsistencies that mar cultural theory. Despite seemingly clear-cut conceptual packaging, on a closer examination cultural theory crumbles into an agglomeration of contradictory propositions which make empirical investigation of the emic dimensions of risk highly problematic.

References

Adams, J. 1995. *Risk*. London: UCL Press.

Almond, G.A. & Verba, S. 1963. *The civic culture: Political attitudes and democracy in five nations*. Princeton, NJ: Princeton University Press.

Beck, U. 1992 [1986]. *Risk society: Towards a new modernity*. London, UK: SAGE.

Benedict, R. 1934. *Patterns of culture*. New York, NY: Mentor.

Benedict, R. 1946. *The crysanthemum and the sword*. Boston, MA: Houghton Mifflin.

Berry, J.W., Poortinga Y.H., Segall M.H. & Dasen P.R. 1992. *Cross-cultural psychology: Research and applications*. Cambridge, UK: Cambridge University Press.

Bock, P.K. 1988. *Rethinking psychological change in the study of human action*. New York, NY: Freeman.

Bourdieu, P. 1977. *Outline of theory of practice.* Cambridge, UK: Cambridge University Press.

Bourdieu, P. 1990 [1980]. *The logic of practice.* Cambridge, UK: Polity Press.

Dake, K. 1991. Orientating dispositions in the perceptions of risk: An analysis of contemporary worldviews and cultural biases. *Journal of Cross-Cultural Psychology* 22(1): 61–82.

Dake, K. 1992. Myths of nature: Culture and the social construction of risk. *Journal of Social Issues* 48(4): 21–38.

Douglas, M. 1966. *Purity and danger: An analysis of concepts of pollution and taboo.* London, UK: Routledge & Kegan Paul.

Douglas, M. 1978. Cultural bias (Occasional paper No. 35). London, UK: Royal Anthropological Institute.

Douglas, M. 1985. *Risk acceptability according to the social sciences.* New York, NY: Russell Sage Foundation.

Douglas, M. 1992. *Risk and blame: Essays in cultural theory.* London, UK: Routledge.

Douglas, M. 1996. *Thought styles: Critical essays on good taste.* London, UK: SAGE Publications.

Douglas, M. & Wildavsky A. 1982. *Risk and culture: An essay on the selection of technological and environmental dangers.* Berkeley, CA: University of California Press.

Fardon, R. (ed.). 2013. *Mary Douglas – culture and crises: Understanding risk and resolution.* London, UK: SAGE.

Garfinkel, H. 1967. *Studies in ethnomethodolgy.* Englewood Cliffs, NJ: Prentice-Hall.

Goffman, E. 1969. *The presentation of self in everyday life.* London, UK: Allen Lane.

Gross, J.L. & Rayner, S. 1985. *Measuring culture: A paradigm for the analysis of social organization.* New York, NY: Columbia University Press.

Harré, R. & Gillet, G. 1994. *The discursive mind.* London, UK: SAGE.

Harris, M. 1976. History and the significance of the emic/etic distinction. *Annual Review of Anthropology* 5: 329–350.

Hilgartner, S. 1992. The social construction of risk objects: Or, how to pry open networks of risk. In *Organizations, uncertainties and risk.* Short, J.F. & Clarke, L. (eds.), pp. 39–53. Boulder, CO: Westview Press.

Jarvie, I.C. 1968. Limits to functionalism and alternatives to it in anthropology. In *Theory in anthropology: A sourcebook.* Manners, R.A. & Kaplan, D. (eds.), pp. 196–203. Chicago, IL & New York, NY: Aldine.

Johnson, B.B. 1987. The environmentalist movement and grid/group analysis: a modest critique. In *The social and cultural construction of risk.* Johnson, B.B. & Covello V.T. (eds.), pp. 147–175. Dordrecht, the Netherlands & Boston, MA: D. Reidel Publishing Company.

Kahan, D.M. 2012. Cultural cognition as a conception of the cultural theory of risk. In *Handbook of risk theory.* Roeser, S., Hillebrand, R., Sandin, P. & Peterson, M. (eds.), pp. 726–759. Berlin & Heidelberg, Germany: Springer.

Kahan, D.M., Braman, D., Gastil, J., Slovic, P. & Mertz, C.K. 2007. Culture and identity-protective cognition: Explaining the white male effect in risk perception. *Journal of Empirical Legal Studies* 4(3): 465–505.

Kahan, D.M., Braman D., Slovic, P., Gastil, J. & Cohen, G. 2009. Cultural cognition of the risks and benefits of nanotechnology. *Nature Nanotechnology* 4(2): 87–91.

Keesing, R.M. 1976. *Cultural anthropology: A contemporary perspective.* New York, NY: Holt, Rinehart & Winston.

Lévi-Strauss, C. & Didier, E. 1991 [1988]. *Conversations with Lévi-Strauss.* Chicago, IL & London, UK: University of Chicago Press.

Marris, C., Langford, I.H. & O'Riordan, T. 1998. A quantitative test of the cultural theory of risk perceptions: Comparison with the psychometric paradigm. *Risk Analysis* 18(5): 635–647.

Rayner, S. 1987. Risk and relativism in science for policy. In *The social and cultural construction of risk.* Johnson, B.B. & Covello, V.T. (eds.), pp. 5–23. Dordrecht, the Netherlands & Boston, MA: D. Reidel Publishing Company.

Rayner, S. 1992. Cultural theory and risk analysis. In *Social theories of risk.* Krimsky, S. & Golding, D. (eds.), pp. 83–115. Westport, CT: Praeger.

Rayner, S. & Cantor, R. 1987. How fair is safe enough? The cultural approach to societal technology choice. *Risk Analysis* 7: 3–9.

Rippi, S. 2002. Cultural theory and risk perception: A proposal for a better measurement. *Journal of Risk Research* 5(2): 147–165.

Schneider, L. 1973. The idea of culture in the social sciences: Critical and supplementary observations. In *The idea of culture in the social sciences.* Schneider, D. & Bonjean, C.M. (eds.), pp. 118–143. Cambridge, UK: Cambridge University Press.

Schwartz, M. & Thompson, M. 1990. *Divided we stand: Redefining politics, technology and social choice.* New York, NY: Harvester Wheatsheaf.

Sjöberg, L. 1997. Explaining risk perception: An empirical evaluation of cultural theory. *Risk Decision and Policy* 2(2): 113–130.

Tansey, J. & O'Riordan, T. 1999. Cultural theory and risk: A review. *Health, Risk & Society* 1(1): 71–90.

Thompson, M. & Wildavsky, A. 1986. A cultural theory of information bias in organizations. *Journal of Management Studies* 23(3): 273–286.

Thompson, M., Ellis, R. & Wildavsky, A. 1990. *Cultural theory.* Boulder, CO & San Francisco, CA: Westview Press.

Verdon, M. 1980. Descent: An operational view. *Man* n.s. 15: 129–150.

Verdon, M. 1981. Kinship, marriage and the family: An operational approach. *American Journal of Sociology* 86: 796–818.

Weber, M. 1958 [1930]. *The protestant ethic and the spirit of capitalism.* London, UK: G. Allen & Unwin.

Wildavsky, A. 1987. Choosing preference by constructing institutions: A cultural theory of preference formation. *American Political Science Review* 81(1): 3–22.

Wildavsky, A. & Dake, K. 1990. Theories of risk perception: Who fears what and why? *Daedalus* 112: 41–60.

4

SITUATED RISK

Culture and the management of uncertainty

Social anthropologist Mary Douglas and political scientist Aaron Wildavsky, in their much-cited book *Risk and culture*, argue that risk is created within culture (Douglas & Wildavsky 1982). They suggest that the meanings, the ontological qualities and the moral implications of risk are socially and culturally constructed by means of collectively shared representations. This theory claims that risk should be viewed as culturally and historically embedded and that there is no single rationality behind the knowledge of risk or the ways in which it is managed. The relativism of cultural theory, however, is not boundless. It is limited to a typology of four basic sociological forms as defined by grid-group theory, namely egalitarianism, individualism, fatalism and hierarchism (Douglas 1978).

As used within risk research, cultural theory has been understood as a paradigmatic break with methodological individualism in that it is not based on assumptions about individuals' following a 'maximisation of utility' rationale (Tansey & O'Riordan 1999). Cultural theory states that it aims to explain risk not from the thoughts, intentions and strategies of individuals but as a phenomenon shaped by social and cultural processes. As noted in Chapter 3, the theory has been highly influential in work by mainly psychologists and sociologists engaged in studies of how – paradoxically – individuals estimate risks, dangers or hazards (Dake 1991, 1992).

Douglas and Wildavsky (1982: 29) raised the question of how generations from before the advent of modern technology regarded risk and danger. In contrast to sociologists such as Beck (1992), Giddens (1990, 1991) and Baumann (1998), adherents of cultural theory acknowledge no principal difference between the explanation of misfortune in modern and in traditional societies. Explanations of risk in modern society are understood to fulfil the same social function as explanations of destiny, supernatural agency or broken taboo in traditional societies. In that they serve to maintain classificatory separations among individuals and among groups, all such explanations have the same function.

Cultural theory has paid particular attention to the phenomenon of taboo in traditional societies. In many traditional societies there are beliefs that certain actions or objects when combined with others will produce catastrophic consequences. An example discussed by Douglas and Wildavsky (1982) – and often cited by advocates of cultural theory to prove the point that risk is culturally 'selected' – refers to the ethnography of the Hima (Elam 1973). The Hima are a subgroup of the Nkole, a Bantu-speaking people occupying south-western Uganda. Traditionally, the Nkole are divided into two quite distinct social groups: the pastoral Hima, who make up about one-tenth of the population, and the agricultural Iru, who constitute the remainder. Hima subsistence depends on cattle products such as beef, milk and butter, but their diet is complemented by millet exchanged with their cattle-less agricultural neighbours. Hima cosmology revolves around a set of clear-cut pollution beliefs. A fundamental organising principle of their cosmology is that women should be strictly separated from cattle, lest any contact should cause sickness and death among the cattle. There is also a strict dietary prohibition stating that plant foods and milk products must never ever be mixed, since this too will cause sickness and death. According to Douglas and Wildavsky (1982: 47), Hima ideas about pollution are instruments of social control and constitute a way of resisting change.

This functionalist explanation of taboo emphasises the maintenance of social structure. Misfortune – such as the illness of a cow – demands an explanation, so a process begins immediately to search for agency and establish responsibility. Explanations in terms of taboo have a characteristic social dimension, because individuals or groups must be separated into categories such as victim(s) and culprit(s), the latter to be punished. Taboo therefore supports and maintains social order – gender divisions, social hierarchies, labour divisions and power relations – by suppressing actions that could lead to fission (Douglas 1966; Tansey & O'Riordan 1999: 74). According to cultural theory, risk, much like taboo, is a mechanism for social categorisation and division, so they structurally serve the same function although there is a 'difference of degree' (Tansey & O'Riordan 1999: 75).

It is notable that according to Hima beliefs, breaking a taboo has inevitable catastrophic consequences. It is not the case that the presence of a woman in a cattle pen brings the possibility of harm; it is a matter of certitude. As Douglas and Wildavsky (1982: 42–44) note, the Hima do not ask questions such as: Does one really get ill by eating vegetables in combination with milk? Would life be more prosperous if agriculture were to be practised together with animal husbandry? In fact, one could argue that their culture does not even allow the formulation of such questions. If a person becomes ill, or if a cow dies, such events post facto start a process of questioning in order to establish what taboo has been broken and by whom. Observance of a taboo therefore has little in common with risk management as a set of strategies to reduce uncertainty. Taboo expresses fate, a certainty about future events, while risk deals with possible bad outcomes (Rosa 1998). Risk can be managed, reduced or increased; it can be taken or it can be avoided. Risk and taboo therefore are analytical counterparts rather than belonging to the same generic conceptual category. A taboo spelling out the certainty that a cow dies if a woman comes into contact with it is fundamentally different from a scientific statement that women bear a contagious infection and that there is a five per cent probability the cow will become infected and die. Cultural theory simply fails to make this distinction between the accounts of an unwanted, negative event (Douglas 1992). As a consequence, cultural theory fails to address risk as a culturally specific mode of the epistemological ordering of contingency in modern society.

What is risk?

Sociologists such as Anthony Giddens (1990, 1991) and Ulrich Beck (1992) have addressed risk as a crucial feature of late modern society. A central theme in their work is that modern Western society has entered a new phase of historical development. Industrial production and the market have assumed novel structural features because of the great mobility of capital, people and technology all over the globe. The progression of late modernity has witnessed an erosion of traditional social relationships, groupings and identities. New concerns have emerged that reframe the relationship between humans and the environment and question the assumptions of industrial society regarding ecology and nature (Lash, Szerszynski & Wynne 1996). An era characterised by trust in social and political institutions and authentic being is over. The embedment of the individual in a firm order of meanings and expectations is disappearing. According to Giddens (1990), certainty has given way to uncertainty, resulting in a state of collapsing 'ontological security', a sense of fundamental vulnerability and a lack of faith.

Zygmunt Bauman (1998) points to a growing fear and a heightened sensitivity to all kinds of threats to meaningful existence as a characteristic of late modernity. So the food we eat, the water we drink, the air we breathe, our habits and lifestyles and, not least, the many technologies that we increasingly depend upon are more or less all imbued with an uncertainty as to what their effects might be. While some consequences are taken for granted as desired benefits, others lurk as possibly harmful outcomes. Yet citizens in modern nation states intuitively believe that they have a moral right not to be put at risk unwittingly unless there is good reason (Hansson & Peterson 2001). Governments and industry are also understood widely to have a moral obligation not to impose risk on the unsuspecting public. Many institutional contexts are crucial for how risk is framed and communicated. Science and technology map causes and effects, and the various news media disseminate information that often conveys that the world is a dangerous place to inhabit.

Issues of risk and safety become political and controversial because interests invariably diverge, whether between individuals or, more importantly, between social groups, corporations and organisations. The identification, definition and management of risk is subject to the hidden or declared strategies of political actors trying to achieve their goals: to win confidence, support and votes. The South African government's policy towards AIDS, the British government's handling of BSE (bovine spongiform encephalopathy – 'Mad Cow Disease'), the colza oil scandal in Spain (Mairal Buil 2003) and the environmental scandal of the

Hallandsås railway tunnel in Sweden (Boholm 2005; Boholm & Löfstedt 1999; Ferreira, Boholm & Löfstedt 2001; Löfstedt and Boholm 1999; Sjölander-Lindqvist 2004) illustrate how concerns about risk to human health and the environment can mushroom into intensely contested political affairs. Such events spotlight the distribution of benefits and disadvantages of modern technology and lifestyles, as well as the legitimacy and trustworthiness of government policy or the lack thereof. Questions on the management and distribution of risk can be expected to become even more intensely debated topics in the political arenas of the world.

Risk analysis focuses on how future conditions can be calculated as the results of cause and effect relationships. Risk assessment answers questions about the probability of getting cancer if exposed to a certain chemical, the chances of a catastrophic reactor breakdown at a nuclear plant or the likelihood of dying in a car accident. Framed as a risk, a hazard is assessed and an estimate is made of possible negative outcomes, together with strategies of mitigation. Using risk as a conceptual framework, modern science can compare hazards to arrive at conclusions such as whether there is a greater risk of death or injury when travelling by motorcycle than there is when travelling by train. This dimension of calculated risk can then be incorporated into societal risk management strategies as well as into individual decision making. For some, such risk assessments might be decisive in choosing a means of transport. The concept of risk can be understood as a framing device which conceptually translates uncertainty from being an open-ended field of unpredicted possibilities into a bounded set of possible consequences.

Risk commonly is defined in mathematical terms as the statistical probability of an outcome in combination with severity of the effect of the outcome, expressed as a cost given in terms of money, deaths or instances of ill health. As we have seen in Chapter 1, value is central to risk, and human health is a value *par excellence*. To cite an example, an article in a Swedish newspaper under the headline 'Polluted air makes many people sick' (Göteborgs-Posten 2000) presented a medical study of 380,000 individuals living in Gothenburg who had either died from or been hospitalised due to respiratory illness. The scientists established a statistical correlation between instances of death or sickness and the incidence of polluted air. The article concluded as follows: 'The risk of dying of lung or trachea diseases increases with the concentration of sulphates. Every increase of 1 microgram per cubic meter increases the risk by 5 per cent' [translation mine]. Here 'risk' refers to the statistical probability of an adverse event that has a known or hypothesised cause. By applying this probabilistic perspective, scientific analyses of risk allow comparisons between what may be very different risk issues. A low-probability risk that carries very severe consequences for a large population – say, a reactor meltdown in a nuclear power plant – can be compared to a high-probability risk with lesser consequences for a large population – such as a car accident. Under the paradigm of cost-benefit analysis and rational choice theory, these kinds of estimates and comparisons can serve as guidelines for decision makers, national regulatory bodies and policy makers as well as for individual citizens in their daily lives.

A distinction between objective (real) and subjective (perceived) risk has served as a conceptual baseline for much of the research on risk within the social and behavioural sciences (Hansson 2010; Lupton 1999; Renn 1998). 'Objective risk' refers to phenomena and causality in the natural world that can have harmful effects. It is the task of science to identify and assess sources of potential harm, to identify measurable correlations and then to assess the probabilities of the harmful outcome. The concept of subjective risk acknowledges that people's beliefs and opinions often deviate from scientific assessments. As revealed in Chapter 2, psychological studies have shown that non-technical assessments of risk are not based purely on a calculation of the product of the estimated statistical probability and the estimated adverse effect. The psychometric model of risk perception involves dimensions such as the amount of knowledge, the degree of novelty and familiarity, the degree of personal control and the catastrophic potential (see Slovic 2000).

As discussed in Chapter 1, categorising something as a 'risk' implies the presence of value. By definition, the concept of risk integrates descriptive/factual and normative components (Hansson 2010; Möller 2012). Thus, in stark contrast to taboo, what is and what is not a risk is open intrinsically to negotiation and contestation (Renn 1998; Shrader Frechette 1991). Statistical probability is a mathematical concept that quantifies the chances of an event's or occurrence's coming to pass, but it has limited relevance for a non-technical understanding of risk. People do not always make rational decisions about risk that take into account scientific assessment and abstract principles of rationality (Renn *et al.* 2000) so as to arrive at the optimal response prescribed by the rational actor paradigm of decision theory. Rational choice theory focuses on decision-making problems in an idealised, isolated context where every new piece of information will be undisturbed by associations with contradictory knowledge. Decisions are never made in a social and cultural vacuum; on the contrary, they emerge from culturally framed 'horizons of choice' (Boholm, Henning & Krzyworzeka 2013). Decisions about risk and its management are socially embedded, shaped by culturally based notions about the state of the world, what the world consists of and how it works (Purcell, Clarke & Renzulli 2000). Cultural notions tell us intuitively what is potentially dangerous and harmful and what is not, and provide us with explanatory models as well as moral guidelines as to why certain things or actions are good or right whilst others are bad or evil.

A conundrum of risk and culture

As shown in Chapter 2, a major objective of comparative cross-national studies has been to test current theories, such as the psychometric model or cultural theory, in addition to examining risk perception in various countries and across continents. One lesson from cross-national research is that there are similarities as well as differences in the perception of risks (Kleinhesselink & Rosa 1991: 22). Some reported differences can be accounted for by the presence or absence of actual risks that are peculiar to a country or a region. Poor drinking water, environmental pollution, terrorist attacks or heavy and dangerous road traffic are simply more prominent threats to some populations than to others. Nevertheless, other findings of difference are puzzling and less easy to dismiss as circumstance specific.

There are many examples of different national responses to risk. For instance, Portugal has had nearly as many cases of BSE as has the United Kingdom, yet there has been a notable absence of public concern or debate about health risks to humans from eating beef. In neighbouring Spain, on the other hand, where actual cases of BSE have been comparatively few, there has been vigorous debate and public distrust in government regulation, with a concomitant decrease in meat sales. In another food-related example, growth hormones in milk or beef are permitted in the United States by the authorities and there has been little active consumer opposition. Quite to the contrary in Europe, neither consumers nor regulators accept such hormones, construing them as dubious additives and a risk to health. The list of examples could be made longer with ease.

In the home environment, the French have shown little interest in the child safety products of the IKEA company, whereas such products make up a salient segment of IKEA's sales in Sweden. Why is that so? The factual risk of children coming to harm in their everyday environment is fairly universal, since children are accident prone. But how the risks relating to children are identified is far from being the same everywhere. One way of answering the question about why the French and the Swedes differ in their views on how to manage child safety would be to look for underlying conceptualisations of risk as it relates to children. One possible framing of such a conceptualisation would be in terms of potential danger in the environment surrounding the child; an unsafe environment constitutes a setting of 'risk objects' potentially threatening the child's well-being (Boholm & Corvellec 2011; Hilgartner 1992). If a child falls out of a window, the accident might be understood to have been a result of a poor design or unsafe construction of the window. In this conceptual framework, risk reduction management for children would then single out electrical appliances, steep stairs without railings, windows without locks, toys that could be swallowed or stoves without barriers to hinder the spillage of boiling water. Strategies will be developed to control all kinds of environmental features to make them less dangerous, less unpredictable.

There are, however, other ways to conceptualise children's relationships with their everyday environment. In a Spanish study in applied anthropology, the focus was on child safety with special regard to traffic risk in urban environments (Buxó i Rey 1996; Buxó i Rey & Torrijos 1999). The essence of this project was that children are conceived of as the primary risk objects to themselves rather than features of the environment. Viewed in this way, considerable effort is made to teach children to act responsibly by paying attention to safety matters in all kinds of contexts: playing on the playground, walking on the sidewalk of a street or riding a bicycle. If children are understood to be inherently unreliable, acting impulsively and therefore constantly at risk from all sorts of accidents, risk management strategies will focus on strict supervision of the child, in combination with educational measures to teach them how to behave safely. If a child falls out of a window, the accident is not seen primarily as a result of the state of the window but as a case of inadequate adult supervision combined with insufficient effort to teach the child to act in a safer way. From this perspective, it might even be argued that making the environment physically safer, for example, by means of furnishing the home with child safety equipment, could actually increase rather than diminish the risk of injury to children, since they will not get the opportunity to learn about the dangers of life. Teaching children moral and practical responsibility for their actions so that they learn to foresee the conse-quences, in terms of risk to themselves and others, will therefore be the basic risk management strategy. Examples like those mentioned here indicate that what is considered as a risk in any particular social context depends on relationships construed between a value at stake and culturally informed assumptions about potential threats.

Coping with uncertainty

Uncertainty is a fundamental dimension of risk (Rosa 1998). If people perceive that their livelihood, health or well-being is threatened, they will respond with various coping strategies, be they technical, political, religious or economic mobil-isation or combinations of such activities (Rappaport 1996). In everyday life, the boundary between certainty and uncertainty seldom is razor sharp, and vagueness and ambiguity tend to be the rule rather than the exception. The dynamic shift between certainty and uncertainty constitutes the core of the matter in any cultural conceptualisation of risk.

Economic anthropology often distinguishes between two aspects of uncertainty (Cancian 1980; Cashdan 1990). On the one hand, there are known risks which people are prepared for and for which they have adopted preventative strategies, and on the other, there are things about which knowledge is inadequate and for which there are no established management procedures. If both outcomes and probabilities are accepted as known, risk can be calculated by weighing probabilities against outcomes to arrive at a 'rational' decision. In contrast, when outcomes and probabilities are seen as uncertain, rational choice clearly has limited value as a strat-egy for decision making. Many risk issues facing late modern society fall into the latter category. In these instances, it is likely that other culturally informed strategies to cope with risk will be developed.

Cultural strategies to cope with poorly resolved risk issues will build on what is conventionally accepted in a community as true, valid, customary and normal and will not involve unprejudiced, full-scale assessments of alternative decisions (Bloch 1998: Ch 1; Boholm *et al.* 2013). Instead, culturally based cognitive short-cuts get activated (Strauss and Quinn 1999) – what cognitive psychologists speak about as *schemata* or *scripts* – and these serve as heuristics that condense prob-lems into much simpler sets of alternatives: for example, a binary structure of morally charged mutually exclusive alternatives, or a situation stipulating one course of action without alternatives. Such schemata, as the child safety example above illustrates, produce contexts which link together a set of terms such as an object of risk (a source of potential harm), an object at risk (a potential target of harm) and an evaluation (implicit or explicit) of human consequences (Boholm & Corvellec 2011). Risk here is regarded not in essentialist terms as a property of things perceived but as an inherently dynamic relational order of meaningful connections between the terms included. The schemata perspective on the cultural nature of risk makes it possible to theorise about variations in the conceptualisation and management of risk among different communities or organisations.

Let us consider an example that was highly amplified in the Swedish media in early 2002. Comparatively strong electromagnetic fields (EMFs) of between 14 and 15 microteslas had been measured at the position of the driver's left foot in the Volvo S60 model and appeared to affect other new models as well (S80, S70). The cause of the problem was the placement of the battery in the back of the car, from where it connected with the engine by means of a floor cable. Most people in Sweden either are or have been Volvo owners, or know someone who owns or has owned a Volvo, so the matter was given a great deal of attention in the Swedish media. The news-boards of the national newspapers featured bold-lettered headlines stating, for example, 'Alarm from scientists – the new Volvo can give you cancer'. Disappointed, angry and worried Volvo owners were interviewed in the press in the public outcry that followed. Volvo responded by stating that they would fix the problem, but customers wanting the remedy would have to pay part of the cost (2,000 kr, equivalent to 200 €). Volvo reasoned that it was not established by science that there was a cancer risk from EMFs,[1] so in their view the cars were safe. The media, however, reported some scientific disagreement with Volvo's conclusion; even so, Volvo continued to insist that they would not bear the whole cost of reducing the electromagnetic exposure. More public outcry followed, and people who had bought new Volvo cars were outraged: they had bought a Volvo especially since they wanted a safe car, but now it constituted a cancer risk; how could Volvo have missed this risk; and why should they pay to mitigate it? Families began to worry about whether it was safe for their children to travel in their cars.

It is unlikely that this 'fault' would have assumed such proportions in Sweden had a different brand of car been involved. The whole matter was very much a question about symbolic meanings relating to the kind of car a Volvo is supposed to be: concern for the environment and high standards of technological safety constitute core themes in Volvo's marketing, both in Sweden and internationally. Addressing an American audience, Volvo made the following statement:

Our care for the environment is a logical extension of our care for people. Volvo is continually exploring ways to lessen its impact on the environment – efforts that include improving the recyclability of cars and eliminating harmful substances from both cars themselves and the production process (Volvo Cars 2002).

The following excerpt from the company's American homepage illustrates how the human dimension of 'automotive safety' was construed (Volvo Cars 2002):

> The driver of the truck lost control of his vehicle and hit me, and my wife, who was five months pregnant.[...] There was much talk that 'the Volvo had saved our lives' and I'm convinced it did.[...] I wish to thank the people at Volvo for the lives of my wife and my child.[...]
>
> *— Joni and Colleen Taylor, November 7, 1989*

The letters have been coming to us for years. Men and women writing about how they believe a car helped save their lives. The Volvo Saved My Life Club recognizes these 'survivors' faith in Volvo, as well as Volvo's dedication to building cars worthy of such admiration. In fact, the only downside to the Volvo Saved My Life Club are the conditions for membership.

Volvo was originally a Swedish company that began to manufacture cars in the late 1920s, although at the time of the story it was a subsidiary of the multinational Ford Corporation. Volvo still operates a big plant at the original factory site in Torslanda north of Gothenburg. A Volvo is understood in Sweden as a traditional Swedish quality car: reliable, practical and adhering to the highest safety standards – the ideal family car (Figure 4.1).

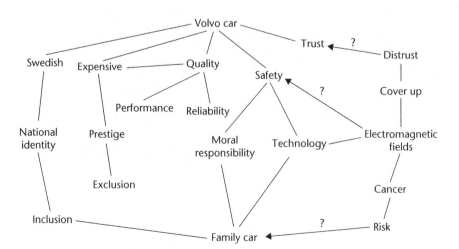

FIGURE 4.1 Web of associations – Volvo car

Media disclosure of possible carcinogenic EMFs in new car models questioned all the taken-for-granted assumptions in Sweden about the nature of Volvo. The episode opened up the possibility that both the safety of the cars and trust in the corporation needed to be re-evaluated; an image of unscrupulous big business that placed profit above the well-being of people threatened to replace the desired image of a caring and responsible corporation driven by the highest moral standards.

Four different reactions can be discerned in the debate in the Swedish media that followed the 'scientific' detection of the EMFs (see for example a feature article 'Deplorable that Volvo tries to get rid of their responsibility' [*Göteborgs-Posten* 2002]):

a. One type of response exemplifies *calculated risk*, in that the risk associated with the EMFs was weighed against benefits and compared with other decision alternatives. – Leif, 53 years: 'The whole thing – compared with commuter trains or microwave ovens – is exaggerated from the beginning. I am not the least worried since it has not been scientifically proven that it is a danger.'

b. Another response type was that there is no reason to worry since Volvo was a highly *trustworthy* company and their assurance that the risk is readily manageable because it is minute or non-existent was reassuring. – Siw, 37 years: 'I am not the least worried! I have full confidence in Volvo and I trust that they will fix this matter. I am not that well-informed but the whole thing seems exaggerated.'

c. A third response type was that there may be a risk but it was manageable by *remedial* measures to better shield the cable leading from the battery – Christer, 34 years: 'We do have a children's chair in the car but no, I am not worried. But I will contact my car dealer to have it fixed.'

d. A fourth response type was that there is a considerable risk and the only appropriate management strategy was to *avoid* using the car as usual. – Niclas, 31 years: 'I do not trust Volvo at all any longer and I will return my V70 and buy a Saab [at the time Volvo's biggest domestic competitor in car manufacturing] instead.' – Maggi, 42 years: 'My husband has got cancer and will absolutely not continue to drive our S60 any longer. We have put it away at Bilia [the official Volvo dealer] and we will not pick it up until the electromagnetic fields are gone. We are now driving a rental car which we have to pay ourselves' [translation and brackets mine].

These four response types provoked by the Volvo episode exemplify various modes of cognitive coping with a risk issue. In the case of calculated risk, the situation is framed as a balancing of fairly well-known stakes and probabilities. If the stakes and probabilities are held to be more uncertain, however, other strategies need to be adopted. One way of coping is to have high trust in those responsible for the management of the risk object; another is to have strong faith in some governing force or principle. But if trust is low or there is only weak faith, the remaining

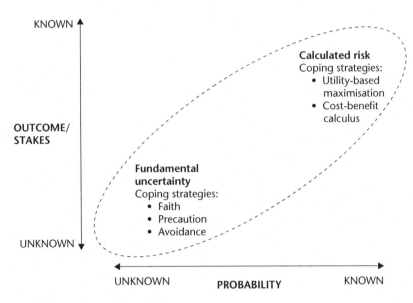

FIGURE 4.2 Contingency: coping strategies

options are precaution or avoidance. Precautionary strategies adopt various measures to mitigate or control risk. Avoidance is different as a coping strategy, in that it implies a dichotomisation of risk versus safety. Any risk object – for example, a Volvo car or foreign beef possibly infected with BSE – is construed as belonging to a bounded category of hazardous objects that are contrasted with a counterpart class of 'safe' objects – such as a Saab car or Swedish beef. Avoidance as a coping strategy entails not engaging in any way with things categorised as hazardous. Such schematisation poses 'risky' and 'safe' as binary categories rather than positions on a continuum. Discussions in risk perception research about 'stigma' with regard to public responses to certain technologies (Flynn, Slovic & Kunreuther 2001) fit well with the avoidance strategy identified here (Figure 4.2).

Knowledge modes and their mediation

Understanding the dynamics of cultural variation in the conceptualisation and management of risk requires insights into how people form relevant knowledge. If risk is to be perceived and managed, it first must be identified and then it must be communicated. Some risk issues, for example, those associated with driving a car, smoking or riding a bicycle, are concrete and familiar. They are well-embedded in the practices of everyday life and likely are personally experienced or witnessed. Other risk issues, like getting cancer from EMFs or loss of biodiversity due to global change, despite often harrowing consequences, emerge as abstract and distant, being disseminated in a formal language of technical expertise. While some risk issues are 'experience-far', beyond the sphere of the everyday, others are 'experience-near' (Geertz 1983). How are experience-far risk issues communicated to and understood by people who are not themselves experts? As noted in Chapters 1 and 2, knowledge of risk issues tends to come from the media, which vividly document mishaps and threats occurring throughout the world. Nowhere is this more pertinent than in the 'virtual risks' category, in which scientific evidence is inconclusive or readily disputable (Adams 1997). Many risks are brought to the attention of the public mainly by means of global media such as television news media and the Internet (Allan, Adam & Carter 2000). In order to understand what role personal, local experience plays in the assessment of information derived from the generalised knowledge of distant expert communities, we need make an analytical distinction among three basic modes of knowledge about risk: everyday experience, science-driven scenarios and collective narratives. These modes structure information by defining risk objects, objects at risk and, crucially, the causal linkage between those objects:

1. Everyday experience takes place in the spheres of ordinary life. Information is disseminated through small talk about health, personal circumstances and local matters; through comments on events near and far but seldom covered by the media; and through gossip regarding mutually known 'others'. Everyday experience covers risk-related issues concerning food, transportation, domestic safety, children, the neighbourhood and various risk factors in the local environment. Knowledge of risk has personal relevance in this mode; risk is clearly context-dependent and is situated socially and in time and space. Risk objects are not dealt with as isolated 'things' but as matters that threaten normative, interpersonally negotiated states of safety (Caplan 2000; Zonabend 1993).

2. In the science-driven mode, results or controversies from science tell about risk framed as the likelihood of undesirable events. Science-driven scenarios tend to offer probabilistic estimates on the likelihood of such occurrences, and this information reaches the general public mainly through the media – TV and printed news, commercials and documentaries, but also through entertainment media (for example, popular movies like *Erin Brockovich* [Ferreira 2004] and the Internet, where there are numerous sites dedicated to the dissemination of scientific information to concerned citizens concerning human health, nutrition, diseases, epidemiology, chemicals, radiation, genetically modified organisms and other risk issues).

3. Collective narratives about events – the Chernobyl reactor breakdown, the sinking of the *Estonia* ferry, September 11, the foot and mouth disease crisis in the UK and the like – are predominantly communicated through news media. Such narratives invite comments by experts who convey scientific information, as well as opinion makers such as Greenpeace and other nongovernmental organisations, which often introduce contradictory scientific evidence or alternative priorities. A narrative, dramaturgical structure is crucial for the media: there must be a story about intentions, motives, victims, villains and heroes, all staged in a specific setting. Human consequences of the drama are spelled out, as are meanings and emotions. Issues of blame, responsibility and trust are topical and intermingled with questions about causation and speculations

on plausible effects. Some episodes even develop sufficient force to impart structure to the interpretation of subsequent events. They become epitomes that are used to label other events that then become subsumed under the interpretative frame of the labelling event. After the failures in the building of an 8.6-km-long Hallandsås train tunnel in southern Sweden, it became quite common to refer to other development plans by saying that they were 'like the Hallandsås'. This simple label implied technological failure, irrational decision making, incompetence, lack of respect for local people and an immoral harm of nature for crude gain ('three minutes of spared travel time') (Löfstedt & Boholm 1999; Boholm 2005).

There are interfaces between all three knowledge modes because information is exchanged between them (Figure 4.3). Results from science are incorporated into everyday experience. The Volvo example well illustrates the convergence of science-mediated propositions and findings, media storytelling based on these science results and everyday experience. Food is another good example. Warnings or other findings about risk aspects of food come from science, like acrylamide in potato crisps (Löfstedt 2003), and may enter into everyday experience and result in changed food habits or a heightened awareness that certain foods or certain elements therein can have negative effects. In cases of food scandals reported in the media – colza oil in Spain, BSE or salmonella in chicken – we can see an interaction between all three modes.

How is information translated from one experience mode to another? Global climate change is for most people a rather abstract idea; they have a vague knowledge, but it engages numerous scientists in a great deal of work. As reported in

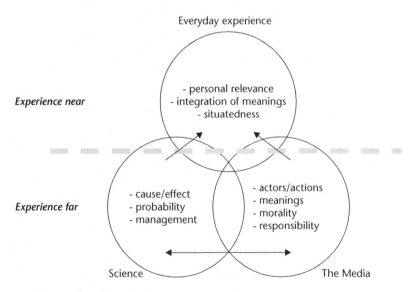

FIGURE 4.3 Modes of knowledge

the media, certain extreme weather phenomena – heavy rains, floods, storms and unusually warm weather – might serve as representations of the risk of climate change. Now translated into experience-near terms, global climate change has emerged as a socially construed risk issue, and abstract scientific models have been imbued with social meanings.

Situated risk – putting risk into context

Social science approaches to risk have shown a tendency to reduce complexity by relying on meta-sociological speculations, idealised simplistic models such as economic rationality, or psychological modelling of attitude. This is problematic, as risk is contextual and fluid; what is or what is not considered a risk issue depends on social relationships, power relations and hierarchies, cultural beliefs, trust in institutions and science, knowledge, experience, discourses, practices and collective memories, all of which shape notions about risk or safety. Risk is a relational term that emerges from context depending on shared conventionally established meanings, that is to say, the context of culture (Rappaport 1996). Social anthropology can contribute by untangling the intrinsic situatedness of risk because, in combination with its ethnographical methods, it has the analytical capacity to expose and problematise taken-for-granted assumptions and given meanings (Caplan 2000).

If risk research focuses exclusively on relativism – that is, on 'subjective', or socially constructed, risk – it will be unable to account for the juxtapositions and amalgamations of 'objective' and 'subjective' perspectives on risk that are part of the problem. The argument in this chapter is for the conceptualisation of risk not as a phenomenon in itself but as a frame that produces contexts that link together a risk object (a source of potential harm), an object at risk (a potential target of harm) and an evaluation (implicit or explicit) of the possible human consequences. Seen in this way, risk is a relational order constituting the connections between people, things and outcomes (Boholm & Corvellec 2011).

References

Adams, J. 1997. Cars, cholera, cows, and contaminated land: virtual risk and the management of uncertainty. In *What risk?*, Bate, R. (ed.), pp. 285–304. Oxford, UK: Butterworth-Heinemann.

Allan, S., Adam, B. & Carter, C. (eds.). 2000. *Environmental risks and the media*. London, UK: Routledge.

Bauman, Z. 1998. *Globalization: The human consequences*. Oxford, UK: Polity Press.

Beck, U. 1992 [1986]. *Risk society: Towards a new modernity*. London, UK: SAGE.

Bloch, M. 1998. *How we think they think: Anthropological approaches to cognition, memory and literacy*. Boulder, CO: Westview Press.

Boholm, Å. 2005. 'Greater good' in transit: The unwieldy career of a Swedish rail tunnel project. *Focaal – European Journal of Anthropology* 46: 21–35.

Boholm, Å. & Löfstedt, R. 1999. Issues of risk, trust and knowledge: The Hallandsås tunnel case. *Ambio* 28(6): 556–561.

Boholm, Å. & Corvellec H. 2011. A relational theory of risk. *Journal of Risk Research* 14(2): 175–190.

Boholm, Å., Henning, A. & Krzyworzeka, A. 2013. Anthropology and decision making: An introduction. *Focaal – Journal of Global and Historical Anthropology* 65: 97–113.

Buxó i Rey, M.J. 1996. Hacia una cultura de la seguridad: Infancia y riesgo. *Revista de Antropologia Aplicada* 1: 113–122.

Buxó i Rey, M.J. & Torrijos, F. 1999. *Riesgo, seguridad vial y cultura cívica.* Barcelona, Spain: Editorial Winterthur.

Cancian, F. 1980. Risk and uncertainty in agricultural decision making. In *Agricultural decision making: Anthropological contributions to rural development.* Bartlett, P.F. (ed.), pp. 171–176. Orlando, FL: Academic Press.

Caplan, P. (ed.). 2000. *Risk revisited.* London, UK: Pluto Press.

Cashdan, E. (ed.). 1990. *Risk and uncertainty in tribal and peasant economies.* Boulder, CO: Westview Press.

Dake, K. 1991. Orientating dispositions in the perceptions of risk: An analysis of contemporary worldviews and cultural biases. *Journal of Cross-Cultural Psychology* 22(1): 61–82.

Dake, K. 1992. Myths of nature: Culture and the social construction of risk. *Journal of Social Issues* 48(4): 21–38.

Douglas, M. 1966. *Purity and danger: An analysis of concepts of pollution and taboo.* London, UK: Routledge & Kegan Paul.

Douglas, M. 1978. Cultural bias. *Occasional Papers/Royal Anthropological Institute of Great Britain and Ireland,* 35.

Douglas, M. 1992. *Risk and blame: Essays in cultural theory.* London, UK: Routledge.

Douglas, M. & Wildavsky, A. 1982. *Risk and culture: An essay on the selection of technological and environmental dangers.* Berkeley, CA: University of California Press.

Elam, Y. 1973. *The social and sexual roles of Hima women.* Manchester, UK: Manchester University Press.

Ferreira, C. 2004. Risk, transparency and cover up: Media narratives and cultural resonance. *Journal of Risk Research* 7(2): 199–211.

Ferreira, C., Boholm, Å. & Löfstedt, R. 2001. From vision to catastrophe: A risk event in search of images. In *Risk, media and stigma.* Flynn, J., Slovic, P. & Kunreuther, H. (eds.), pp. 283–299. London, UK: Earthscan.

Flynn, J., Slovic, P. & Kunreuther, H. (eds.). 2001. *Risk media and stigma: Understanding public challenges to modern science and technology.* London, UK: Earthscan.

Geertz, C. 1983. *Local knowledge.* New York, NY: Basic Books.

Giddens, A. 1990. *The consequences of modernity.* Chicago, IL: Polity Press.

Giddens, A. 1991. *Modernity and self-identity.* Stanford, CA: Stanford University Press.

Göteborgs-Posten. 2000. Förorenad luft ger fler dödsfall. 21 November 2000, p. 6, part 1.

Göteborgs-Posten. 2002. Bedrövligt att Volvo försöker smita undan ansvaret. 22 February 2002, p. 6.

Hansson, S.O. 2010. Risk: Objective or subjective, facts or values. *Journal of Risk Research* 13(2): 231–238.

Hansson, S.O. & Peterson, M. 2001. Rights, risks, and residual obligations. *Risk Decision and Policy* 6:157–166.

Hilgartner, S. 1992. The social construction of risk objects: Or, how to pry open networks of risk. In *Organizations, uncertainties and risk.* Short, J. F. & Clarke, L. (eds.), pp. 39–53. Boulder, CO: Westview Press.

Kleinhesselink, R.R. & Rosa, E. 1991. Cognitive representations of risk perceptions: A comparison of Japan and the United States. *Journal of Cross-Cultural Psychology* 22: 11–28.

Lash, S., Szerszynski, B. & Wynne, B. (eds.). 1996. *Risk, environment & modernity.* London, UK: SAGE.

Löfstedt, R. 2003. Science communication and the Swedish acrylamide alarm. *Journal of Health Communication: International Perspectives* 8(1): 407–432.

Löfstedt, R. & Boholm, Å. 1999. Off track in Sweden. *Environment* 41(4): 16–20, 40–44.

Lupton, D. 1999. *Risk.* London, UK & New York, NY: Routledge.

Mairal Buil, G. 2003. A risk shadow in Spain. *Ethnos* 68(2): 179–191.

Möller, N. 2012. The concepts of risk and safety. In *Handbook of risk theory.* Roeser, S., Hillerbrand, R., Sandin, P. & Peterson, M. (eds.), pp. 56–85. Berlin & Heidelberg, Germany: Springer.

Purcell, K., Clarke, L. & Renzulli, L. 2000. Menus of choice: The social embeddedness of decisions. In *Risk in the modern age: Social theory, science and environmental decision-making.* Cohen, M.J. (ed.), pp. 62–79. London, UK: Macmillan Press.

Rappaport, R.A. 1996. Risk and the human environment. *Annals of the American Academy of Political and Social Science* 545(May): 64–74.

Renn, O. 1998. Three decades of risk research: Accomplishments and new challenges. *Journal of Risk Research* 1(1): 49–71.

Renn, O., Jaeger, C.C., Rosa, E.A. & Webler, T. 2000. The rational actor paradigm in risk theories: Analysis and critique. In *Risk in the modern age: Social theory, science and environmental eecision-making.* Cohen, M.J. (ed.), pp. 35–61. London, UK: Macmillan Press.

Rosa, E.A. 1998. Metatheoretical foundations for post-normal risk. *Journal of Risk Research* 1(1): 15–44.

Shrader-Frechette, K.S. 1991. *Risk and rationality: Philosophical foundations for populist reforms.* Berkeley, CA: University of California Press.

Sjölander-Lindqvist, A. 2004. Local environment at stake: The Hallandsås railway tunnel in a social and cultural context. Lund Dissertations in Human Ecology, 2. Lund, Sweden: Lund University.

Slovic, P. 2000. *The perception of risk.* London, UK: Earthscan.

Strauss, C. & Quinn, N. 1999. *A cognitive theory of cultural meaning.* Cambridge, UK: Cambridge University Press.

Tansey, J. & O'Riordan, T. 1999. Cultural theory and risk: A review. *Health, Risk & Society* 1(1): 71–90.

Volvo Cars. 2002. *Why Volvo?* Retrieved from www.volvocars.com/whyvolvo (now removed; accessed 1 March 2002).

Zonabend, F. 1993. *The nuclear peninsula.* Cambridge, UK: Cambridge University Press.

Note

1. EMFs are officially classified as a potential cancer risk. Childhood leukemia is specifically mentioned. For example, see www.cancer.gov/cancertopics /factsheet/Risk/magnetic-fields (accessed 30 January 2015).

5

RISK AS ORGANISATIONAL PRACTICE

A case of railway planning

The secular, stochastic conception of the world and the concurrent demise of determinism made room for the modern understanding that humans have the power to control nature and society (Hacking 1990). The concept of risk is closely associated with the advent of statistical calculation (Hacking 1990; Jasanoff 1999), which provided a new paradigm for understanding and managing uncertainty. This paradigm originated in a scientific discourse that required a quantifiable analytical vocabulary and demanded validation by empirical data. In employing the concept of 'risk', science approaches uncertainty as analytically distinct from its context (Turner 1994). As a mode of thought, risk is associated with the idea that life is planned on the basis of rational decision making (Luhmann 1993). Sociologists have argued (Beck 1992; Dean 1999; Giddens 1990; Reith 2004) that risk can be understood as a socially, culturally and historically specific meta-discourse about decision making, in which the state embraces a new role as a provider of 'safety' by governing risk by means of regulatory regimes (Hood, Rothstein & Baldwin 2001; Jasanoff 1999).

Risk management today is firmly established on the agenda of government and business. To qualify as legitimate and responsible, organisations must be accountable for their capacity to deal with risk by means of various administrative tools and techniques (Hood, Rothstein & Baldwin 2001; Power 2007; Rothstein, Huber & Gaskell 2006). This need for accountability in the management of risk has given rise to organisational responses (Hutter & Power 2005; Power 2007; Hood, Rothstein & Baldwin 2001) that articulate understanding of risk and its constitution in various ways. The increasing demand for risk management on the part of organisations, businesses and government authorities has been identified as a general societal trend emphasising public accountability and responsibility (Power 2007; Power *et al.* 2009; Rothstein, Huber & Gaskell 2006). It has led to a globally growing body of standards and guidelines for risk management (see Hillson 2007),[1] building on the idea of a standardised model for the systematic, logical treatment of all kinds of risks. A basic assumption is that risks can be compared on a neutral scale and assessed in relation to their costs, leading to clear and reasonable actions about what risks to take or not to take and what mitigation measures to instigate (see e.g. Edwards 1995). Among the cornerstones of formal risk management guidelines and standards are the calculation of risk as the product of measurable consequence and probability (according to the formula $C \times P$), the classification of risks in a typology of size (low, medium and high), the idea that risk management should be based on but be distinct from risk analysis and the idea that risk management comprises a fixed sequence of rationally ordered actions.

Despite the existence of formal standards, several scholars have noted a reluctance to adopt formal, standardised risk management approaches in businesses such as construction (see Uher & Toakley 1998; Flanagan & Norman 1993). Geotechnical experts, for example, prefer case histories to statistical information in risk management (Hartford & Baecher 2004: 353). Respondents in a survey of Australian construction firms 'showed a distinct preference for using qualitative methods in data elicitation and risk analysis techniques' (Uher & Toakley 1998: 169). Studies of the construction business in the United Kingdom (Akintoye & MacLeod 1997) and of industries in Sweden (Kallenberg 2009) came to similar conclusions – namely, that despite the proliferation of standardised manuals and guidelines, the dominant risk management method consisted of informal, pragmatic and intuitive use of experience and inference of subjective probabilities. In the same vein, risk management by government authorities and business organisations has been shown to be quite 'messy' (Boholm 2013a), involving a 'spiralling regulatory logic' (Rothstein, Huber & Gaskell 2006) of interlinked responses to societal and institutional risk, defensive manoeuvring to manage risks to institutional reputations (Power et al. 2009) and concern for internally constructed core values that potentially are at stake (Corvellec 2010).

This chapter focuses on formal risk management as an organisational practice and uses as a central example an examination of formal risk management procedures in the Swedish Rail Administration authority. The aim in studying how risk was identified and assessed in a railway planning project was to shed light on the actual practice of the current, almost globally distributed (ideal) formal model of risk management. More broadly, this ethnographic case study contributes to research into practice-based knowledge (Gherardi 2000) and the cultural dimensions of risk and safety in organisations (Gherardi & Nicolini 2002; Pidgeon 1991). By questioning any taken-for-granted association between norm and practice, between formal risk management guidelines and actual organisational risk management, this chapter addresses the 'decoupling' of risk management in practice from formal risk management standards and models (Corvellec 2009).

The data were gathered between March 2007 and October 2008 by means of participant observation of project planning meetings, reference group meetings (including actors such as the county board, the municipality, the regional public transport company and the Rail Administration and Road Administration) and consultation meetings with stakeholders. Meetings were documented by handwritten notes, and data also included printed documentation (e.g. internal documents, minutes, official reports and Rail Administration handbooks and standards) and notes from informal discussions with officials, planners, designers and consultants. A total of 23 meetings were observed. The risk management process was followed from the risk identification stage to the formulation of the risk management plan, the latter being a standing item on the agendas of the project meetings

Railway planning in Sweden

Railway infrastructure in Sweden is state owned, so the national government decides about investing in new lines and upgrading or closing down existing lines. The Rail Administration is the statutory body responsible for the railway system, including the tracks and related infrastructure, such as stations, crossings, bridges, tunnels, signalling systems and electricity provisioning for the trains. Train engines and rolling stock are run by companies that lease rail capacity from the Rail Administration. Railway planning is regulated by the Railway Building Act (SFS 1995:1649) and the Environmental Code (SFS 1998:808), as well as by numerous other regulations and standards regarding a variety of railway planning responsibilities (technical, organisational, economic, legal and environmental).

Railway planning and design call for specialised knowledge of many matters, including geology, hydrology, ecology, landscape, law, engineering, traffic and sociology. Numerous formal, practical, political, economic, spatial and temporal restrictions on the planning process require the cooperation of a range of governmental authorities and other stakeholders such that the consultation process is of considerable duration (Boholm 2013a, 2013b). Railway planning, like infrastructure planning in general, can be understood as 'the translation of a painstaking arrangement of myriad human and nonhuman elements as a single engineering artefact' (Suchman 2003: 189). A railway plan consists of detailed selection of a route and the design of bridges, tunnels, barriers and road crossings. The plan must consider safety regarding future train traffic, construction specifications, construction processes and facilities (such as working roads or locations for storage of excavated material) and organisational, technical, economic and property rights issues. An environmental impact assessment (EIA), including consultation according to the Environmental Code, is mandatory.

The Railway Building Act requires consultation with affected real estate owners, municipalities, regional boards and 'others who might have a substantial interest in the matter' (SFS 1995:1649, Ch. 2, §5). Matters of property rights are a topic for the railway planning stage, and all land use issues must be legally settled before the plan is accepted. The regional county board is a powerful local government authority at the planning stage; if it objects to the EIA, the planning decision is elevated to the Swedish government, substantially delaying the project. A railway plan can be appealed to the government by citizens or other stakeholders. Although stakeholders are provided with certain legal rights, railway planning adheres to a Swedish technocratic regulatory style of consensual negotiation among government authorities, political interests and elite stakeholders with limited public participation (Boholm 2013a, 2013b; Löfstedt 2005).

The case

The Swedish government decided to invest 10 billion kr (about €1 billion) to upgrade road and rail capacity on the Norway-Väner Link north of Gothenburg in western Sweden. In terms of rail links, the existing single-track railway line would be upgraded to double-track and constructed for high-speed trains. The double-track, high-speed railway promised reduced travel time, shorter intervals between departures, new commuter stations and environmental benefits. Among several subprojects was a route of approximately 14 kilometres of double track, including three tunnels (124–200 m long) and a 400-m-long bridge. The 14-km route traversed farmland and mountainous rural areas with dense conifer forests and passed through two rural communities, each with around 500 inhabitants. The area is rich in archaeological, historical and natural heritage and conservation sites, including the spectacular Slumpån river canyon. The old railway route crossed the canyon on a steel bridge built in the 1950s, which was to be replaced with a new bridge. Construction of the new bridge in such a highly sensitive natural environment presented a major challenge for the project. The local communities and municipality generally favoured the project and the selected route.[2]

Like other railway projects, the studied railway planning project was managed by a project leader from the Rail Administration who was responsible for the budget, time table and management of the consultants and who in turn was accountable to the Rail Administration hierarchy of senior officials. The Rail Administration contracted the firm Rail Administration Consulting (RAC) as head consultants with the responsibility for delivering planning services for the railway plan, the EIA and the systems document.[3] As head consultant, RAC was responsible for planning the route of the railway line (referred to as 'planning in plane and profile'); designing the signal system and the contact cables, bridges, tunnels and road over- or underpasses; and conducting all the legally mandated investigations (regarding risk assessments and impacts on flora and fauna, landscape, heritage, etc.) as well as compiling the EIA document.

By law, all Swedish state authorities must have risk management plans (SFS 1995: 1300); in addition, there are a host of laws and regulations applicable to railway planning concerning workplace safety, electrical safety, crisis management, disaster protection, fire and explosions, environmental protection, planning and building and security. Risk management is specifically mentioned in the Rail Administration's official general 'quality policy' to be led by six statements called 'guiding stars', all formulated as undertakings or promises. The sixth star states: 'We shall identify and in a relevant and cost-effective manner treat those risks that threaten the conditions for reaching set goals. We shall have low acceptance of risk and only take well-considered and deliberate risks' (translation mine).[4]

The Rail Administration issued a risk management regulation (BVF 015 2008) and an accompanying Handbook (BVH 015 2006) that laid out the rules and standards for risk management in the Administration. The stated aim of the regulation is to identify and manage risk in what is said to be a 'cost-effective' manner by means of 'goal-oriented, standardised, and systematic' risk assessment (BVF 015 2008: Ch. 9). It spells out a logical order for handling risk management, starting from risk identification and proceeding through risk assessment and risk analysis to risk management; it requires that this process be documented in a report that meets a set standard.[5] The regulation introduced several definitions of key concepts, a vocabulary to define 'risk' and its consequences and measures by which to manage it. It also established that steering, implementation and auditing of risk management should be systematic and meet external requirements. Risk analyses should be quality controlled, and risks must be managed cost-effectively. The regulation stipulated that work on risk management should serve as a basis for (1) strategic, tactical and operational decisions; (2) risk management decisions; and (3) decisions about how to reduce total costs associated with risks (BVF 015 2008: Ch. 11).

The Handbook recognised risk identification as a key component of risk management (BVH 015 2006: 13) and stated that the aim was to 'identify risks of an activity that threaten the fulfilment of stated strategic goals' (translation mine). The Handbook's interest in risk was therefore oriented to that which threatened a project rather than that which emanated from it (unless these resulted in blowback that threatened the project indirectly). Very little guidance was given in either the regulation or the Handbook about how risks should be identified. When it came to risk assessment, the Handbook was more instructive (BVH 015 2006: 13–15). It states that the probability of a risk can be estimated in three ways: *empirical estimation, logical estimation* and according to *expert judgment*. While empirical estimation built upon statistics of actual occurrences – requiring the existence of relevant and adequate data – logical estimation was said to derive from calculating the probabilities of individual causes and then summing them. Expert judgment was simply insight based on experience – and, as we will see, this was the dominant approach used.

The remainder of this chapter considers how this regulation, building on risk management as a formal and standardised approach, is enacted in the social practice of railway planning. The quotes referred to in the text are taken from the project planning meetings.

Risk identification as social practice

A one-day meeting dedicated to risk management issues was held early in the railway planning phase of the project (March 2007). The objective was the identification and assessment of risks relevant to the railway planning phase by a broad group of specialists. The meeting was the first stage in formulating an overall risk management plan for the project. Fifteen experts attended the meeting, and proceedings began with a brief introduction from the RAC project leader, who explained the objectives. All participants introduced themselves: eight were from the Rail Administration (with expertise in expert support, technical coordination and real estate), and seven were consultants, including two from RAC. Competencies in the consultant group included writing EIAs, geotechnology, contaminated soil management, construction, real estate, tunnel building and security and bridge design.

The first item on the agenda was the concept of risk, defined as the outcome of the consequences of an event. The product of the consequence of an event and the probability of those consequences yielded the estimate of the risk. A PowerPoint presentation gave the definition $C \times P = R$, with a comment saying that C (consequence) and P (probability) needed to have quantifiable measures.[6] There was neither questioning nor discussion of this definition. The need for risk management was justified by reference to organisational demands; namely, it was included in the project commission and was mandatory due to 'general system requirements'. The project leader commented that it is 'easy to forget about risk' and that it is better to 'think first', which increases 'the probability that the project will run well'. The project leader then spoke about the project's scope and goal, characterised according to five focal areas: time plan, budget, constructability, good consultation climate and environmental considerations. She continued with a summary of the project, specifically noting that 'geotechnology is very difficult' and that 'many come and tell us about Småröd'. Småröd was the site of an unexpected landslide that had occurred four months earlier, north of Uddevalla and not far from the project route. A newly built stretch of road on the E6 motorway, along with 13 vehicles, simply collapsed into a big hole, and it was sheer luck that just one person was injured. The project leader then mentioned that the river canyon at Slumpån is a national conservation site governed by the Swedish Environmental Protection Agency and concluded by emphasising that 'We have no time not to cooperate well with the county board and the municipality'.

The quality coordinator from expert support in the Rail Administration then explained the process of 'systematic risk management', stating that 'communication' was central, so that 'all those involved know what is going on'. She stated that risk identification was to be done by means of 'brainstorming',[7] with the intention of subsequently assessing risks with regard to probability and consequence, calculating risk estimates and compiling this information in a risk management planning document. The whole idea of the exercise was so that 'everything should be brought to the table' and that it was fine to be 'a little crazy and come up with odd things'.

The quality coordinator explained that risk management means drawing up priorities and choosing strategies for the management of risk by action plans and follow-ups throughout the project. She emphasised a number of areas with notable risks, such as geotechnology, bridges, cost estimates, environment and landscape, constructability, steering and organisation, formal administration and information. She also referred to various 'consequence areas', such as time, economics, quality, environment, work environment and trust, noting that 'not everyone is accustomed to these being important parameters' and that there might be other issues such as 'third parties', residents or travellers, 'but we have to establish numbers and then choose those with the biggest consequences'. Such a distinction between risk sources and their effects or consequences recalls much of the literature on risk management in construction (Flanagan & Norman 1993: 8).

Scales ranging from 1 to 5 used to measure consequences were presented next, along with time consequences ranging from 'less than ½ month' to 'above 3 months', economic consequences from 'less than 1 million kr' to 'more than 30 million kr' and other consequences from 'very small' to 'very big'. Similarly, a probability scale of 1 to 5 was introduced, ranging from 'not likely, 1 per cent' to 'will occur, 100 per cent'. Nobody questioned this measure, despite the fact that something with a 100 per cent probability did not qualify as a 'risk' by any current definition. The quality coordinator noted that the risk inventory document might become very extensive and that another project had come up with 80 different risks. She described the risk management planning document, which outlined an administrative routine for identifying risks in which each risk is numbered, categorised depending on consequence area(s), described in words and associated with numbers for C, P, and $C \times P$. Each risk was categorised depending on the response strategy chosen, of which there were essentially six: avoid/eliminate, transfer, minimise C, minimise P, actively accept and passively accept. Columns for responsibility, the date and comments were included. The risk management plan document was said to be a 'living document' that could be changed and revised as the project continued: 'It can be a standing item on the agendas for the project meetings'.

During the discussion, the participants were somewhat hesitant at first but soon began to talk. A first question was 'What about risks that we cannot control?', to which someone responded, 'Real risks are always things that we cannot control! The contractor is broke, for example, or the weather'. The issue of control is crucial to how planners interpret risk and risk management, and this will be discussed in more detail below. Another issue had to do with what the literature describes as 'reputational risk' (Power et al. 2009); one participant asked:

> What about risks having to do with trust? What is relevant? A contractor makes a mess of things and the Rail Administration is blamed. What do the media write about? Public opinion accuses the Rail Administration, but in our business, everyone knows that the contractor has failed.

This remark reflects something of the 'messiness' of practical risk management, where risks tend to 'spill over' into reputational risk for the organisation, since the line of demarcation in terms of responsibility and accountability can be contested in the public domain (Boholm 2013a, 2013b; Power et al. 2009; Rothstein, Huber & Gaskell 2006).

The attendees next were divided into two smaller groups, and participants were asked to write down each identified risk on a yellow sticky note, together with specified consequence area(s). The risk estimate calculations were to be made by the sub-group so as to sort the identified risks according to the standardised two-dimensional ($C \times P$), four-square table.[8] This analysis enabled the categorisation of risks as low, medium and high, graphically indicated by the colours green, yellow and red, respectively. This exercise gave rise to several questions, and again the issue of control was brought up: 'What about risks that the Rail Administration cannot influence?' – traffic risks being cited as an example. 'What about the planning stage in relation to the building stage?' 'If it rains a lot, is that a risk that should be counted?' The quality coordinator answered that the focus should be on those matters that the Rail Administration could influence and that experience from earlier projects was important in this regard. Her comment resonates with a basic distinction drawn between controllable and uncontrollable risks in the literature on construction risk management (Flanagan & Norman 1993: 49–50).

After a period of individual identification of risks, the notes were assembled and discussed in the sub-groups as the next step of the exercise. The sub-group leader acted as a chair and read out all the recorded risks. Some risks were commented upon and discussed intensely, while others were noted just in passing. The exercise was carried out following a set order: (1) each noted risk was read aloud to the sub-group (in the extract below, the risk as originally noted is shown in square brackets), (2) the probability and consequence of the risk were discussed and (3) numbers were agreed on. The following extract from the notes exemplifies the procedure:

> About the risk [different technologies do not form a functioning whole], the participants acknowledged that the forecasting stage is important and that 'some things might be missed' and that the 'coordinated study must work'. Then the question about probability. One answer was that this could happen but it could be managed: 'The consequences are not very great. But can be very high if it happens on inauguration day!' No one however, thought that this was very probable but even so, measures between 2 and 3 to 4 were suggested for probability. Someone argued that the consequences 'depend', since the risk is not so complex technically but there are other complications; the risk was then categorised as medium-sized and of 'little significance'. The group was asked to decide on a degree of consequence and settled for 3, with the comment 'which does not lead to any action' (Project planning meeting, March 2007, translation mine).

The one-day meeting ended with the official in charge noting the importance of the meeting and that the discussions had served as a 'knowledge-building process of great value'. She also said that the identified risks would be further assessed outside of the meeting and that new risks might be added. She explained that the identified risks would be recorded on a checklist and that those identified as pertaining to the building stage would be dealt with in the forecasting stage and in the examination of the railway planning document. An important matter for future work would be to assign responsibility for the identified risks to either the project commissioner or one or more of the consultants.

The next meeting took place three weeks later (April 2007), and this time the group was smaller, consisting of the project leader, the coordinators of the consultants and the quality coordinator from the Rail Administration. The yellow sticky notes had been compiled into a list of 125 different risks all entered into the Rail Administration risk management planning document template. The document contained columns for each risk issue (with a short description of the risk); a column for 'consequence areas'; and numbers for consequences, probability and the calculated risk estimate. The document also had columns for management action, assigned responsibility and the date. The magnitude of risk was calculated (as noted above) as the product of consequence and probability; since the measurement scales of consequence and probability each ranged from 1 to 5, the highest risk estimate was 25 and the lowest was 1.

The task for this meeting was to assess and sort the list and to specify mitigatory measures for each risk. The project leader suggested that the group should go through the list quickly to see if something had been forgotten. Nothing was identified. Questions then arose about how the risks should be sorted. After some remarks, the project leader said that the 'risk estimate is very subjective'. Someone suggested that two risks could be merged into one and asked the quality coordinator if she had any objection. She did not, and stated that merging risks in some cases might make things clearer and easier to follow. The list was read through and commented on, but with little discussion of specific risks. Once done, the group discussed whether a person's name should be entered in the responsibility column. Someone said that the important thing was that the process be traceable, so that it was clear how the group had worked. The discussion mainly concerned how to compile the risk management planning document in terms of its form, with action plans and checklists, and how the document was to be used. At a later project meeting (May 2007), the risk management plan was presented; by then it contained 86 identified risks.

Identifying risk

The risk management planning work, resulting in the list of 86 identified risks to be managed by the project, focused on several risk themes. These themes reflected uncertainty deriving from organisational interdependency and the systemic complexity inherent to railway planning, and they included issues perceived as uncertain, yet nonetheless the responsibility of the Rail Administration. Railway planning is quite complex due to the great number of interrelated elements it deals with; many things can go wrong in a railway project and for many different reasons, since negative effects can emerge from complex causal conditions (Boholm 2009) involving the interactions of humans, organisations, technology and nature (Suchman 2003). In discussions during the March 2007 meeting, planners described the situation thus: 'There is a tremendous uncertainty in project planning – a guessing competition'; '[No matter] how good a job one does, there is always great uncertainty'; and 'Things will always happen!' Railway planning depends on the cooperation of a number of expert planners, entrepreneurs and builders and puts great demands not only on expert knowledge, skill and practical experience, but also on coordination of the project's many parts and dimensions (i.e., technical, organisational, social, legal, environmental and administrative). Creation of a stable organising 'alignment' of all elements involved is crucial for reaching the project goal of creating a certain 'engineering artefact' – the plan for a new railway line (Suchman 2003). The desired stable alignment of the project can be jeopardised due to misunderstandings and failures of cooperation, coordination and communication, as well as lack of trust.

A number of the risks in the risk management plan concerned resource uncertainty: matters of economics and the continuity of staff, expertise and the internal priorities of the Rail Administration. From a project perspective, decisions being made at higher administrative levels might mean funds running out or priorities changing. Another worry concerned the financing of later stages of building in terms of various costs for compensating stakeholders or for restoration work. Technical coordination and matters of traffic disturbance, construction problems and construction logistics in relation to ongoing road and rail traffic during building were also noted; these matters prompted considerable discussion, as did disturbances due to weather.

Continuous reconciliation of a multitude of interests was a major task for the rail planning officials. They can be regarded as 'negotiation bureaucrats', since 'negotiations are the most essential prerequisites for the accomplishment of their tasks, in relation both to working conditions and the fragmented implementation structure governing the decisions they need to make' (Johansson 2012). Consequently, it comes as no surprise that planners and designers recognise numerous legal and administrative barriers to railway planning; they know from experience that matters of law and administration can have a decisive impact, resulting in time delays, increased costs and demand for new technical solutions. Regulatory obstacles and areas where other authorities had responsibility (e.g., the municipality, county board or sectoral government administrations) were noted as risk issues, for example, in cases of archaeological remains or new animal or plant species. Due to legislation for archaeological heritage and nature conservation, discoveries of these items require the involvement of other authorities and the implementation of investigations and fieldwork that may threaten the time plan and budget of the project. Similarly, local landowners whose properties will be crossed by the new rail line and who would have a legal right to compensation for the alienation of ownership or loss of use of land or buildings are also identified as risk objects in the implementation of railway planning.

One category of identified risks had to do with various forms of negligence (in case of poor investigations, calculations or coordination; human error; or even outright violations of agreements). A salient issue identified as a risk was the failure of contractors to live up to the expectations of Rail Administration officials; as one planner said, 'If the consultant does not think correctly, everything can be affected'. The relationship between the Rail Administration and contractors, such as builders or consultants, was sensitive. The Rail Administration's power to manage the actions of the contractors is indirect and vested in the conditions of the business agreement between the authority and the private company in terms of the commission and contract specifications. Such indirect, legal-contractual steering somewhat restricts the entrepreneur's freedom of action, but since control is indirect and the contractor carries out the actual work, the Rail Administration officials have no guarantee that negligence will not feature in the contracted work. The contractor may still fail by not adhering to the specifications of the contractual instructions from the Rail Administration or by adhering to faulty or inadequate instructions. Therefore, the Rail Administration officials have little choice but to trust the contractor (Kadefors 2004). This division of responsibility results in an awareness among railway designers and planners of the limits of legal-contractual control. Furthermore, Rail Administration designers and planners are very aware that the media, the public and even other authorities may not acknowledge a strict division of public-private responsibility, so that failure by a contractor might 'spill over' and tarnish the reputation of and trust in the Rail Administration.

Assessing and calculating risk

This section considers in greater detail how risks were assessed and calculated, using the observation data from the brainstorming exercise (the March 2007 meeting). Expert judgement is crucial for the risk assessments, since the relevant knowledge largely resides in specialised professional experience – in land management, environmental protection, engineering or hydrogeology. In some cases, a single expert makes the assessment or leads the process; experts in other fields simply delegate much of the assessment to the specialist, since they know little of the matter. Sometimes expert knowledge is negotiated in the group so as to arrive at a consensual position. This is clear from observation 1:

> 1. A risk that led to some discussion was [it is forgotten that traffic on the existing line is affected]. The specialist who identified this risk used the term 'KTrav',[9] about which the others seemed to know little. He explained that KTrav consists of contracts between the Rail Administration and rail transport companies that serve to regulate capacity of and access to the railway, and that these conditions must be described 18 months ahead of time: 'Transport companies like to know about any reduction of speed, loss of power and how long interruptions will be in advance, and such interruptions must be carefully justified'. Participants discussed this risk, and the consequence was suggested to be between 3 and 5 (Project planning meeting, March 2007, translation mine).

In this instance, the knowledge of a single specialist was dominant in the identification and description of the risk and in attributing prominence to it. Specialist competence is vital in establishing the substance of a claim that something is (or is not) a risk and how it should be assessed according to consequences and probability. The brainstorming exercise can therefore give rise to widely different suggestions concerning probability or consequence (in this case, ranging from 3 to 5), since the participants have highly variable knowledge of and different frames of reference for the risk issue at hand.

As noted, a crucial observation is that the planners associated risk with circumstances over which they lacked control. Contrary to the ideals of formal risk assessment, risk was not analysed independently of its management. The following observation is illuminating:

> 2. The risks [ill-conceived planning] and [lack of competence] were met with the usual question, 'What about probability?', which in turn gave rise to laughter and lively discussion. It was commented that this is 'a likely risk, but also one likely to be managed'. The city tunnel in Malmö was brought up for comparison, and it was noted that the present project 'after all is in the countryside', presumably understood to mean that there are other, much more complex railway projects than this one (Project planning meeting, March 2007, translation mine).

This observation indicates that here the distinction between risk treatment and risk analysis has collapsed in practice, since risk treatment (what can or cannot be controlled) framed the risk analysis. The conflation of risk analysis and treatment evident in this meeting goes against the prescribed risk management procedural logic, which states that risks should *first* be analysed on the basis of the $C \times P$ calculus and that *only then*, as a rational second step in the risk management chain of actions, should treatments be identified.

The observations from the meetings reveal that the process was consensual overall; any initial disagreement over the analysis was resolved via negotiations that ensured that a group decision was achieved without dissent among the experts (as in observation 3 below). This may be attributed to a consensus-oriented 'Swedish way' of working in groups:

> 3. Discussion continued on the noted risks [landslide in Slumpån] and [Slumpån is affected by process water]. The Rail Administration environmental expert said that such risks have major consequences. The project leader suggested that the risks might be subdivided so that it would be clearer what was collapsing, the foundations of the old bridge or land masses. It was agreed that the consequences were major and warranted an estimate of 5, but that the probability was unclear. No one had an answer, and it was suggested that the risk should be classified as yellow (with a medium-sized risk estimate), with probability of 3. The project leader then asked, 'Can we agree on this?' Someone thought that the probability was too high, since 'such things occur several times every month, but there are protection measures' (Project planning meeting, March 2007, translation mine).

Another finding was that risk assessment was dependent on the specific situation in which the matter of concern was embedded. The planners had difficulties estimating risk in the abstract, since they needed to have a frame of reference in which to situate the issue. The following observation of a discussion of the risk of traffic problems when building the railway bridge over the river Slumpån illustrates how risk analysis depended on a situated framing of the issue:

4. Attention then turned to the risks [road and rail are to be built whilst under traffic] and [traffic over Slumpån on the existing railway bridge]. Answering the question, 'What is the risk of traffic problems?' someone stated that simultaneously building and maintaining traffic would be 'complex to build and difficult to plan', since it would be necessary to adapt the existing rails so that they could continue to be used. The question was raised, 'What about the probability for Slumpån?' The answer was that this 'will depend on where the bridge will be located'. The probability was estimated to be 4, and it was discussed whether it should even be 5. 'At [location X] it is possible to plan, but probability will depend on the exact location of the line'. What about probability? Nobody seemed to know, and it was said that 'it can occur' [i.e., traffic problems]. The probability 3 was then suggested (Project planning meeting, March 2007, translation mine).

In observation 4, the framing was implicit and seemed to change as the discussion progressed, shifting the probability from 5 to 3. The discussion in the group served to negotiate a shared frame of reference for assessing probability and consequence. A lesson from this observation is that probability estimates tend to be meaningless unless the framing of the problem is made explicit.

These observations illustrate how planners actually proceeded with risk calculation. They did not actually calculate risk by assessing probability and consequence ($C \times P$), as is prescribed by standardised risk management guidelines. Risk was approached not analytically but 'practically', by sorting the forecasted events into those that could and could not be controlled. The observations also indicate the contextual sensitivity and dependency of risk assessment and how planners must shoe-horn the knowledge they have of contingencies in railway planning and design into the $C \times P$ calculation.

Measures of probability and consequence tended to be produced in a rather *ad hoc* fashion. On occasion, probabilities and consequences were (as in observation 3) even established *post hoc*, after the risk was first classified according to the red–yellow–green risk management typology. In practice, therefore, risk calculation was the product of an intuitive risk assessment rather than the result of a calculation of consequence and probability. In practice, the formula for estimating risk ($R = P \times C$) was not applied. Consequence was equated with control: if the project team and Rail Administration were in control, the probability and risk were both deemed low.

These snapshots of actual practice in the identification and assessment of risk in railway planning reveal that statistical analysis (based on calculated incident frequency or modelling based on causal and probabilistic parameters) did not play an independent role in the process of measuring and codifying risk. Practical experience of railway planning and knowledge of what had or had not worked in past projects outweighed formal procedure. Planners' knowledge of the history of other projects derived from both personal experience and storytelling among planners, consultants and designers about the lessons learned elsewhere. Risk management in railway planning therefore has a narrative organisational dimension (see Czarniawska 1998; Law 1994).

Although conducted in a group as a 'brainstorming' exercise, risk identification was linked to individual professional expertise. The experts seldom disagreed with each other; possible differences were negotiated away so that agreement was reached. This consensual style was linked to accountability, since if an expert argues for a particular risk and this risk is turned down by the group, this might lead to problems should the risk come to pass. The actors collaborating in the project, whether consultants or Rail Administration officials, had a shared interest in acting in unison, to maintain a united front protecting the project from various threats. Although the participants might have had different agendas deriving from their specific competencies and interests, they had a shared goal in that all had an interest in a smooth planning process and attaining the goal of an officially approved railway plan. They collaborated to produce a 'stable organisational alignment' that would hold the project together (Suchman 2003).

The risk identification exercise that followed the formal risk management guidelines served as input into the risk management plan. This framed risk management as a collection of actions regarding numerous specific risks, each dealt with separately, which is very similar to how risk is treated in EIAs (Corvellec & Boholm 2008). The approach was bureaucratic, defining phenomena as discrete and amenable to labelling, categorising and sorting into slots associated with a specific rule-bound action or measure. Awareness of the complexity of railway planning cropped up in the discussions among the planners and revealed a world of systemic interdependencies between interacting people, machines and biological and physical matter, all bound together as the 'project'. The planners used the formal management model – the bureaucratic ordering of the risk management plan – in their own way by translating it into the practical reality of railway planning as they knew it.

This case study of railway planning demonstrates how risk analysis was embedded in expert practical knowledge. As practised in that setting, probability assessment lacked even a remote affinity with statistical calculation; it derived from practical experience, what the planners knew from past projects and the inferences they drew about the success or failure of future events and actions. A major conclusion is that there was a creative tension in railway planning between a bureaucratic mode of organising in terms of a formal (rule-bound, standardised and context independent) ordering and an informal (intuitive, practice-based and context-dependent) ordering.

Discussion

Risk management guidelines and tools are ultimately abstract. The ideal is that the model is applicable to any risk in any context and that every risk can be approached within a single framework, by a single procedural logic that moves in a sequence from identification, analysis and evaluation through to treatment and monitoring. The practice of risk management is about managing specific, identified risks in some way or another: a risk is always a danger *of* something (sometimes natural, sometimes social) *for* somebody in a given social nexus (Gregersen 2003: 356). Organisations are expected to relate to and manage specific risks identified from values, assets or governmental responsibilities, not 'risk' in general. Furthermore, the reality that officials, experts and practitioners engage with is often complex, involving diverse goals and competing priorities. Therefore, general rules and standards are invariably negotiated and adapted in context to be applicable to practical cases and concerns (Johansson 2012). The fact of organisational complexity and the relativity of perspectives on risk – the meanings of a risk for a stakeholder living in the vicinity of the new line being different to those for a local politician or municipal official, a technical expert or a Rail Administration representative – calls for reflective approaches (Pidgeon 1998) that acknowledge the context and framing of a risk issue as important parts of organisational risk management (Turner 1994).

Another problem with risk management guidelines is the idea that risk has an objective existence independent of interpretations, values and ethics (Turner 1994). Risk management manuals construe risk in mathematical terms as the statistical probability of an outcome in combination with the severity of its effect as measured in terms of economic loss, death, injury, ill health or other negative consequences. The 'natural attitude' of policy makers and regulators (Bradbury 1989) is that risk is located 'out there' in the external world, ready to be detected by adopting procedural rules to identify and measure sources of potential harm, to establish causal relationships and to assess probabilities. A positivistic perspective on risk takes meanings, interpretations, interests, values and ethics for granted. It concentrates on the empirical description, measurement and calculation of causal relationships to produce 'accurate' risk assessment but ignores the fact that knowledge of risk has practical, cultural, social and political dimensions. Despite criticism from anthropology, science and technology studies, psychology and philosophy (see for example Hansson 2010; Jasanoff 1995, 1999; Slovic 1999; Shrader-Frechette 1991), the view of risk and risk management as a matter of objective facts and rational assessment maintains a stranglehold when it comes to managerial models of organisational risk.

We have seen how risk management is mainly done by experts who might be regarded as 'proficient performers' with substantial practical experience of solving relevant problems that allows them to 'operate from a mature, holistic, well-tried understanding, intuitively and without conscious deliberation' (Flyvbjerg 2001: 18). Flyvbjerg notes that the intuition of the expert performer is not a matter of 'guesswork' or 'irrationality'. The freedom from rules can be taken as a sign of 'virtuosity', since the expert performer has a holistic and intuitive understanding of a wide repertoire of cases and problems encountered and managed in the past, knowledge that can be immediately activated in in relation to any current problem (Dreyfus 1997; Flyvbjerg 2001: 20). If this is the case, the argument that the imposition of bureaucratic, rule-bound formal models will lead to better risk management (see Akintoye & MacLeod 1997; Flanagan & Norman 1993; Uher & Toakley 1998) loses some persuasive power.

Lessons from organisational studies regarding the practical and social constitution of safety (Turner & Pidgeon 1997; Vaughan 1996) need to be brought into consideration in the mainstream risk management field. The present study argues, as do Gherardi and Nicolini (2003: 208), that risk management is a 'situated practice'. If risk management guidelines and tools do not resonate with the practical mode of organising the management of risk and safety, they will live a life of their own in some distant abstract, normative realm detached from the practical reality of actors. Consequently, much more attention should be paid to how risk management is contextualised from a practical organisational perspective, where responsibility, expertise, accountability, trust, coordination and communication are fundamental to effective management.

References

Akintoye, A.S. & MacLeod, M.J. 1997. Risk analysis and management in construction. *International Journal of Project Management* 15(1): 31–38.

Beck, U. 1992 [1986]. *Risk society: Towards a new modernity*. London, UK: SAGE.

Boholm, Å. 2013a. Messy logic: Organisational interactions and joint commitment in railway planning. In *Organisational anthropology: Doing ethnography in and among complex organisations*. Garsten, C. & Nyqvist, A. (eds.), pp. 169–186. London, UK: Pluto Press.

Boholm, Å. 2013b. From within a community of planners: Hypercomplexity in railway design work. In *Elusive promises: Planning in the contemporary world*. Abraham, S. & Weszkalnys, G. (eds.), pp. 57–75. New York, NY: Berghahn.

Boholm, M. 2009. Risk and causality in newspaper reporting. *Risk Analysis* 29(11): 1566–1577.

Bradbury, J. 1989. The policy implications of differing concepts of risk. *Science, Technology and Human Values* 14(4): 380–399.

Corvellec, H. 2009. The practice of risk management: Silence is not absence. *Risk Management* 11(3–4): 285–304.

Corvellec, H. 2010. How organisational risk derives from what managers value. *Journal of Contingency and Crisis Management* 18: 145–154.

Corvellec, H. & Boholm, Å. 2008. The risk/no-risk rhetoric of environmental impact assessments (EIA): The case of off-shore wind farms in Sweden. *Local Environment* 13(7): 627–640.

Czarniawska, B. 1998. *A narrative approach in organization studies*. Thousand Oaks, CA: SAGE.

Dean, M. 1999. *Governmentality: Power and rule in modern society*. London, UK: SAGE.

Dreyfus, H.L. 1997. Intuitive, deliberative, and calculative models of expert performance. In *Naturalistic decision making*. Zsambok, C.E. & Klein, G. (eds.), pp. 17–28. Mahwah, NJ: Lawrence Erlbaum Associates.

Edwards, L. 1995. *Practical risk management in the construction industry*. London, UK: Thomas Telford Publications.

Flanagan, R. & Norman, G. 1993. *Risk management and construction*. Oxford, UK: Wiley-Blackwell.

Flyvbjerg, B. 2001. *Making social science matter: Why social inquiry fails and how it can succeed again*. Cambridge, UK: Cambridge University Press.

Gherardi, S. 2000. Practice-based theorizing on learning and knowing in organizations. *Organization* 7(2): 211–223.

Gherardi, S. & Nicolini, D. 2002. Learning the trade: A culture of safety in practice. *Organization* 9(2): 191–223.

Gherardi, S. & Nicolini, D. 2003. To transfer is to transform: The circulation of safety knowledge. In *Knowing in organizations: A practice-based approach*. Nicolini, D., Gherardi, S. & Yanow, D. (eds.), pp. 204–224. London, UK: M.E. Sharp.

Giddens, A. 1990. *The consequences of modernity*. Chicago: Polity Press.

Gregersen, N.H. 2003. Risk and religion: Toward a theology of risk taking. *Zygon* 38(2): 355–376.

Hacking, I. 1990. *The taming of chance*. Cambridge, UK: Cambridge University Press.

Hansson, S.O. 2010. Risk: Objective or subjective, facts or values. *Journal of Risk Research* 13(2): 231–238.

Hartford, D.N.D. & Baecher, G.B. 2004. *Risk and uncertainty in dam safety*. London, UK: Thomas Telford Publications.

Hillson, D. 2007. Surveying the risk management universe – Where are we now? In *The risk management universe: A guided tour*. Hillson, D. (ed.), pp. 1–9. London, UK: The British Standards Institution.

Hood, C., Rothstein, H. & Baldwin, R. 2001. *The government of risk: Understanding risk regulation regimes*. Oxford, UK: Oxford University Press.

Hutter, B. & Power, M. (eds.). 2005. *Organizational encounters with risk*. Cambridge, UK: Cambridge University Press.

Jasanoff, S. 1995. Procedural choices in regulatory science. *Technology in Society* 17(3): 279–293.

Jasanoff, S. 1999. The songlines of risk. *Environmental Values* 8: 135–152.

Johansson, V. 2012. Negotiating bureaucrats. *Public Administration* 90(4): 1032–1046.

Kadefors, A. 2004. Trust in project relationships: Inside the black box. *International Journal of Project Management* 22: 175–182.

Kallenberg, K. 2009. Operational risk management in Swedish industry: Emergence of a new risk management paradigm? *Risk Management* 11: 90–110.

Law, J. 1994. Organization, narrative and strategy. In *Towards a new theory of organizations*. Hassard, J. & Parker, M. (eds.), pp. 248–268. London, UK: Routledge.

Löfstedt, R. 2005. *Risk management in post-trust societies*. New York, NY: Palgrave Macmillan.

Luhmann, N. 1993. *Risk: A sociological theory*. New York, NY: Aldine de Gruyter.

Pidgeon, N. 1991. Safety culture and risk management in organizations. *Journal of Cross-Cultural Psychology* 22(1): 129–140.

Pidgeon, N. 1998. Safety culture: Key theoretical issues. *Work & Stress* 12(3): 202–216.

Power, M. 2007. *Organized uncertainty: Designing a world of risk management*. Oxford, UK: Oxford University Press.

Power, M., Scheytt, T., Soin, K. & Sahlin, K. 2009. Reputational risk as a logic of organizing in late modernity. *Organization Studies* 30(2–3): 301–324.

Reith, G. 2004. Uncertain times: The notion of 'risk' and the development of modernity. *Time & Society* 13(2–3): 382–402.

Rothstein, H., Huber, M. & Gaskell, G. 2006. A theory of risk colonization: The spiralling regulatory logics of societal and institutional risk. *Economy and Society* 35(1): 91–112.

Royal Society Study Group. 1983. *Risk Assessment. Report of a Royal Society Study Group*. London, UK: The Royal Society.

Shrader-Frechette, K.S. 1991. *Risk and rationality: Philosophical foundations for populist reforms*. Berkeley, CA: University of California Press.

Slovic, P. 1999. Trust, emotion, sex, politics, and science: Surveying the risk-assessment battlefield. *Risk Analysis* 19(4): 689–701.

Suchman, L. 2003. Organizing alignment: The case of bridge building. In *Knowing in organizations: A practice-based approach*. Nicolini, D., Gherardi, S. & Yanow, D. (eds.), pp. 187–203. London, UK: M.E. Sharp.

Swedish Rescue Agency (Räddningsverket). 2003. *Handbok för Riskanalys*. Karlstad, Sweden: Räddningsverket.

Turner, B.A. 1994. The future of risk research. *Journal of Contingencies and Crisis Management* 2(3): 146–156.

Turner, B.A. & Pidgeon, N. 1997. *Man-made disasters*. London, UK: Butterworth Heinemann.

Uher, T.E. & Toakley, A.R. 1998. Risk management in the conceptual phase of a project. *International Journal of Project Management* 17(3): 161–169.

Vaughan, D. 1996. *The Challenger launch decision: Risky technology, culture, and deviance at NASA*. Chicago, IL: University of Chicago Press.

Regulations

SFS 1998: 808. Miljöbalk [The environmental code].

SFS 1995: 1649. Lag om byggande av järnväg [The railway building act].

SFS 1995: 1300. Förordning om statliga myndigheters riskhantering [Regulation on government authorities' risk management].

SFS 1996: 734. Förordning om statens spåranläggningar [Regulation on the government's rail track facilities].

SFS 1997: 756. Lag om tilldelning av spårkapacitet [The distribution of rail track capacity act].

BVF 015. 2008. Riskhantering i Banverket [Risk management in the Rail Administration], F07-14965/AL20, 1 Feb. 2008.

BVH 015. 2006. Banverkets riskhantering: Handbok [Rail Administration risk management handbook], HK06-967/AL 20, 1 July 2006.

Standards

A Risk Management Standard. Association of Insurance and Risk Management (AIRMIC), Institute of Risk Management (IRM) & National Forum for Risk Management in the Public Sector (ALARM). 2002. London, UK.

A Risk Management Standard. Federation of European Risk Management Associations (FERMA). 2003. Brussels, Belgium.

Risk Management. Standards Australia and Standards New Zealand. AS/NZS 4360: 2004. Sydney & Wellington, Australia.

Risk Management Guidelines. Standards Australia and Standards New Zealand. HB 436: 2004. Sydney & Wellington, Australia.

Notes

1. For example, see standards issued by the Federation of European Risk Management Associations (FERMA), the UK-based Institute of Risk Management (IRM), the Association of Insurance and Risk Management (AIRMIC) and the National Forum for Risk Management in the Public Sector (ALARM), as well as the Australian Risk Management Standard formulated by a number of academic institutions and government authorities.

2. Building was planned to commence in 2009, with completion in 2012. The railway investigation report was completed in June 2006; the matter was referred by the National Rail Administration to the government in March 2007 for permitting, which was finally granted in May 2008. Meanwhile, the Rail Administration project management team of planners and designers continued to work on the railway plan for the selected route. The budget for the sub-project was 1.2 billion kr.

3. Rail Administration Consulting (RAC) was founded in 1998 as part of the Rail Administration. Since 2001, RAC has operated on the free market in competition with other consultancy companies to win contracts for rail planning projects from the Rail Administration.

4. Banverket. Kvalitetspolicy. www.banverket.se/sv/Amnen/Om-Banverket /Verksamheten/Policydokument/Kvalitetspolicy.aspx (accessed 1 June 2009).

5. The Rail Administration regulation for risk management (BVF 015 2008) and its risk management handbook (BVH 015 2006) have much in common with international risk management standards, such as the AIRMIC, ALARM, IRM 2002, and FERMA 2003 standards. The Swedish Rescue Agency (2003) has also published a handbook for risk analysis for Swedish authorities based on similar ideas.

6. This well-established approach to risk assessment traces back to The Royal Society (1983).

7. 'Brainstorming' exercises are noted in the risk management literature as instances of 'what-if' analysis that encourage 'brainstorms of destructive thinking' as antidotes to overconfident enthusiasm (Flanagan & Norman 1993: 5).

This tool is often recognised although seldom problematised in international risk management standards and handbooks (see e.g., *Risk Management Guidelines Handbook, Standards Australia and Standards New Zealand*, pp. 37–40).

8. For example, see *Risk Management Guidelines Handbook, Standards Australia and Standards New Zealand*, pp. 49–56.

9. KTrav comprises short-term traffic agreements, according to the regulation governing the Swedish state's rail track installations (SFS 1996: 734) and the regulation governing allocation of rail track capacity (SFS 1997: 756).

6

THE PUBLIC MEETING AS A THEATRE OF DISSENT

Risk and hazard in environmental decision making

Participation in land-use planning depends on the category of participants and the roles they have in the planning process (Petts 1999). A developer, a governmental authority, a local resident, a stakeholder group and an environmental group each have different interests and motives that will be brought to bear. Also, the scope of options for participation may vary, from being solely a recipient of information about a project to becoming a participant in planning and decision making in ways that can actually influence the outcome of a project. Public meetings are one of several formats used by government agencies, municipalities and companies to inform the public and stakeholders about local projects or planning ventures. These meetings facilitate the dissemination of planning alternatives and the goals and objectives, including risks and benefits, associated with decision alternatives. However, being consulted does not automatically imply having power within the decision-making process (Soneryd 2003).

According to the Swedish Environmental Code,[1] consultation meetings are mandatory in environmental planning processes. An environmental impact assessment (EIA) must include 'consultation' (*samråd* in Swedish), held at several stages of the project, with the affected authorities and municipalities and the county administrative board, as well as the public and interested organisations. The Environmental Code does not specify the form of consultation; it states only that consultation should be held and documented at certain junctures in the planning process. The Code distinguishes between early and late consultation; the rationale for early consultation is the provision of inputs into the EIA at the stage of applying for necessary permits.

Public trust in government is relatively high in Sweden (Löfstedt 2005). The various tiers of public administration favour a consensual style of risk regulation with expert advice playing a key role in decision making. The public often has a very limited effective role in the planning process, and the consultation process prescribed by the Environmental Code mainly serves as a forum for negotiation between different authorities (Päiviö & Wallentius 2001; Rönnborg 2006). The common format for consultation with citizens is a public meeting where information is delivered by authorities and project managers. The public and identified stakeholders are invited to comment, discuss, ask questions, criticise and voice consent or dissent. Although suggestive of an open political arena, consultation in practice offers little deliberation between government and citizens. There also are requirements for consultation according to the Planning and Building Act, but at this stage municipal plans are usually advertised so that people may take part in the scheduled presentations and deliver commentaries in writing before a set date.

Consultation meetings as part of an EIA related to infrastructure development invariably address a multitude of risk issues (Corvellec & Boholm 2008). Risks arising from, for example, a new road, railway line, wind farm, cell phone mast or airport extension may be identified in such diverse areas as construction technology, groundwater flows, animal and plant life, landscape aesthetics and human health. What are the risks? How big are they? How can risk be assessed? What priorities should be set? What values are at stake? How should those values be prioritised? Should there be more or less concern about birds at risk than about flowers? Is causing physical harm to humans worse than causing psychological trauma? These kinds of questions tend to arise when major projects are planned even in a local-scale setting. It is not just the sheer number of issues and perspectives that adds to the complexity. Knowledge of any of these issues necessarily is knowledge from a certain standpoint (van den Hove 2006), and standpoints may be divergent, sometimes dramatically so. Such 'coexistence of irreducible standpoints' (van den Hove 2006: 11) has two possible solutions: either one standpoint establishes a hegemonic position vis-à-vis all others or the proponents of the standpoints must communicate and exchange views, arguments and facts in order to arrive at some form of consensus solution to the common problem.

The multitude of specific consequences and risks of policy decisions about land use, environmental planning and natural resource management offers rich nourishment for heated local debate. When locations need to be found for infrastructural facilities or industrial plants, the voicing of conflicting interests, values, demands and wishes regarding the uses and meanings of a particular landscape will follow (Boholm & Löfstedt 2004). Planning sets in motion processes of counter-planning, which likely will give rise to rhetorical battles between the opposing forces, each side seeking arguments to destroy the other in a power contest over what the decision alternatives are and which of them will be chosen. Ultimately, the legitimacy of power over the local environment is at stake (Binde & Boholm 2004; Corvellec 2001; Hobbs 2011; Sidaway 2005).

The heated and long-drawn disagreements that result sometimes continue for many years. Arguments in favour of one point of view or another are embedded in a broader discourse on trust and mistrust, responsibility and accountability of authorities and regulatory bodies (Binde & Boholm 2004; Boholm 2000, 2005a; Corvellec 2001). Such debates display a rhetorical organisational logic very different from any ideal model of decision making characterised by 'perfect dialogues between rational actors convincing each other on the mere virtue of their arguments' (Corvellec 2001: 37–38).

Face-to-face interaction among participants over a set period of time is characteristic of meetings for risk communication. They spend time together in the same room and communicate verbally and non-verbally, the course of interaction unfolding as an interplay among the participants. Despite the fact that public meetings and other forms of face-to-face discussions and interactions are prominent and often-used arenas for risk communication and environmental management (Chess & Purcell 1999), there is a surprising lack of research on the subject, particularly on deliberate efforts to involve the public in democratic processes (Fiorino 1990; McComas 2003a, 2003b; Ryfe 2005). The literature is mainly prescriptive and normative, discussing how ideals such as dialogue and participation – taken to be conducive to trust-building and to conferring the legitimacy for which government agencies yearn – can be achieved in practice (Renn 2004). Many public meetings fail due to open conflict, distrust and, sometimes, lack of interest (very few citizens show up). Noted problems include the substance of the meetings and what is accomplished by them (McComas 2003a, 2003b). Public meetings as a forum for consultation with the public have been criticised both for over- and under-representation. Strongly voiced stakeholders or citizen interests can use the opportunity to exercise undue influence. However, there are very few published empirical studies of actual meetings and the communication taking place in them. In one such study of participants' views of meetings held regarding two proposed waste sites in upstate New York, a major conclusion was that most felt the meetings to be quite meaningless (McComas 2003a) and that those attending, especially the more active participants, tended to distrust the organisers (McComas 2003b).

This chapter aims to fill part of this gap by means of an ethnographic case study of communication at local public meetings concerning the Hallandsås railway tunnel project in southern Sweden. The study was conducted over a period of almost seven years; within this time the tunnel project was followed continuously from early 1998 to mid-2004. Field observations were made by the author between January 2000 and 1 June 2004 of almost 20 official public meetings that dealt with the railway tunnel. There were basically three types of local meetings, although they were similar in organisational structure: consultation meetings as mandated by the Environmental Code, information meetings ('consultation forums') called by the Rail Administration and court hearings held by the Environmental Court and the Supreme Environmental Court.[2] Notes taken at the meetings documented the key participants who were present; the topics that were introduced and discussed; and the statements, arguments and verbal expressions that were used, as well as the emotional tone and attitude and other features that pertained to the context in which the communication took place. Most of the meetings were taped[3] to supplement the notes. In addition, each meeting was officially documented and these minutes were later published on the Hallandsås tunnel project's home page on the Internet.[4] Other sources have been used, including informal talks with and spontaneous questions asked of participants at the meetings (officials, experts, stakeholders and citizens). Local media[5] reports from the meetings served as another source of information. It needs mentioning that research on the Hallandsås tunnel project was conducted by a small team of researchers from University of Gothenburg, Sweden, and that three to four individuals often were present at meetings and could therefore check and compare observations, notes and impressions.

A brief outline of the theoretical framework is needed before proceeding to the presentation of the case. Communication about risk at consultation meetings is approached from a pragmatic perspective addressing the context of communication, including the assumptions, knowledge, experience, intentions and actions of participants. Communication is understood as a situated social activity (Allwood 2000). People attend consultation meetings for different reasons: A public official goes to a meeting to present a proposal for a new landfill site because this is part of their work as a representative of the decision-making and regulatory authority, while a local resident attends the same meeting because they live near the proposed site and it will affect their neighbourhood (see Luhmann 1993: Ch. 6). So from the onset the participants have very different roles in the communication that will ensue at the meeting. Therefore, we need to address not only the factual content communicated but the manner of presentation of that content to the audience. Communication is a complex process of creation and interpretation of meaning, situated in social life. The process includes the participants in terms of the roles they have, their motivations and their practical rationality, as well as the structures and procedures that condition communication and how 'relevance' in communication is established – that is to say, what relationships are considered meaningful and how interconnections between messages are made (Allwood 2000; Sperber & Wilson 2003).

The present study addresses how cooperation is established and maintained in communicating about risk, how conflicts are managed and how participants with different roles and status interact – as experts and laypersons, decision makers and stakeholders – particularly as there can be no expectation that they will share assumptions and knowledge or have convergent interests and communicative intentions.

Back on track – the Hallandsås railway tunnel

The railway tunnel project[6] commenced in 1992 and was strongly contested for a number of reasons, most of which emerged from the unexpectedly difficult hydrogeological conditions of the Hallandsås ridge. The Hallandsås ridge is partly an agricultural area, with many farms specialising in vegetable growing and dairy and animal husbandry, but also encompasses a nature reserve. The Hallandsås tunnel belongs to a category of mega-projects – complicated multibillion-kronor investments in infrastructure (tunnels, bridges, airports, railways and roads) – that systematically become far more expensive than originally budgeted (Flyvbjerg,

Bruzelius & Rothengatter 2003). In most cases, such works are publicly funded and promise huge benefits for society, in terms of growth, quality of life, regional development and national or international integration. Characteristically, these projects are technically and organisationally complex and depend on the mobilisation of networks of diverse participants over long periods of time. The projects also draw heavily on symbolism and give rise to motivational arguments to legitimate the project and to prove its merits (Boholm 2005a; Darian-Smith 1999; Latour 1996).

Tunnel construction started in October 1992, but it encountered considerable technical problems in 1995-1996 when groundwater leaked uncontrollably from the excavations in quantities far greater than those permitted by a decision from the Water Rights Court. Attempts at sealing the flow did not work properly, and in 1996 a dramatic lowering of the water table was noticed as wells above the tunnel areas began to dry out. This caused inconvenience and expense for local residents and farmers who depended on a reliable supply of water for irrigation, cleaning and a drinking source for their animals. An attempt was made to deal with the leaking tunnels using the chemical sealant Rhoca-Gil, but this procedure dispersed acrylamide – a component of the sealant and a known toxin – into the groundwater, wells and streams (Baier 2003; Boholm & Löfstedt 1999; Löfstedt & Boholm 1999; Sjölander-Lindqvist 2004).

The project was stopped in October 1997 after the toxic leak and the dramatic losses of groundwater. Several government commissions and investigations were launched to establish what had gone wrong. Various court proceedings also were initiated to investigate the legal aspects of the project and to determine legal responsibility for the violation of the water permit, the toxic leak and the acrylamide poisoning of some of the tunnel workers (Heiefort 2004). In 2001 the Swedish government decided that, on condition that the relevant authorities gave the necessary permits, the tunnel should be built despite the past problems and the fact that it had become much more expensive. A new water permit deemed necessary by the Rail Administration to complete the tunnels was granted by the Environmental Supreme Court in 2003, and the Båstad municipality granted the building permit. Construction by the contractors Skanska (previously on the project) and Vinci (newly appointed) began in 2004–2005 using new technology, including deep-freezing the unstable parts of the ridge and using a new, specially designed state-of-the-art tunnel-boring machine. A final breakthrough in the tunnel-boring process was achieved on 4 September 2013. In the original plan, the tunnel was to be inaugurated in 2000, but given the history, the opening was postponed until 2015.

Leaking groundwater from the tunnel and of course the culminating poisoning were sources of concern for local residents. Most were worried about the long-term effects on the surrounding environment and the local landscape and about how agriculture would be affected in the future (Sjölander-Lindqvist 2004). Environmental investigations and environmental court proceedings were initiated in order to assess risk and decide what was 'acceptable'. While some institutions and actors were in favour of the tunnel, others were hesitant and still others decidedly against it, especially, and understandably, the local residents and farmers who had been most severely affected. Since the tunnel was being built in a democratic society, dialogue and consultation among various stakeholders and interests were essential.

A great number of participants were involved in the process – government agencies, companies, experts, members of nongovernmental organizations (NGOs), local citizens and the news media. Communication was profuse and enlivened by means of an array of media: information brochures; political, administrative and legal documents; EIAs; expert reports; newspaper articles; films and photography; speeches at information meetings; and informal commentaries. Goals, aims and reasons for decisions were formulated, explained, deliberated and criticised. Since 1998, the Rail Administration's Hallandsås project arranged a number of local consultation meetings at which these kinds of information about the project were conveyed to the general public, who in turn had the opportunity to discuss it, ask questions and express their opinions.

Public consultation – forums for communication

Between the project's commencement in October 1992 and the toxic leak in October 1997, the Rail Administration did not arrange any meetings or information activities for the local public. Beginning in 1996, home owners and farmers having problems with wells going dry were dealt with individually. There was no concerted effort to address the issues adversely affecting local people and environments or to incorporate these issues into the scope of the project (Sjölander-Lindqvist 2004). Following the toxic leak in October 1997, the municipality of Båstad declared parts of the Hallandsås ridge a risk area and initiated a crisis group to handle residents' worries. Turbulent days followed. The Environmental Assessment Group (Miljögranskningsgruppen [MGG]) – commissioned by the Rail Administration to assess the environmental impacts of the tunnel project and composed of experts in hydrogeology, chemistry and ecology – soon assumed the role of communicators of facts and risk assessments, while the Rail Administration's project management team stepped into the background. At the time, public trust in the Rail Administration was low (Boholm & Löfstedt 1999; Palm 1998) whilst MGG and the Båstad municipality fared better in perceptions. Between October 1997 and January 1998, MGG had a number of formal and informal contacts with individuals, organisations, interest groups and local residents.[7] Most of these contacts came in the form of informational meetings arranged in collaboration with stakeholder organisations like the local branch of the Swedish Society for Nature Conservation, three resident road associations from the northern side of the ridge and residents on the southern side, represented by their lawyer.

Issues discussed at these meetings ranged from the effects of the tunnel-building on water resources and the risk of acrylamide contamination and of further spread of the chemical to complaints by residents about the management of the situation by the authorities and about matters regarding water distribution. At first, these meetings and information efforts were not announced publicly and were targeted at affected groups to deal directly with their issues and problems. In January 1998, MGG acknowledged the value of having a more formal forum for providing information about various aspects of the tunnel project to those affected when it announced that the tunnel project was gradually moving from a stage of acute mitigation to one of planning for continuation.[8] The group noted that such a continuation of the tunnel project would need a consultation process (*samrådsprocess* in Swedish) in accordance with the demands of the Environmental Code (§§ 4 and 5); MGG considered the contacts and meetings held during the last three months of 1997 to be a good start.[9]

Regarding the consultation process (*utökat samråd* in Swedish) required ahead of an eventual restart of the tunnel building project, MGG noted 'a great need for public transparency and opportunity to influence'.[10] The group considered various models for the organisation of such a process. One was the open public meeting (*stormöte* in Swedish) with a panel of experts. The stated advantage of this format was that it excluded no one from participation. Some drawbacks were also noted, namely that the experts might play too prominent a role and that aggressive voices and extreme opinions might dominate the discussion at the cost of more moderate opinions. Another option discussed was a 'limited consultation' (*begränsat samråd* in Swedish), which would be publicly announced but would require special invitation to attend. The rationale for such restricted meetings was that representatives of the Rail Administration, the municipality, the building contractor and specially invited experts could then communicate with affected local residents and other stakeholder groups. This more exclusive meeting format was never used.

The first consultation meeting, called a consultation forum (*samrådsforum* in Swedish) was held on 9 March 1998 in the municipality office in Båstad. Sixteen citizens were present (several of whom had been active in attending meetings and following the tunnel project for an extended period of time), together with two local journalists, representatives from the Båstad municipality and a representative from MGG. The official minutes from the meeting note the following: MGG should be the organiser of the meetings; MGG should see that minutes are taken; the Rail Administration and Skanska (the building contractor) can be represented but should not be the organisers; the meeting should be based on dialogue and not on one-way dissemination of information; there should be printed announcements of the meetings; and the national mass media should not be allowed to attend. In addition, the meeting defined a number of tasks for MGG to fulfil: establish the amount of acrylamide remaining in a local stream and in private wells, assess the risk of damage to buildings due to the lowered water table, assess the risk from altered flows of groundwater when the levels were restored and answer questions about whether local residents had any legal mechanisms and grounds to ask for the water permit to be revoked.[11]

The next meeting was held three weeks later (30 March 1998) in a school in Båstad.[12] Attendance at this meeting was as before, with the addition of a few newcomers, including additional representatives from the municipality and a representative of the Rail Administration. The formal procedures and aims of the meetings were restated; the topics for discussion concerned acrylamide in agricultural produce and the legal status of the water permit. The Rail Administration's newly recruited project manager noted that as he was new to the job, he had limited experience of events before October 1997. Noting that the relationship between the Rail Administration and the local public was strained, he suggested that 'we' should now look forward. The project manager declared that tunnel construction in the future would continue only on the condition that it would not harm the environment or the residents of the area. He explained that the Rail Administration had learned a lesson from 'the events' (referring to the acrylamide incident). Several people at the meeting enquired as to what guarantees there were that mistakes would not be made in the future. To this the project manager answered that the project would be certified and have external audits. A number of questions were then raised, such as: Who will be responsible for judging future risk? How big is the potentially affected area? How should the currently permitted limit of 33 litres of water discharged per second be interpreted? How will the water quality in wells be affected? What about alternative routes for the new railway? How will streams, springs and groundwater be affected? Have wild animals and farm animals been affected by drinking contaminated water, and if so, how? These questions from the first two meetings became recurrent themes of communication in the consultations held in the years that followed.

In 2000 the Rail Administration undertook an EIA of the tunnel project that was to serve as a basis for a decision by the Swedish government as to whether the project should continue and, if so, under what terms, conditions and budgetary limits. The local community now was included in the project.[13] More than 30 consultation meetings were held between October 1997 and June 2003. Six of these meetings were consultations held as part of the Rail Administration's EIA process in 2000, and their minutes were eventually presented as a report to the government.

Another major arena of communication about the tunnel project was the hearings in Båstad held by the Environmental Court (which had replaced the old Water Rights Court) and by the Environmental Supreme Court during 2002–2003. The matter in front of the Environmental Court was that the Rail Administration needed a new and considerably more generous water permit (the old one permitted a discharge of 33 litres per second, and proved to be technically unfeasible) in order to resume building the tunnel, and the Rail Administration accordingly had applied for a new limit of 100 litres per second. These proceedings were held in public and included numerous public and private stakeholders. The majority of private stakeholders were local residents and farmers who strongly opposed the proposed new permit. At these hearings the applicant and the various stakeholders were allowed to present arguments for or against the application, with special focus on the environmental consequences of the 100-litres-per-second proposal. The hearings were very well attended by Rail Administration personnel, concerned local residents, interested citizens, various experts called in to give statements, lawyers, representatives of national and local NGOs and media reporters. During the hearings, the environmental aspects of the tunnel were debated both in general terms and in minute detail. In addition to debates and presentations, the hearings included visits to a select number of sensitive local environments or biotopes so that the court obtained a more 'practical' view of what was discussed (Boholm 2005b).

The staging of a public meeting

During the meetings a variety of people spoke, argued, explained and made slide presentations that included maps and animations; decisions and their alternatives were demonstrated and explained by authorities and experts and then discussed, questioned and criticised by members of the audience. The meetings tended to have a standardised structure divided into three consecutive stages:

1. The opening, which presented the perspective of the authorities (especially the Rail Administration) and experts. An obligatory part of this stage was to present arguments proving that the tunnel project contributed to the 'greater good of society'.
2. A coffee break in the middle of the meeting.
3. The questioning, which presented various arguments against the project; dissent; and counterarguments, including claims that arguments from perspectives other than those of officials and experts must be considered. This stage could include speeches of local residents who felt victimised by the project.

Looking at the meetings over time – a period of nearly seven years from early 1998 to mid-to-late 2004, – there was surprisingly little variation. New topics emerged, of course – for example, numerous technical matters referring to the intricacies of tunnel-building technology – and individual experts as well as specific evidence came and went, but overall the communication themes remained stable and so did the conflict lines in the debate. The thematic issues concerned the legality of the project, the status and interpretation of the old and new water permits, the reasons for the project, the history of the project, the credentials and credibility of the Rail Administration, risk assessments and judgements, what was included in or should be excluded from the project environment, future scenarios, risk management operations and routines and of course, many technical matters.

The opening of the meeting

A meeting always opened with an official representative of the project (such as the project manager representing the Rail Administration) explaining the project from the point of view of the concerned authority. The national perspective and broader policy goals were made explicit. These arguments built on a number of assumptions about rail traffic, the environment, good governance and the role of the Rail Administration in society: that the railway was a safe and environmentally friendly means of transport; that the Rail Administration promoted the railway and therefore it followed (seemingly in a logical fashion) that the Administration gave priority to environmental values; that the Administration made wise decisions based on a meticulous scrutiny of decision alternatives; and that its officials worked towards a just cause ('a better society'). Another cornerstone of the argument was that the national objectives had been decided by the democratically elected government. Decision making about the Hallandsås tunnel was embedded in a broader context of more substantial decisions within the context of national environmental policy and the decision to upgrade the West Coast Railway Line (Boholm 2000). An obligatory part of the opening of a meeting was the assertion that the decision to build the tunnel was a just and rational one (because the tunnel is needed) and that the Rail Administration and project management were trustworthy (having the necessary competence and a suitable frame of mind). Here, for example, is the opening statement of the project manager at the April 2002 hearing:

> The West Coast Line is a highly prioritised railway route in Sweden. The reason for this is that capacity of rail traffic must be increased, linking Norway with the European continent. Traffic must be relocated from road to rail. Never before have so many people travelled by rail; there is a five per cent increase per year of rail travel in Sweden. There is a lack of capacity on the rail. In the region of Mälaren, for example, there has been a tremendous expansion, and we have seen a decrease in road traffic. We must counteract the increasing road traffic on the E6 motorway. With the Hallandsås tunnel we will have an increased capacity – 24 trains per hour. The single track meanders over the ridge and is a typical railway of the nineteenth century that does not live up to the requirements of today. The Hallandsås tunnel will offer a long-term opportunity to direct traffic from road to railway. This will improve the environment and road safety (Project manager, introductory address to the court, Environmental Court hearing, Båstad, 22 April 2002, notes taken and translated by author).

Over one year later, the same project manager stated:

> The project started ten years ago, and it has been standing still for over six years. The lorry traffic has doubled on the E6 motorway and will double one more time. It will be difficult to accomplish the government's environmental goals. Hallandsås is the biggest bottleneck. We have a functioning railway net, and we should be anxious to get the railway system in order. We must benefit from investments already made. The building project will be carried out as a well-planned activity, with concern for the environment. We have discussed shortcomings. But this does not mean that nothing works. It is healthy to be really self-critical from time to time. This also holds for the contractors. The investigations underlying the decisions are of high quality. [...] The environmental impact is acceptable. The entire investigation is reliable and has been commended by Naturvårdsverket (the Swedish Environmental Protection Agency) and the Statens Geotekniska Institut (Swedish Geotechnical Institute)

(Project manager, concluding address to the court, Environmental Supreme Court hearing, Båstad, 5 September 2003, notes taken by author).

The next step was presentations by experts (representing sciences such as geology, hydrogeology, ecology, biology, chemistry and the engineering technologies) on the subjects of technical matters, risk identification and risk management. These presentations tended to be structured as factual, technical expositions of states of affairs and causal relationships. They sometimes were interrupted by members of the audience who questioned a particular fact or a suggested causal relationship, or who disagreed about which facts mattered and how they should be interpreted.

The coffee break

Coffee was served with sandwiches or cakes, and the assembly would split up into small, informal gatherings of attendees who exchanged greetings and small-talk, but also held discussions on the matters at hand. Food has social meaning, and eating together is a marker of belonging and inclusion in most societies. In Swedish culture, the coffee break (*fika* in Swedish) is an institution at workplaces and at home, attended by colleagues, neighbours, visitors and friends. Drinking coffee together opens up an informal way of interacting both with those you know and with strangers and promotes small talk, personal comments and gossip. The informality of the event does not, however, mean that it lacks capacity for social structuring. The coffee break serves to 'bond' participants, making visible the borders of a social group or constellation, differentiating those who belong from those who do not belong, and indicating which actors constitute the core of the group. Serving coffee with sandwiches or cakes also expresses hospitality on the part of the host. Such hospitality may be understood as a token of social respect and recognition that people have devoted time and effort to come to the meeting.

The questioning

After coffee, the meeting re-assembled for the concluding part, which consisted of discussion followed by questions. This part characteristically displayed a number of polarised themes: factual evidence versus emotions, risks versus benefits, experts versus locals, scientific knowledge versus local experience, economic versus environmental values and trust versus suspicion. While the authorities and experts were most active during the first stage, the members of the audience became more active during this last stage of the meeting. People in the audience raised questions; made statements; reported contrary evidence; suggested alternative solutions; and often engaged in emotional outbursts born of personal frustration, anger or despair. Some such contributions received spontaneous applause. Critical speakers tended to focus on their unique competence and knowledge as a result of local residence, for example:

The former speaker [a university professor called in as an expert] does not live here. I do. We should learn from history, as history repeats itself.

> The residents are very worried. Trust in the Rail Administration is very low since they exceeded the old water permit (Resident, Environmental Court hearing, Båstad, 25 April 2002, notes taken by author).

Especially notable was a recurrent form of speech that expressed the point of view of the 'innocent victim'. At almost every meeting, one or more local residents delivered speeches with a strong moral and emotional tone, focusing on their sufferings, the destruction of unique values (losses of water, landscape and local nature) and their lack of trust in the Rail Administration and the tunnel project. These monologues could be more or less elaborated, occasionally prepared in advance and read aloud as statements. The core message was always the same: local residents had been mistreated by the authorities. The tone was quite emotional and personal and brought to the fore the suffering and despair of those who felt themselves to be victims of the decisions made by the authorities. The themes focused on perceived lack of control, lack of trust, suffering and feelings of vulnerability. For example:

> The environment, fish and water, has been on the agenda. This is good. But where is the individual person? The residents? They are shut away in the background. I want to tell about our experiences. Maybe it is a bit tedious. But it is needed. How we have been living now for several years. It has been great pressure since 1996. A foreign power has occupied our yard. 'Move, or we will drive over you!' During the summer of 1997, when the groundwater was at its lowest, we did a questionnaire covering six square kilometres including many objects, dams, brooks and wells. We compiled the answers and made a map with dates. It was a terrible sight. There was no water! We approached the county board for help. Nobody bothered. In October 1997 it stopped. The Rail Administration had exceeded the water permit for several years by 80–100 litres per second. That was done deliberately. Otherwise the project would have been stopped. The great lowering of the groundwater – that is the big crime! As a consequence of the toxic leak, we ended up living in a risk area. We were not allowed to deliver milk and animals for slaughter for a period of six weeks. We were lucky; we did not have to put down any animals. Then there was the water tank. Twice a day we had water delivered to our farm. It was an endless traffic of experts, people to take samples and workmen. Meetings after meetings. Still poor water, it was called 'serviceable but with comments', from a new drill. Not one week without contact with the Rail Administration during these years. [...] We cannot take additional problems. We want our fresh water back, and then we want to be left in peace (Farmer, concluding address to the court, Environmental Court hearing, Båstad, 25 April 2002, notes taken by author).

Such speeches, putting emotions into words, were strongly applauded by members of the audience expressing solidarity with the speaker. Confronted with such counter-rhetoric in the form of criticism, questioning of project logic and reason and projection of victimisation, the Rail Administration project management and the experts it had summoned usually adopted a position of deference. In response, they tended to repeat the project's 'reason' by presenting once again the factual arguments and statements, explicating the project's legitimacy in broad terms and emphasising the political mandate to act, but avoided answering directly any emotional or personal misgivings or grievances. Nor did they in any way discuss the planning solutions and options already excluded from the decision process. These consultative meetings thus can be described as basically two sets of monologues, separated by a coffee break. Matters were indeed very far from the participatory dialogues prescribed in the risk communication literature as being the ideal format for 'rational discourse'.

Victims versus decision makers

A recurrent observation from attending a considerable number of consultation meetings on the subject of the Hallandsås tunnel was that the meetings had a strong element of built-in conflict. This feature also is an often-reported feature of contested facility siting projects, where over time the views of those involved tend to become increasingly polarized in a continuing debate about the pros and cons of a project (Binde & Boholm 2004; Corvellec 2001). A facility siting process can give rise to a myriad of conflicts, including colliding interests and goals, diverging priorities and experiences and disputes about existing evidence and evidence needed. But what will be discussed here is not conflict in terms of opposing interests, values or standpoints deriving from either expert or lay knowledge. The interest instead is whether behind some conflicts there lies a much more profound divide between modes of agency: how individuals and groups perceive themselves in terms of agency (or lack of it) in relation to the outside world, including other people (Stoffle & Evans 1990).

Action is linked to intentionality, the capacity to act and to make things happen as planned in the world. The concept of agency distinguishes events caused by physical factors from actions caused by prior intentions:

> An agent is one who 'causes events to happen' in their vicinity. . . . An agent is the source, the origin, of causal events, independently of the state of the physical universe (Gell 1998: 16).

To have agency means that a being has a capacity to do things and get things done; there is a self-movement that is monitored from the inside ('the internal self'). It should be noted that agency is not an absolute feature of a being. It is a quality that is attributed by an observer (observing oneself or others) according to conventionalised expectations:

> The idea of agency is a culturally prescribed framework for thinking about causation, when what happens is (in some vague sense) supposed to be intended in advance by some person-agent or thing-agent (Gell 1998: 17).

Agency, as directed intentionality, has a goal that is outside of the acting being. The object acted upon is the 'patient' of the actor (Gell 1998: 21–23). Agency and 'patiency' therefore, comprise two relationally constituted states: the one who acts and the one acted upon (Gell 1998; Karlsson 2002). Decision making is a form of agency; without agency there can be no decisions. A decision can be understood as a specific form of human action and reasoning in which alternatives are assessed and computed in a systematic and deliberate process (Boholm, Henning & Krzyworzeka 2013). As shown in Chapter 1, the notion of risk is closely related to that of decision making (Luhmann 1993). Without agency and the capacity for making a deliberate choice from among alternatives, there would be no risk. Decisions, however, do not affect only the decision maker, since actions arising from decisions often have consequences for other people. Those affected find themselves in a different position than that of the decision maker; they are patients of the decision maker's agency (capacity to act).

Luhmann's distinction (1993) between risk and danger (hazard) relates to agency and lack of agency. To label something a hazard implies that it is imposed from outside a realm of decision and action. A risk, on the other hand, is considered to have an internal cause, since it presupposes agency, i.e., choice between decision alternatives (Boholm 2012). The distinction between risk and hazard, and the associated distinction between agent and patient, depends on identification of inner dispositions like intentions or on external factors (Fölsterling 2001; Heider 1958). An observer (observing self, others and the relationship between self and other) identifies agency, its source and its direction. Whether or not something is considered a risk or a hazard therefore depends on the stance of the observer, and 'if we wish to know which is which, we must observe the observer and if necessary develop theories on the conditioning of his observation' (Luhmann 1993: 27).

In the modern state, many decisions which affect citizens as individuals are delegated to other people: politicians, public officials and regulators. The relationship between decision maker and those affected by a decision (who may be called 'stakeholders') often is asymmetrical. In most cases, stakeholders find themselves in a different position to that of the decision maker; they are affected by a decision which might endanger their interests, values, identity or assets (Luhmann 1993: Ch. 6). For the stakeholder the potential negative consequences of a decision are framed in terms of hazard (as potential negative outcomes beyond the influence of the one adversely affected), while for the regulator/decision maker such consequences are framed as risk (as deliberate acts of weighing potential negative outcomes with benefits). This means that it is not the issue as such – the substantial outcome of a decision – that defines whether or not something counts as hazard or risk, but who the observer is (Table 6.1). Consequently, 'One man's risk is another man's danger' (Luhmann 1993: 153).

Risk and hazard are distinctions within the same schema (Luhmann 1993) – risk is contingency in the agency mode; hazard is contingency in the patiency mode. This means that an issue can oscillate between risk and hazard depending on how a relationship is framed in terms of agency and patiency (Gell 1998).

TABLE 6.1   Distinction between regulator/decision maker and stakeholder positions

Regulator/Decision maker	Stakeholder
Makes decisions	Affected by decisions
Agent	Patient
Calculated contingency (intentionality)	Causality
Risk mode	Hazard (danger) mode

How do these distinctions help in understanding the consultation meetings in which the Rail Administration's project managers, other officials and experts and the affected stakeholders as well as the local public met and communicated? As noted, an obligatory part of those meetings was a demonstration by the Rail Administration and contractors of their capacity to act by means of rational and well-founded decisions that the democratically elected Swedish government supported and thus politically legitimated. Such demonstrations included a display of facts to be assessed in the decision-making process that required a myriad of technical, legal and organisational decisions. The focus on aspects of risk made the decision process of building the tunnel a transparent process, and in this way, the consultation meetings can be seen as instances of 'performative governance' (Futrell 1999):

> Performative governance is a situation in which impressions of committed governance are displayed by officials yet effective inclusion of citizenry in the decision-making processes – the principal objective of the occasion – is negligible (Futrell 1999: 502).

The Rail Administration and its contractors made an effort to convince their audience of their capacity to make properly qualified decisions and to act competently on the basis of them. They claimed both competence and agency as rational decision makers, as is necessary to sustain a 'license to operate' as tunnel builders (Corvellec 2007). The other obligatory stage of the consultation meetings involved the stakeholders who used the 'concluding questions and discussion' session to voice their distrust of the Rail Administration and the tunnel project, and their long-term suffering due to the project. In terms of the meetings, the stakeholders occupied very different positions to those of the Rail Administration and associates: the former were affected directly by the decisions made by the latter; the stakeholders were the suffering party – they were the ones acted upon. They had no state-sanctioned licence with regard to the building of the tunnel and had little authority over how their own property was affected by the construction or used by the builders. Local resident stakeholders clearly identified themselves as victims of the operations. Quite simply, the tunnel for them was a hazard and not a risk.

Conflict generation in communication

'Schismogenesis' is a term introduced by Gregory Bateson (1935) in his analysis of ritual interaction and interpersonal communication. It refers to processes of social differentiation and opposition (including phenomena such as contestation, hierarchies and domination) in which the reactions of individuals to the actions of others influence and modify any future actions (Bateson 1935, 1958, 1973; Nuckolls 1995). For Bateson, interaction is the interplay of coordinated action or behaviour. Individual A reacts to the actions or behaviour of individual B, and A's reactions modify and influence B's actions or behaviour in the future, and so on in recursive fashion. Bateson distinguished analytically between two possibilities: either A and B respond to each other with similar behaviour (for example, an angry retort to an angry challenge, leading to further anger) or they respond with functionally complementary behaviours (for example, by means of contrast pairs such as dominance–submission).[14]

The consultation meetings regarding the Hallandsås tunnel developed according to a process of complementary schismogenesis revolving around risk and hazard – agency and patiency modes of existence, which differentiated the regulators from stakeholders. The more the Rail Administration officials emphasised their agency through decision-making capacity and a sustained licence to operate, the more the affected stakeholders responded by demonstrating their patiency and their consequent victimisation due to this lack of agency. The Rail Administration's discourse of risk was responded to by the stakeholders' discourse of hazard. When stakeholders argued against the tunnel project in terms of their lack of agency, it being a hazard to them, the Rail Administration officials responded by intensifying the risk discourse in an effort to convince the audience of their capacity to act and to make wise decisions. Such demonstrations of agency and decision-making capability, however, only made local residents feel more vulnerable and more exposed to the consequences of the decisions of others. This deprivation of agency *vis-à-vis* their own land and their own local and everyday environment greatly added to their frustration and increased their hostility towards the entire project (Grimes 2005; Sjölander-Lindqvist 2004).

In fact, the schismogenetic structuring of the consultation meetings resulted in a breakdown at a meeting on 27 October 2003 when the most vocally critical group of residents read a statement that expressed their feelings of victimisation at the hands of the Rail Administration and the tunnel project. During an earlier part of this meeting, the Rail Administration project manager had reported that the Environmental Supreme Court had approved the application of the Rail Administration for a new water permit. This was followed by a presentation from project management and the contractors about how an especially difficult section of the planned tunnel (with highly problematic geological conditions) could be dealt with by various technical solutions (one decision alternative being deep freezing of the surrounding materials). It was after this matter was concluded that the group of disgruntled stakeholders read a statement ending in a declaration that they would not attend any future meetings. The group of about 30 people then rose and left the room before the meeting was formally concluded. The statement was also delivered to the meeting as a written document signed by the action group

Save Lya (*Rädda Lya* in Swedish).[15] The first part of the statement consisted of a summary of the concerned stakeholders' experiences of the tunnel project:

> Let us summarise our experiences of the tunnel project together with our conclusions. There is probably no other building project in our time that has treated local residents so badly over such a long period. We have lived with the Rail Administration's illegal draining of groundwater, their betrayed promises and legal tricks since 1995, when Skanska took over the project. We have endured toxic contamination, dried-up wells, wetlands, streams and springs, diminished yields from agriculture, processes of compensation, difficulties in planning our economy and our future, recurrent intrusion and negotiations with the Rail Administration. Our lives are a continuous worry over what the Rail Administration will do next. These meetings are called Consultation Forums. But consultation requires a little bit of humility. But that has not been the attitude of the Rail Administration. They have presented biased information on decisions already made. The Rail Administration's Consultation Meetings are just plays to the galleries. We have no influence on the decision process (Spokesperson from Save Lya, MGG PM 296, Grevie, 2003, translation mine.)

In this way the stakeholder group effectively renounced their patiency to the Rail Administration's agency as the decision makers, so the subsequent meetings lost legitimacy as a consultation forum. This circumstance prompted the Rail Administration project management to rename the meetings '*Forum Hallandsås*', rather than *Samrådsforum Hallandsås*' (Hallandsås Consultation Forum). This renaming, however, did not change the essence or content of the subsequent meetings, apart from the fact that they lost much of their earlier schismogenetic dynamic, since the tussle between those in agency mode and those in patiency mode had ceased. In a conflictual interaction system, each new move – action or communication – is framed by the conflict; in an escalating conflict, the move will trigger a conflictive response. Meanings are integrated so that events, actions and communications in an escalating development are incorporated and interpreted in light of the conflict – which means that it is nearly impossible to solve conflicts from within such a system (Luhmann 1995: Ch. 9).

Discussion

Risk communication as a practice often takes for granted that other people's ideas about risks can be managed by means of skillfully designed dissemination of information – by means of pedagogical presentation of facts (Lundgren & McMakin 2004). Such efforts, however, are likely to fail, since the context of communication – the concepts and assumptions, the knowledge, experiences, expectations and social and cultural conventions that guide speaker and hearer in understanding the meanings of messages – are not taken into account sufficiently. A pragmatic perspective on risk communication shifts focus from the technical aspects of information transmission – what is to be communicated, to whom and in what way – to communication as action and interaction (Allwood 2000). Communication is not something that stands apart from interaction systems or social systems (Luhmann 1995).

Communication involves assumptions that people have about themselves, other people and the world. These assumptions steer the interpretation of messages; many assumptions are shared between those communicating, but not all. Messages there-fore can be understood differently. There is no neutral, assumption-free position from which information is interpreted. A risk communicator, in fact, has little control of the ways in which messages are understood unless the assumptions that guide the interpretation of meanings by an audience are known (Chess, Burger & McDermott 2005). Risk issues are inherently open to interpretation from diverse standpoints. Risk is observed and judged; there is no absolute risk as such. Risk is judged in relation to another state in which the risk could be the same, bigger or smaller. As we have seen in Chapters 1 and 4, the concept of risk is a *relative* term, constituted by what we know and do not know regarding potentially harmful influences between entities (Reith 2004).

In risk communication, participation often is advocated as a road towards mitigating conflicts by means of creating shared expectations, consensus and respect for other viewpoints. It is assumed that participation works through com-munication, by intensifying and broadening communication, by inviting more participants to have a say and by encouraging dialogue (Renn 2004). However, communication as such lacks a capacity to make people more cooperative and disposed to agree on a common characterisation of the world. Participation works not by enabling people to communicate but by altering or modifying existing agency-patiency relationships (Luhmann 1993: 152 ff). Participation procedures in public policy (for example, in the implementation of decisions having considerable consequences for local groups who are not the decision makers) could empower stakeholders with a capacity to act and make decisions on matters of concern to them. Such empowerment would enable stakeholders to move from a hazard mode to a risk mode of relating to an issue. But for this to occur, some of the decision-making power has to be transferred from regulators to stakeholders (Stoffle & Evans 1990).

Communication alone will not abate schismogenetic differentiation in risk communication. If mutual understanding (or an approximation of it) is a desired result, stakeholders and regulators must come to share fundamental assumptions about the context at hand – and that will require a meaningful transfer of deci-sion power from regulator to stakeholder. Such a transfer weakens the contrast between a risk mode and a hazard mode and, concomitantly, between the regula-tor's and the stakeholder's positions as adversaries. For these positions to converge (by deliberative and participatory processes), the power to make and act upon decisions must be diffused. A somewhat provocative conclusion, therefore, is that risk communication will never lead to understanding in a society that accepts the rule of the majority's view (and interests) over that of the minority. Attaining an understanding between regulator and stakeholder through risk communication is therefore a democratic paradox. On occasion, the majority may want to make decisions that will have negative side-effects for a minority, without allowing the affected minority effective agency in relation to the matter (wildlife conservation and natural resource management abound with such examples). The (democratic) principle of concentrating decision-making power in the majority means that there will always be minorities deprived of agency over matters of direct concern to them. Irrespective of the effort spent on communication, a proper understanding will not be achieved as long as the existence modes of the respective parties differ fundamentally – one party with agency making the decisions and the other with patiency taking the consequences.

References

Allwood, J. 2000. An activity-based approach to pragmatics. In *Abduction, belief and context: Studies in computational pragmatics*. Bunt, H. & Black W. (eds.), pp. 47–78. Amsterdam, the Netherlands & Philadelphia, PA: John Benjamins Publishing Company.

Baier, M. 2003. *Norm och rättsregel: En undersökning av tunnelbygget genom Hallandsås*. Lund, Sweden: Sociologiska Institutionen, Lund University.

Bateson, G. 1935. Culture contact and schismogenesis. *Man* 35: 178–183.

Bateson, G. 1958. *Naven: The culture of the Iatmul people of New Guinea as revealed through a study of the 'naven' ceremonial*. Stanford, CA: Stanford University Press.

Bateson, G. 1973. *Steps to an ecology of mind: Collected essays in anthropology, psychiatry, evolution and epistemology*. Frogmore, UK: Paladin.

Binde, P. & Boholm, Å. 2004. Schismogenesis in a Swedish case of railway planning. In *Facility siting: Risk, power and identity in land-use planning*. Boholm, Å. & Löfstedt, R. (eds.), pp. 160–176. London, UK: Earthscan.

Boholm, Å. (ed.). 2000. *National objectives – local objections: Railroad modernization in Sweden*. Gothenburg, Sweden: Cefos, University of Gothenburg.

Boholm, Å. 2005a. 'Greater good' in transit: The unwieldy career of a Swedish rail tunnel project. *Focaal – European Journal of Anthropology* 46: 21–35.

Boholm, Å. 2005b. Riskbedönningars ontologi och epistemologi: Hallandsåsen och dess vatten. In *Risk och det levande mänskliga*. Brinck, I., Halldén, S., Maurin, A.-S. & Persson, J. (eds.), pp. 9–43. Nora, Sweden: Doxa.

Boholm, Å. & Löfstedt, R. 1999. Issues of risk, trust and knowledge: The Hallandsås tunnel case. *Ambio* 28(6): 556–561.

Boholm, Å. & Löfstedt, R. (eds.). 2004. *Facility siting: Risk, power and identity in land use planning*. London, UK: Earthscan.

Boholm, Å., Henning, A. & Krzyworzeka, A. 2013. Anthropology and decision making: An introduction. *Focaal – Journal of Global and Historical Anthropology* 65: 97–113.

Boholm, M. 2012. The semantic distinction between 'risk' and 'danger': A linguistic analysis. *Risk Analysis* 32(2): 281–293.

Brox, O. 2000. Schismogenesis in the wilderness: The reintroduction of predators in Norwegian forests. *Ethnos* 65(3): 387–404.

Chess, C. & Purcell, K. 1999. Public participation and the environment: Do we know what works? *Environmental Science and Technology* 33(16): 2685–2692.

Chess, C., Burger, J. & McDermott, M.H. 2005. Speaking like a state: Environmental justice and fish consumption advisories. *Society and Natural Resources* 18: 267–278.

Corvellec, H. 2001. Talks on tracks – debating urban infrastructure projects. *Studies in Cultures, Organisations and Societies* 7: 25–53.

Corvellec, H. 2007. Arguing for a license to operate: The case of the Swedish wind power industry. *Corporate Communications: An International Journal* 12(2): 129–144.

Corvellec, H. & Boholm, Å. 2008. The risk/no-risk rhetoric of environmental impact assessments (EIA): The case of off-shore wind farms in Sweden. *Local Environment* 13(7): 627–640.

Darian-Smith, E. 1999. *Bridging divides: The Channel Tunnel and English legal identity in the new Europe.* Berkeley, CA: University of California Press.

Fiorino, D.J. 1990. Citizen participation and environmental risk: A survey of institutional mechanisms. *Science, Technology & Human Values* 15(2): 226–243.

Flyvbjerg, B., Bruzelius, N. & Rothengatter, W. 2003. *Megaprojects and risk: An anatomy of ambition.* Cambridge, UK: Cambridge University Press.

Fölsterling, F. 2001. *Attribution: An introduction to theories, research and applications.* New York, NY: Taylor & Francis.

Futrell, R. 1999. Performative governance: Impression management, teamwork, and conflict containment in city commission proceedings. *Journal of Contemporary Ethnography* 27(4): 494–529.

Gell, A. 1998. *Art and agency: An anthropological theory.* Oxford, UK: Oxford University Press.

Grimes, M. 2005. Democracy's infrastructure: The role of procedural fairness in fostering consent. *Göteborg Studies in Politics*, 97. Gothenburg, Sweden: Department of Political Science, University of Gothenburg.

Heider, F. 1958. *The psychology of interpersonal relations.* New York, NY: John Wiley & Sons.

Heiefort, R. 2004. When complexity becomes a problem: "Law" and "fairness" on separate tracks in Sweden. In *Facility siting: Risk, power and identity in land use planning.* Boholm, Å. & Löfstedt, R. (eds.), pp. 177–188. London, UK: Earthscan.

Hobbs, E. 2011. Performing wilderness, performing difference: Schismogenesis in a mining dispute. *Ethnos* 76(1): 109–129.

Karlsson, M. 2002. Agency and patiency? Back to nature. *Philosophical Explorations* V(1): 59–81.

Latour, B. 1996. *Aramis or the love of technology.* Cambridge, MA: Harvard University Press.

Löfstedt, R. 2005. *Risk management in post-trust societies.* New York, NY: Palgrave Macmillan.

Löfstedt, R. & Boholm, Å. 1999. Off track in Sweden. *Environment* 41(4): 16–20, 40–44.

Luhmann, N. 1993. *Risk: A sociological theory*. New York, NY: Aldine de Gruyter.

Luhmann, N. 1995. *Social systems*. Stanford, CA: Stanford University Press.

Lundgren, R. & McMakin, A. 2004. *Risk communication: A handbook for communicating environmental, safety, and health risks*. Columbus, OH: Battelle Press.

McComas, K.A. 2003a. Trivial pursuits: Participant view of public meetings. *Journal of Public Relations Research* 15(2): 91–115.

McComas, K.A. 2003b. Public meetings and risk amplification: A longitudinal study. *Risk Analysis* 23(6): 1257–1270.

Nuckolls, C.W. 1995. The misplaced legacy of Gregory Bateson: Toward a cultural dialectic of knowledge and desire. *Cultural Anthropology* 10(3): 367–394.

Päiviö, J. & Wallentius, H.G. 2001. The Hallandsås railway tunnel project. In *EIA, large development projects and decision making in the Nordic countries*. Hilding-Rydevik, T. (ed.), pp. 55–94. Nordregio Report, 6. Stockholm, Sweden: Nordregio, Nordic Centre for Spatial Development.

Palm, L. 1998. *Hallandsåstunneln som tvistefråga, kris och förtroendeproblem*. Stockholm, Sweden: Styrelsen för Psykologiskt Försvar.

Petts, J. 1999. Public participation and EIA. In *Handbook of environmental impact assessment*: Volume 1. Petts J. (ed.), pp. 145–177. Oxford, UK: Blackwells.

Reith, G. 2004. Uncertain times: The notion of 'risk' and the development of modernity. *Time & Society* 13(2–3): 382–402.

Renn, O. 2004. Participatory processes for designing environmental policies. *Land Use Policy* 23: 34–43.

Rönnborg, P. 2006. *Finding the right place: The story about an offshore wind power project*. Gothenburg, Sweden: School of Business, Economics and Law, University of Gothenburg.

Ryfe, D. M. 2005. Does deliberative democracy work? *Annual Review of Political Science* 8: 49–71.

Sidaway, R. 2005. *Resolving environmental disputes: From conflict to consensus*. London, UK: Earthscan.

Sjölander-Lindqvist, A. 2004. Local environment at stake: The Hallandsås railway tunnel in a social and cultural context. Lund Dissertations in Human Ecology, 2. Lund, Sweden: Lund University.

Soneryd, L. 2003. Public involvement in the planning process: EIA and lessons from the Örebro airport extension, Sweden. *Environmental Science & Policy* 7: 59–68.

Sperber, D. & Wilson D. 2003 [1986]. Relevance: Communication and cognition. Malden, MA, Oxford, UK, Melbourne, Australia & Berlin, Germany: Blackwell Publishing.

Stoffle, R.W. & Evans, M.J. 1990. Holistic conservation and cultural triage: American Indian perspectives on cultural resources. *Human Organization* 49(2): 41–49.

van den Hove, S. 2006. Between consensus and compromise: Acknowledging the negotiation dimension in participatory approaches. *Land Use Policy* 23: 10–17.

Source documents

Banverket 2000. Projektutredning Hallandsås: Miljökonsekvensbeskrivning. Banverket: Borlänge. [The Swedish Rail Adminstration, Project investigation Hallandsås: Environmental impact assessment].

Banverket 2004. Årsredovisning. Banverket: Borlänge. [The Swedish Rail Administration 2004: year report].

MGG PM 024 1998-02-25. [The Environmental Assessment Group PM meeting protocol]

MGG PM 107 1998-03-09. [The Environmental Assessment Group PM meeting protocol]

MGG PM 108 1998-03-30. [The Environmental Assessment Group PM meeting protocol]

MGG PM 015 1998-01-08. [The Environmental Assessment Group PM meeting protocol]

MGG PM 296 2003-10-27. [The Environmental Assessment Group PM meeting protocol]

Miljöbalk (SFS 1998: 808). [The environmental code].

Notes

1. Miljöbalk (SFS 1998:808) Ch. 6, §§4–6.
2. The author was a participant observer of 15 out of a total of 16 'consultation forums' and 'consultation meetings' and was present during all three Environmental Court Hearings regarding the tunnel project, in April 2001 (the Environmental Court), in November 2001 (the Environmental Court) and in September 2003 (the Supreme Environmental Court). Each of those hearings extended for several full days.
3. The Environmental Court Hearings were not taped by the author, since neither audio recording nor photography is allowed during proceedings. The Court, however, tapes the hearings and releases them as official public documents that were used here.
4. www.banverket.se/sv/Amnen/Aktuella-projekt/Projekt/1869/Hallandsas.aspx (now removed; accessed 10 July 2007).
5. *Nord Västra Skånes Tidningar* (NST) has reported regularly from the meetings.
6. Two parallel tunnels, 8.6 kilometres long, now drilled in their entirety. The Hallandsås is a horst, an upfaulted geological formation created 70–100 million years ago by movements of the earth's crust. The interior of the ridge consists partly of clay, intersected by huge water-filled crevices. It contains enormous amounts of groundwater, and in certain places at 170–180 metres above sea level, water emerges naturally from the ground through ponds, brooks and springs. The area above ground is fertile and ideal for farming. The landscape is varied, partly pastoral with grazing animals and fields with vegetables or grain; there are pastures, farmsteads intersected by small roads and areas of beech or alder forest and of moor. The north side of the ridge is a nature reserve, and on the Hallandsås there are several dispersed *Natura 2000* habitats protected by the European Union.

7. MGG PM 015, 8 January 1998.

8. MGG PM 024, 25 February 1998, p. 3.

9. MGG PM 015, 8 January 1998, p. 7.

10. MGG PM 024, 25 February1998, p. 3.

11. MGG PM 107, 9 March 1998.

12. MGG PM 108, 30 March 1998.

13. Banverket, Miljökonsekvensbeskrivning 2000, p. 14.

14 Bateson's concept has been used to explain conflicts in land-use planning and wildlife management (Binde & Boholm 2004; Brox 2000; Hobbs 2011).

15. Aktionsgruppen Rädda Lya. Lya is a little village on the ridge above the tunnel.

7

VISUAL IMAGES AND RISK MESSAGES

Commemorating Chernobyl

Two events in particular stand out in the history of Swedish news reporting on environmental issues (Djerf-Pierre 2011). One is the Hallandsås tunnel scandal, which between 1997 and 2010 generated a total of 99 stories on national television. The other notable event is the nuclear accident on 25–26 April 1986, in reactor number four at V.I. Lenin Chernobyl Nuclear Power Station in Ukraine, which up until 2011 had generated altogether 279 stories. Both events are the top-scoring environmental issues in Swedish national television news reporting.

The Hallandsås tunnel was a major event for local news media reporting (Håkansson 2000). In the first four weeks following the toxic leak in October 1997, the *Nordvästra Skånes Tidningar* (a daily local newspaper) published in total 285 news articles on the tunnel project (an average of ten articles per day). This massive media coverage focused on issues of responsibility and blame – directed foremost at the National Rail Administration, which was in charge of the project – as well as on the themes of social conflict between those involved and of the dimensions of human impact in terms of the direct consequences for residents and the economic implications (Håkansson 2000).

This surge of national and local media reporting on the Hallandsås environmental scandal (Djerf-Pierre 2011: 506) included both textual and visual information. Ferreira, Boholm and Löfstedt (2001) analysed the photos and the texts of captions included in a 12-page supplement of a national daily tabloid issued in the aftermath of the environmental scandal (*Expressen*, 23 October 1997). They noted that, in relation to the accompanying captions, the photos served to visualise an invisible risk object, namely the Rhoca-Gil chemical sealing agent that leaked into wells and streams and poisoned water. The photos presented a comprehensive narrative about risk objects and victims (farmers, local residents, etc.) within a specific environmental setting.

The interplay of media communication and risk perception constitutes a field of research of tremendous complexity (Dunwoody & Peters 1992; af Wåhlberg & Sjöberg 1997). The reasons are several: the media is itself diverse; the audiences of the media are not passive receptacles but active processors of information, with divergent perspectives, interests and modes of engagement; and there are many dimensions to messages about risk. Consequently, an exploration of the ways in which messages about risk are produced, dispersed and construed in society will require refined models of communication. In this respect, models such as the social amplification of risk framework (Kasperson *et al.* 1988; Pidgeon, Kasperson & Slovic 2003; Renn *et al.* 1992) are too limited, because they are based on a natural science, technical paradigm of the transmission of a physical signal from sender to receiver. Risk issues are not simply signals; they are socially construed conceptual schemata, embedded in public discourse, of which the activities of the media form a part.

The media and the visualisation of risk

Media discourses actively construct problem issues in a given cultural context, by identifying and characterising issues of concern and also by exposing conflicting perspectives, drawing attention to new and divergent information and experiences, which in turn help to redefine and give new meanings to a problem (Gamson & Modigliani 1989). What is to be considered 'risky', why and how, is not established from some independent perspective – whether termed that of 'science' or 'the media' – that stands apart from social organisation. As argued in this book, risk issues are structured by a cognitive schema that encompasses the risk object(s), the associated value(s) at stake and the assumed causal linkage(s) (Boholm & Corvellec 2011). Answers to questions about risk are shaped by the interactions among actors, the meanings, the taken-for-granted conventions and the assumptions that govern and elucidate social intercourse within an institutional setting (Wynne 1992). The mass media must therefore be understood as active agents in the public construction of messages about risks (Allan, Adam & Carter 2000; Carvalho & Burgess 2005; Gamson & Modigliani 1989; Kitzinger 1999; Flynn, Slovic & Kunreuther 2001; Stallings 1990).

Many messages about risk in the media focus on risk at a societal level, in terms of estimates by scientific experts of harmful outcomes, such as the numbers of deaths or the prevalence of illness. If laid forth in the dry language of science, such risk issues in the eyes of the public might seem abstract and vague, distant and difficult to grasp (Sharlin 1987). By portraying the consequences of catastrophic events and environmental hazards with images – of devastated landscapes, people crying over destroyed homes, a grief-stricken mother and her suffering child, a forlorn domestic pet or an emaciated wild animal – the uncertainty of future risk is rendered with concrete form and content (Hansen & Machin 2013; Tulloch & Blood 2012). Visual images have a particular potential to communicate emotive and intuitive knowledge, to impart veracity and to permit projection of identification, and this makes them an effective medium for the social construction of messages about risks (Nicholson-Cole 2005).

For example, during the mid-1980s in Sweden there was increasing concern about environmental issues such as the pollution of the sea. Public debate took a new direction when the news media in the summer of 1988 began to circulate pictures of dead or seriously ill seal cubs that had been found around the coast. These photographs of dying seals (later proved to be affected by a viral infection rather than by pollution), with their large, sad, suffering eyes, strongly influenced public understanding of risk to the natural environment. In the October election of that same year, the Swedish Green Party was voted into the parliament for the first time. What had been construed previously as an abstract scientific issue about concentrations of chemicals and toxic substances in a marine environment was now turned into a tangible, authentic, emotionally charged political matter; photographs of suffering animal victims played a key role in bringing the concrete consequences of environmental risk to the foreground (Johannesson 1991).

This chapter explores the role of visual images in communication about risk in printed news media, drawing on material from the European news media's commemorative coverage in 1996 of the accident at the Chernobyl nuclear plant ten years earlier. I argue that visual images have a strong capacity to represent risk as being subjectively relevant, even when the threat is remote from everyday experience. Visual images can therefore be expected to boost messages about risk, giving support to emotionally charged conative perceptions imbued with personal and emotional concern that is relevant to action (Hilgard 1980).

Text and pictures

Pictures served as conventional aids to memory in earlier times in European society, when people outside of the educated classes of the aristocracy, clergy, public officials, scholars and merchants had not mastered reading and writing. Pictures in an illuminated manuscript helped the reader to memorise the text, so that its contents might be recalled even outside of the library and without access to the book itself. Visual images in churches served educational and commemorative purposes; they reminded illiterate members of the congregation of the stories of the Gospels, the principles of Christian faith and religious customs (Carruthers 1990; Yates 1966). The visual image has indeed lost nothing of its potency with the passing of the centuries: 'Ours is a visual age', as E.H. Gombrich commented (1970: 82). Today, the media and the Internet produce an ever-increasing flow of pictures and other images of various kinds, depicting authentic as well as constructed visual realities, which are accessible to an ever larger proportion of the population. As a mode of communication, visual representation seems to be taking over more and more from the written word.

The commonplace experience that visual representations help people to remember a message has been confirmed by research into the media and psychological studies of perception. Communication tends to be all the more effective if visual and textual information are combined, provided that the two modes of information are consonant with regard to the messages conveyed. In the literature on visual representations of environmental problems and risk issues, it is suggested that pictures add context and enhance understanding and that they make complex and abstract issues relevant to everyday experience and daily life (Léon & Erviti 2013; Nicholson-Cole 2005). Functioning in this manner, pictures serve to make messages about risk more concrete to an audience (Smith & Joffe 2009); a photograph of a melting iceberg shows climate change actually taking place, that it is a fact and not a matter of scientific conjecture involving uncertainty (Smith & Joffe 2009: 658). Pictures are especially effective in communicating 'content that is important, hard to understand and new' (Pettersson 1997: 127). News stories which employ both text and pictures are perceived as being more interesting, and they are also recalled better afterwards (Katz, Adoni & Parness 1977; Graber 1996).

Reviewing research on the role of visual representations in coverage of environmental issues by the media, Hansen and Machin (2013: 155) noted that the 'invisibility and slow development of many environmental problems pose particular difficulties for their news construction and communication generally, and for their visual representations specifically'. Similarly, Ferreira, Boholm and Löfstedt (2001: 292) noted that 'Stereotypes are pervasive in media mediated risk events, not least due to the difficulties inherent in visualizing concepts and immaterial sources of danger – how does one visualize, for example, radiation? Or the depletion of the ozone layer? How is the toxic substance acrylamide to be pictured?' While written text has a communicative capacity for formulating logically interrelated propositions about states of affairs – propositions that could be proven true or false – visual images are effective in stirring emotions, in conferring aesthetic qualities and coherent patterns of meanings. While the comprehension of a text demands formal skill, training and education, the understanding of a visual image can expand based on intuitively reasoned processes of culturally informed interpretation (Ferreira 2004).

A visual image has the potential to accommodate complex information that can be condensed effectively into a pattern (Gombrich 1970). While language requires logical consistency for intelligibility, a picture with ambiguous and puzzling features can create messages of great richness and depth. An allusive image is often perceived as being more interesting, since it demands a great deal more interpretative contribution from the viewer. In a similar fashion to texts, visual images are subject to alternative readings depending not only on the internal complexity of the picture itself but also on the perspective of the viewer, a point well demonstrated by the 'rabbit-duck' illusion famous from psychology textbooks, where the image of the rabbit can also be seen as one of a duck (Gombrich 1960: 2–8).

Analysis of visual images in the media calls upon other methodological considerations than the common procedures for quantitative analysis of written texts. A picture is communicative to the degree that it shows an object or image by means of resemblance of relations, association, contrasts, metaphor and metonym. Study of visual images has slowly become part of the agenda of research into how risk is perceived and communicated, along with the realisation that it must be conducted in depth to be productive and take into account state-of-the-art semiotic theory on non-verbal communication (Hansen & Machin 2013; Léon & Erviti 2013; Nicholson-Cole 2005; Smith & Joffe 2009; Tulloch & Blood 2012).

The media and the tenth anniversary of the accident at Chernobyl

Investigation of the content of news media was on the research agenda of an EU-funded project launched in January 1996 as a cross-national, comparative investigation of public attitudes to risks in five European countries: Sweden, Norway, the United Kingdom, France and Spain (Sjöberg 1999). One expectation of the project was that in April 1996, on the tenth anniversary of the explosion and consequent meltdown at Chernobyl, the news media in all five of these European countries would pay a great deal of attention to the accident and its effects, as well as to the risk more generally from nuclear power and radiation.

The content of major newspapers in each country was collected and coded in the spring of 1996. This material from the news media has been used for quantitative analyses of content not only concerning the Chernobyl accident and risk from nuclear power, but also with respect to a number of other types of hazard. The analyses of this vast body of material were focused on the 'framing' of issues of risk for the various types of hazard – like the attribution of blame; arguments about consequences, costs and benefits; the degree of individual control; the presence of conflict; and measures taken by society that mitigate circumstances that imply risk (for Swedish data see Nilsson, Sjöberg & af Wåhlberg 1997).

Photographs and other visual images from the press were also collected during the period of study. Quite clearly, the Chernobyl accident was a topic which produced a considerable amount of visual representation in the news media. In the Swedish case, it was clear that photographs were far more prominent in the presentation of stories concerning Chernobyl than they were in coverage of the other types of hazard, such as bovine spongiform encephalopathy (BSE), traffic accidents, air pollution, chemical waste and domestic nuclear power plants. Compared to the other stories, coverage about Chernobyl on the whole tended to have a much more alarming tone and devoted proportionately more space to photographs. In the case of Chernobyl, there were 11 times as many alarming messages as reassuring ones, and this ratio was nearly twice as high as the ratio for the next two most alarmingly presented hazards – alcohol consumption and Eastern European nuclear power plants (Nilsson, Sjöberg & af Wåhlberg 1997).

Events at Chernobyl were indeed commemorated in all five countries, and there were feature stories that emphasised both the historical catastrophe and its present-day consequences. The big national newspapers of all five countries carried extensive articles about Chernobyl, including large collections of pictures. But the scale of coverage by the media was not equal in all cases, as the proportion of material relating to Chernobyl, out of the total number of stories about hazards, varied among countries. In the United Kingdom, during the weeks of the study, 'Mad Cow Disease', or BSE, became a dominant issue on the political agenda and a huge amount of media coverage was devoted to it. Although BSE also attracted substantial attention from the media in the other countries, the reporting of the risk was more varied, and substantial attention was devoted instead to Chernobyl and nuclear related topics.

Photography as certified presence

A photograph can portray, realistically and in great detail, humans in various circumstances, their 'body language' – for example, postures, gestures and facial expressions – their general appearance, their social attributes and their surroundings. Photographs can capture moments in a dramatic episode, and from them a viewer can infer a range of emotions and attitudes by relying on non-verbal cultural codes. Like a painting by a Renaissance master, a photograph can serve as a vehicle for vicarious experience that invites viewers to project their own interpretations onto the objects of representation, thereby achieving subjective identification (Gombrich 1972).

Photographs constitute the most salient category of images in the news media. Photography, most basically, is a physical process of registering a visual 'imprint' of a particular time and place on a sensor. In contrast to other kinds of images, such as paintings or drawings, which are taken to represent an artist's subjective perspective, photographic images serve to verify objectively the event that is depicted (on the epistemology, aesthetics and morals of photography, see Sontag 1973; Berger & Mohr 1995). A news story that is accompanied by photographs tends to be understood by readers as more trustworthy and authentic than one without them (Graber 1996: 89–90). Or, as Roland Barthes (1984: 87) put it in his intriguing investigation of the phenomenology of photography, 'Every photograph is a certificate of presence', and, more expansively:

> Photography's inimitable feature (its *noema*) is that someone has seen the referent (even if it is a matter of objects) in *flesh and blood*, or again *in person* (Barthes 1984: 79).

Photography documents reality, a moment of 'truth' in the strict positivistic sense. The image depicts a frozen fragment of time, factual evidence of what was:

> A photograph arrests the flow of time in which the event photographed once existed. All photographs are of the past, yet in them an instant of the past is arrested so that, unlike a lived past, it can never lead to the present. Every photograph presents us with two messages: a message concerning the event photographed and another concerning a shock of discontinuity. Between the

moment recorded and the present moment of looking at the photograph, there is an abyss (Berger & Mohr 1995: 86–87).

As an 'ectoplasm of "what had been"' (Barthes 1984: 87), a photograph raises many questions regarding the context of the phenomena and the situation depicted. If answers are not provided, the picture might seem strange or absurd, its content a mere accidental configuration of people and or objects, devoid of meaning. Factual evidence is not necessarily the same as meaningful information. To be understood, photographs need to be accompanied by clues that prompt the unfolding of the story of which the photographs are part so that the images are 'read' as illustrative of the narrative. If a photograph is explained verbally or by a caption or headline that provides the historical or biographical context, the viewer can reach imaginatively across the 'abyss' to link the photographed past with their present. The frozen instance of factual evidence becomes intelligible as part of a narrative, and by these answers the inherent ambiguity of the photograph – the when, where, who and why – is resolved to some extent:

> The photograph, irrefutable evidence but weak in meaning, is given meaning by the words. And the words, which by themselves remain at the level of generalisation, are given specific authenticity by the irrefutability of the photograph. Together the two then become very powerful; an open question appears to have been fully answered (Berger & Mohr 1995: 92).

The symbiosis of the photographic image and words is therefore crucial for photography to serve as a means of communication, and it is in this coexistence that the cultural construction of messages operates.

'Cultural studies' is a diverse academic movement that examines the processes of communication used by the modern forms of highly visual mass media in both popular entertainment and commercial advertising; it incorporates insights from structuralism, semiotics and literary studies (Fiske 1987; Hall *et al.* 1980). Text and image are employed in the modern media's complementary and mutually enforcing modes of communication. The nature of these interdependencies, and their role in the interpretation of messages, needs to be understood more fully, however.

Since pictures in the news media generally are accompanied by text, be it an article and or a caption, a key issue for analysis of the construction of risk is to explore how visual representations and text actually interact with one another. Di Francesco and Young's (2010) study of the visual representation of global warming in Canadian news media suggests that the relationship between text and image is a loose one. Text content and visual meanings seem to constitute two disconnected voices, since 'image and article frequently refer to completely different dimensions of the climate change issue, thus presenting multiple and sometimes even competing narratives to readers' (Di Francesco & Young 2011: 532). The analysis of how text and image co-constitute risk messages is currently in its infancy but offers a challenging area for future research.

Images of Chernobyl: themes and topics

There are several ways in which the visual material might be categorised. One scheme would be by genre, or type of story. Drawing on the classical notions of Aristotle, Nordström (1996) analysed images relating to the sinking of the passenger ferry *Estonia* in 1994, with nearly 900 dead, according to four categories of representation: (a) dramatic representation, a story with a tragic or comic point, including the actions of actors and the setting; (b) lyrical representation, emphasising mood, feelings and – often transcendental – reflection; (c) epical representation, a perspective of events over a more extended time; and (d) didactic representation, the intention being to teach and to convince by means of logical arguments based on facts.

This scheme of general categories can be applied to media representations of the Chernobyl accident, as there are many examples of stories that are dramatic, lyrical, epical or didactic. However, the present aim is to focus on specific salient issues in the deployment of visual imagery by the press during the period of commemoration, and this required a methodology with a stronger focus on visual genre and overall semantic content or story than Nordström's more formalistic approach.

Portraits and landscapes have constituted prominent genres in the history of Western painting from the Renaissance up to the present. Traditional portraiture, depicting a person or a group of people posed in a realistic setting with objects having significant, easily recognisable social and cultural attributes, tells a story about the subject's social position and roles, their achievements and claims to authority and their moral worth. Another prominent genre of the early modern period is landscape painting. Representations of natural scenery and landmarks, along with buildings, artefacts, people and/or animals, in the form of either a painting or, later, a photo, are dense with symbolic meanings (Schama 1995). Landscape representations inscribe the surroundings with symbolic meanings by using conventionalised codes that often are specific to a particular time or social and cultural setting (Cosgrove & Daniels 1988). Such representations convey ideological messages not only concerning society but transcendental forces as well as moral and existential issues.

Since 'landscape' and 'portrait' are such dominant conventional modes of visual representation in Western culture, these two categories were used as heuristics for the present analysis of risk messages in modern media. A listing by country of all photos, including captions and headlines, provided an overview of the extensive collection of visual material relating to the commemoration of the Chernobyl accident. The message content of this material was then analysed with regard to the kinds of actors or environments that were portrayed. Portraits of people in specific settings – for example, a patient in a medical clinic, a farmer in a field, an old woman in front of her house or a child playing with a toy – were sorted into categories of story topics. Closer examination of these portraits and topics suggested that the actors could be divided further into a category of victims – those who had been exposed to the negative effects of the accident (like cancer patients and people who had had their homes and life situations destroyed) and a category of various types of 'managers' of radiation or its negative effects (like technicians, medical doctors and sanitation workers). The gaze of the subjects portrayed – whether directed at the viewer or away, so crucial for the medium of photography – served as the principal element in the deconstruction of the meaning of these 'Chernobyl portraits'.

A substantial number of the pictures do not have people as the major subject but instead highlight a specific surrounding, a natural scene shown with or without human traces (monuments, buildings or artefacts). Many of the examples are aesthetic and highly suggestive representations of such 'Chernobyl landscapes'. The following sections provide an overview of some of the themes and topics discernible in the imagery of Chernobyl in newspapers. The photographs and the accompanying headlines from the media of all five countries comprise approximately 200 items.

The interior of the Chernobyl nuclear plant

Reactors one and three at the Chernobyl nuclear plant were still in operation in 1996. That fact was the subject of some stories about Chernobyl, describing personnel of the nuclear plant, mainly men wearing white protective clothing, going about their tasks ('Impossible to shut down Chernobyl', *Gävle Dagblad* [Sweden], 22 April; 'Chernobyl—a closed world', *Gävle Dagblad* [Sweden], 23 April [see Figure 7.1]; 'Expensive to close down Chernobyl', *Göteborgs-Posten* [Sweden], 10 April; 'OMS for the first time links Chernobyl with leukaemia', *El Pais* [Spain], 11 April; 'Atom problems', *Oppland Arbeiderblad* [Norway], 9 April). These operators are depicted from a distance, and close-up shots are not used. They are represented not primarily as individuals but rather as components of a closed and specialised technological environment – a de-personalisation emphasised by their white uniforms. The operators appear preoccupied and do

REPORTAGE *tisdag 23 april 1996* Gefle Dagblad

Kontrollerar processen. *I kontrollrummet sker övervakningen av Tjernobyls äldsta reaktor, enhet 1. Rutinerna har ändrats så gott som totalt efter olyckan, men så långt som till att förbjuda rökning vid kontrollpanelerna har man inte gått.*

Tjernobyl – en sluten värld

FIGURE 7.1 Chernobyl – a closed world

not gaze towards the camera, but instead they look at the various instruments and tasks at hand. The interior of the reactor shows huge control panels, with immense numbers of buttons, controls and instruments.

Entrenched in the complicated technological world of the reactor, the operators seem detached from the mundane world outside. Viewing such pictures, one could if so inclined imagine how easy it would be to commit a mistake: to press the wrong button, to misread some number or to overlook some vital indicator. Such an error is only too human, and if it happens, who (or what) should be blamed? On the other hand, someone more trustful of technology viewing these pictures might make quite different associations, namely that the 'high tech' interior of the reactor suggests that nuclear power is controllable and safe. The visual representations of these interiors raises questions about trust and responsibility, and the possible answers will closely depend on pre-existing attitudes to technology and nuclear power.

Chernobyl landscapes

Derelict empty houses; neglected gardens or fields; and car parks filled with trucks, cars and other radiation-contaminated vehicles are favoured motifs in the portrayal of the surrounding landscape ('Monument to an incomprehensible catastrophe', *Göteborgs-Posten* [Sweden], 20 April; 'The world's most dangerous junk heap for cars'; *Aftonbladet* [Sweden], 23 April; 'The volcano is still alive' *El Pais* [Spain], 7 April). One image that reoccurred in several countries shows an amusement park covered in snow, with dilapidated bumper cars and a Ferris wheel standing still without a person in sight ('An amusement park contaminated by radioactivity', *Göteborgs-Posten* [Sweden], 20 April [see Figure 7.2]; 'In

FIGURE 7.2 An amusement park contaminated by radioactivity

the sarcophagus of radiation death', *Dagbladet* [Norway], 21 April; 'Chernobyl, ten years after', *El Pais* [Spain], 7 April). This image draws its force from symbolic contrasts: normally, an amusement park is a place of intense activity, with crowds of people enjoying and safely thrilling themselves. It is a place for childish, innocent play and wonder and where family members interact. The message conveyed is that this social, active, playful and innocent side of existence was destroyed by the accident at Chernobyl. The amusement park, broken and abandoned, is a graveyard, serving as a metaphor for doom and decay, for collapsed, eroded civilization, all caused by the failure of nuclear power.

Another favoured visual topic is the clean-up of the contaminated landscape. Workers are shown either as regiments of white-clothed, depersonalised figures or as a lone figure using some kind of equipment or instrument to clean away or measure radioactivity. No close-ups are used, and people, concentrating fully on their tasks, are represented in a similar way to those working inside the still-functioning reactors ('Break in the growth of the world's nuclear energy', *El Pais* [Spain], 18 April; 'Ten years on, dead zone of Chernobyl', *The Times* [UK], 18 April). In another photograph ('Deadly shadow hangs over Europe', *The Guardian* [UK], 13 April [see Figure 7.3]) a crowd of white-uniformed radiation clean-up workers are lined up in front of the camera, reminiscent of some kind of alien occupying power. They just stand there in a large group, nearly all gazing at the camera, and this imparts a puzzling, even sinister, impression. Why have they stopped working? What does their gaze mean? What are their intentions? Here a story has to be invented that might ascribe meanings to the photographs.

FIGURE 7.3 Deadly shadow hangs over Europe

What is common to the pictures of Chernobyl landscapes – excluding those focusing on the destroyed reactor (the 'sarcophagus') – is emptiness and decomposition, a landscape divorced from human inhabitants. Not only has the space been evacuated, but it has also lost cultural meaning, tradition and history; it has been rendered as quite enigmatic and strange.

We were victims

The county of Gavleborg on the east coast of Sweden was one of several areas seriously affected by radioactive fallout following the Chernobyl accident in the spring of 1986. For this reason, a local newspaper (*Gävle Dagblad*) was included in the survey of Swedish media. This publication gave quite substantial coverage to the anniversary of the Chernobyl accident, emphasising its effects on the local area. Several of these stories included substantial photographic material, often showing groups of children who are busy cycling, fishing or enjoying themselves out-of-doors. One story ('I am not so worried any more' (*Gävle Dagblad*, 27 April [see Figure 7.4]) depicts a farmer in a barn together with his apparently healthy and thriving cows. He is shown standing close to one of the cows, with his arms around it, whilst looking directly at the camera. The messages conveyed by these pictures of Swedish victims are quite reassuring – all look healthy and confident. Ten years after the accident, order and nature have been restored in Sweden, and things are back to normal.

FIGURE 7.4 'I am not so worried any more'

They are victims

The overwhelming majority of the photographs dealt with the fate of human victims abroad. The messages conveyed by these alarming pictures and the accompanying headlines stood in sharp contrast to the ways in which Swedish victims were portrayed. These remote victims are people who lived close to the plant or in the areas of Ukraine, Belarus and Russia most badly affected by the radioactive fallout. As a result of the accident, some have become ill and now are dying, whilst others are waiting to become ill. Some have been left alone to live as outcasts in the radioactive zone. In contrast to the reactor personnel and the clean-up workers, these victims were all presented as individuals, perhaps in the company of relatives or friends, and the accompanying captions often included their names and elements of their personal biographies. The camera views are close-ups, with the subjects often looking straight into the lens, the nuances of their faces shown in detail. These victims are *persons*, not personnel like those who managed the reactor or cleaned up the landscape. Nonetheless, a distancing is still apparent in the focus on the desolate looks of the subjects and their poor living conditions; they are not 'Us' but 'Them', construed as geographically and socially distant others.

Most frequently, the victims chosen for photography are children of various ages, the surroundings often being hospital-like. Typically portrayed in various stages of advancing illness and approaching death, they often stare directly at the camera with a sad or serious gaze. In one case there is no gaze; a close-up shows an unconscious child whose head is covered in cables and medical equipment ('The fires, the ashes, the scars of Chernobyl', *The Guardian* [UK], 20 April, see Figure 7.5). This child

18 | FOCUS/UKRAINIAN DISASTERS

It was a Soviet Eden for the power workers. Then their reactor exploded, and the USSR collapsed.
James Meek discovers how Ukrainians are coping with the fallout and, below, the continuing risks of meeting their energy needs

The fires, the ashes, the scars of Chernobyl

FIGURE 7.5   The fires, the ashes, the scars of Chernobyl

seems to be morphing into a machine, losing his or her humanity and becoming an object; there is no consciousness, and no gaze. Another child is shown in a strange tub, undergoing a medical examination under the supervision of a white-coated doctor and surrounded by instruments ('Chernobyl ten years after', *Expressen* [Sweden], 21 April). Elsewhere, a child sits on a bed playing all by himself, apparently quite contentedly, while in the background a group of adults (perhaps parents) are shown sitting together with their backs turned towards the child ('The cancer clinic', *Göteborgs-Posten* [Sweden], 20 April). Looking at this picture, a viewer understands that shortly the child will die and that his parents cannot bear this sight. When adults are portrayed as victims, they notably tend to be shown as parents of an afflicted child.

Very old people, most of them women, shown in front of their dilapidated houses or fields or carrying out simple domestic chores like collecting water from a well, form another category of frequently depicted adult victims. Two elderly sisters, for example, are depicted in front of their house ('In the zone of death – better to die from radiation than from starvation', *Göteborgs-Posten* [Sweden], 23 April). They have no future, no continuity; they stayed in the contaminated area and will die there. Without spouses or children, they are in a sense already dead, although their bodies continue to exist.

'Little Anja and her family chose to stay in the radioactive village' (*Göteborgs-Posten* [Sweden], 24 April) shows a young child, approximately three or four years old, playing outside her home. Her mother and grandmother are standing in the background, and we also see a few chickens, a dog and some furniture in the yard. Little Anja, smiling, is quite happily looking directly into the camera. The effect is quite eerie, drawing on the inherent ambiguity of the circumstances. A viewer of the picture knows what Anja does not: that she surely will die from cancer; that contrary to its healthy appearance, her body already is contaminated and deteriorating. Here a symbolic contrast operates: this is an already old young body, anachronistically in a state of approaching death and decay.

Overall, the victims of the Chernobyl accident are presented as being in a state of heightened expectation of death. Victims linger in limbo, undergoing death while still alive. This ambiguity of victimised existence derives from a loss of control of the body. The body becomes like an enemy, developing all kinds of unpredictable malignant ailments, painful and horrible. The victims of Chernobyl are also presented as socially marginalised in a very concrete way: many people – the elderly as well as children who lost their parents due to the catastrophe – have returned to the contaminated zone to carry on their existence (Knorre 1992).

The accident at Chernobyl brutally forced people in Ukraine to reconsider their own mortality as well as their perception of their own bodies, being unable to fulfil their life roles as parents, husbands, mothers or children (Petryna 1995: 211). These are the images of Chernobyl and its aftermath, projected as 'a theater of mortified flesh' and 'bodies that gaze' (Petryna 1995: 199). A striking example of this imagery is to be found in *El Pais* [Spain], from 26 April: 'Chernobyl commemorates its drama with another radioactive leak' (see Figure 7.6). The accompanying photograph was taken in a hospital in 1986 and shows a hairless person with a

FIGURE 7.6 Chernobyl commemorates its drama with another radioactive leak

naked torso who stares directly at the camera, festooned with medical tubes and partially secluded by drapes within a room. The image is slightly blurred, such that it is impossible to know if this ghostly figure is a man or a woman, young or old; all that is left is a pair of staring eyes.

Discussion

By reproducing stereotypical patterns of visual content and composition – such as a suffering child grasping her teddy bear on her grieving mother's lap or a devastated and depopulated landscape – conventionalised, idiomatic messages with regard to the meanings of the Chernobyl accident are being constructed. Broadly speaking, what may be concluded about the messages conveyed through pictures in the news media is that 'Chernobyl' emerges as a meta-meaning: the accident is but an example of fate and a warning of a need for redemption (Paine 1992: 269). Chernobyl here serves as an apocalyptic vision of doomsday and the end of humanity on earth; some invoked a New Testament prophecy in the Revelation of St. John (8: 10–11) about a falling star called Wormwood ('chernobyl' in Russian) that, when it hit the earth, poisoned the waters and so killed many people (Knorre 1992). Visual material presented in the media seems very much to challenge the idea of Chernobyl as an 'accident', an event accountable for in terms of 'science'. It instead is portrayed as an event preordained by divine forces striking at sinful humanity.

Some images do not fit into themes identified and analysed, being neither portraits, landscapes nor interiors. These images are more enigmatic and intuitive and seem to involve more complex conceptions. In some of these cases, captions or headlines give some guidance regarding the intended meaning of the images, in others, less so. For example, with the headline 'If Chernobyl had been located in a Western country' a Swedish tabloid (*Aftonbladet* [Sweden], 23 April) showed a photograph of three dogs, two of which are lying stretched out in the middle of a road and the third lying beside the road. This image is an illustration of the inherent problem of ambiguity in photography and the medium's dependency on accompanying verbal explications discussed above. The picture, together with the headline, raises a number of questions to which no explanations are provided. What are the dogs doing? Are they dead, or are they just sleeping? If dead, how did they die? From some dreadful disease caused by radiation? In what ways is the fate of these dogs related to the implied accident? In contrast to the image of a suffering child with a teddy bear, the newspaper reader in this case must try to invent their own story by using intuitive reasoning as well as more rationally based knowledge to answer these questions.

As Ferreira, Boholm and Löfstedt (2001: 292) noted in their analysis of media representation of the Hallandsås disaster in Sweden, one class of photos works as a stereotype, building (iconically) on conventional, romantic meanings and associations regarding the 'open, agrarian, pastoral landscape' with idyllic scenery of pastures, meadows, groves and the historical traces of human inhabitants. Stereotypical representations of nature draw on conventionalised assumptions about immanent value. Visual representations of stereotypical nature – a 'pristine landscape' or a striking animal – in the context of risk invoke an inherent concern because of the juxtapositioning of inherently valued nature – the value at stake – with the claim that it is under threat from the risk object (Meisner & Takahashi 2013: 267).

Once established, stereotypic (iconic) images may become 'portable' bits of communication: an image of a smoking industrial chimney represents not just a risk object but the risk issue schema of pollution or global warming, even without accompanying textual commentary; an image of a polar bear, irrespective of context, represents an object at risk. In this way images become abstracted from their specific local and temporal context and so bear messages in general, serving as representations of some global environmental problem or risk issue (Hansen & Machin 2013: 158).

Visual metaphors are another type of representation discussed in the literature. An example is a front cover of a *Time* magazine issue on 'Global Warming', 9 April 2001, which depicted 'the earth as a fried egg in a cast-iron frying pan' (Meisner & Takahashi 2013: 267, date of issue given in error as 2011). By drawing meanings symbolically from associations of resemblance, such graphic metaphors can establish risk objects. In case of the Hallandsås tunnel, the 'Underground Hell' metaphor represents the tunnel's depths as a dark and sinister cavern, a subterranean repository of diabolical machinations that brought about the 'poisoning of water' (Ferreira, Boholm & Löfstedt 2001: 291–295). This example illustrates how risk objects and objects at risk (values) and their causal relationship are established by the combination of the visual elements of the photos and the written content of the captions that guide interpretation.

In the case of the Chernobyl catastrophe, the imagery of risk and disaster presents highly conventionalised understandings of the varied meanings that can be drawn from the event. However, success in researching the use of imagery and the topics of risk and hazard calls for the development of systematic qualitative semiotic approaches. Such developments must be concerned with contextual meanings and also must account for the conventionalised sets of codes which organise visual and verbal signs into messages (see Bruhn Jensen 1995; Bruhn Jensen & Jankowski 1991; and specifically with regard to television, Selby & Cowdery 1995). It is hoped that insights from symbolic anthropology, semiotics and cultural studies might be combined in the future into a theoretical and methodological perspective that will illuminate the connection between the way risk is perceived and the presentation of pertinent visual images.

References

Allan, S., Adam, B. & Carter, C. (eds.). 2000. *Environmental risks and the media.* London, UK: Routledge.

Barthes, R. 1984 [1980]. *Camera lucida: Reflections on photography.* London, UK: Fontana.

Berger, J. & Mohr, J. 1995. *Another way of telling.* New York, NY: Vintage Books.

Boholm, Å. & Corvellec, H. 2011. A relational theory of risk. *Journal of Risk Research* 14(2): 175–190.

Bruhn Jensen, K. 1995. *The social semiotics of mass communication.* London, UK: SAGE.

Bruhn Jensen, K. & Jankowski, N.W. 1991. *Handbook of qualitative methodologies for mass communication research.* London, UK & New York, NY: Routledge.

Carruthers, M. 1990. *The book of memory: A study of memory in medieval culture.* Cambridge, UK: Cambridge University Press.

Carvalho, A. & Burgess, J. 2005. Cultural circuits of climate change in U.K. broadsheet newspapers, 1985–2003. *Risk Analysis* 25(6): 1457–1469.

Cosgrove, D. & Daniels, S. 1988. *The iconography of landscape.* Cambridge, UK: Cambridge University Press.

Di Francesco, A. & Young, N. 2011. Seeing climate change: The visual construction of global warming in Canadian national print media. *Cultural Geographies* 18(4): 517–536.

Djerf-Pierre, M. 2011. Green metacycles of attention: Reassessing the attention cycles of environmental news reporting 1961–2010. *Public Understanding of Science* 22(4): 495–512.

Dunwoody, S. & Peters, H.P. 1992. Mass media coverage of technological and environmental risks. *Public Understanding of Science* 1: 199–230.

Ferreira, C. 2004. Risk, transparency and cover up: Media narratives and cultural resonance. *Journal of Risk Research* 7(2): 199–211.

Ferreira, C., Boholm, Å. & Löfstedt, R. 2001. From vision to catastrophe: A risk event in search of images. In *Risk, media and stigma*. Flynn, J., Slovic, P. & Kunreuther, H. (eds.), pp. 283–299. London, UK: Earthscan.

Fiske, J. 1987. *Television culture*. London, UK: Methuen.

Flynn, J., Slovic, P. & Kunreuther, H. (eds.). 2001. *Risk media and stigma: Understanding public challenges to modern science and technology*. London, UK: Earthscan.

Gamson, W.A. & Modigliani, A. 1989. Media discourse and public opinion on nuclear power: A constructionist approach. *American Journal of Sociology* 95(1): 1–37.

Gombrich, E.H. 1960. *Art and illusion: A study in the psychology of pictorial representation*. London, UK: Phaidon.

Gombrich, E.H. 1970. The visual image: Its place in communication. *Scientific American* 272: 82–96.

Gombrich, E.H. 1972. Action and expression in Western art. In *Non-verbal communication*. Hinde, R.A. (ed.), pp. 391–401. Oxford, UK: Oxford University Press.

Graber, D.A. 1996. Say it with pictures. *Annals of the American Academy of Political and Social Sciences* 54: 85–96.

Håkansson, N. 2000. Framing the tunnel: Local news media and the Hallandsås toxic leak 1997. *Cefos Working Paper*, 27. Gothenburg, Sweden, Gothenburg University, CEFOS.

Hall, S., Hobson, D., Lowe, A. & Willis, P. (eds.). 1980. *Culture, media, language*. London, UK: Hutchinson.

Hansen, A. & Machin, D. 2013. Researching visual environmental communication. *Environmental Communication* 7(2): 151–168.

Hilgard, E.R. 1980. The trilogy of mind: Cognition, affection and conation. *Journal of the History of the Behavioral Sciences* 16: 107–117.

Johannesson, K. 1991. *Retorik och konsten att övertyga*. Stockholm, Sweden: Nordstedts.

Kasperson, R.E., Renn, O., Slovic, P., Brown, H.S., Emel, J., Goble, R., Kasperson, J.X. & Ratick, S. 1988. The social amplification of risk: A conceptual framework. *Risk Analysis* 8: 177–188.

Katz, E., Adoni, H. & Parness, P. 1977. Remembering the news: What pictures add to recall. *Journalism Quarterly* 54: 231–239.

Kitzinger, J. 1999. Researching risk and the media. *Health, Risk & Society* 1 (1): 55–69.

Knorre, H. 1992. 'The star called Wormwood': The cause and effect of Chernobyl. *Public Understanding of Science* 1: 241–249.

Léon, B. & Erviti, C. 2013. Science in pictures: Visual representation of climate change in Spain's television news. *Public Understanding of Science*, 6 September 2013, doi: 10.1177/09636625135001962013.

Meisner, M.S. & Takahashi, B. 2013. The nature of *Time*: How the covers of the world's most widely read weekly magazine visualize environmental affairs. *Environmental Communication* 7(2): 255–276.

Nicholson-Cole, S.A. 2005. Representing climate change futures: A critique on the use of images for visual communication. *Computers, Environment and Urban Systems* 29: 255–273.

Nilsson, Å., Sjöberg, L. & af Wåhlberg, A. 1997. *Ten years after the Chernobyl accident: The reporting of nuclear and other hazards in six Swedish newspapers.* Rhizikon: Risk Research Report, 28. Stockholm, Sweden: Center for Risk Research, Stockholm School of Economics.

Nordström, G.Z. 1996. *Estonia: Bilder av en katastrof.* Stockholm, Sweden: Styrelsen för Psykologiskt Försvar.

Paine, R. 1992. 'Chernobyl' reaches Norway: The accident, science, and the threat to cultural knowledge. *Public Understanding of Science* 1: 261–280.

Petryna, A. 1995. Sarcophagus: Chernobyl in historical light. *Cultural Anthropology* 10(2): 196–220.

Pettersson, R. 1997. *Verbo-visual communication.* Gothenburg, Sweden: Valfrid: Research Center for Library and Information Studies, University of Gothenburg.

Pidgeon, N., Kasperson, R. E. & Slovic, P. (eds.). 2003. *The social amplification of risk.* Cambridge, UK: Cambridge University Press.

Renn, O., Burns, W., Kasperson, R.E., Kasperson, J.X. & Slovic, P. 1992. The social amplification of risk: Theoretical foundations and empirical application. *Journal of Social Issues* 48: 137–160.

Schama, S. 1995. *Landscape and memory.* New York, NY: Alfred A. Knopf.

Selby, K. & Cowdery, R. 1995. *How to study television.* London, UK: Macmillan.

Sharlin, H.I. 1987. Macro-risks, micro-risks, and the media: The EDB case. In *The social and cultural construction of risk.* Johnson, B.B. & Covello, V.T. (eds.), pp. 183–197. Dordrecht, the Netherlands: D. Reidel Publishing.

Sjöberg, L. 1999. Risk perception in Western Europe. *Ambio* XXVIII(6): 543–549.

Smith, N.W. & Joffe, H. 2009. Climate change in the British press: The role of the virtual. *Journal of Risk Research* 12(5): 647–663.

Sontag, S. 1973. *On photography.* New York, NY: Farrar, Straus & Giroux.

Stallings, R.A. 1990. Media discourse and the social construction of risk. *Social Problems* 37: 80–95.

Tulloch, J. & Blood, W. (eds.). 2012. Icons of war and terror: Media images in an age of international risk. Abingdon, UK: Routledge.

af Wåhlberg, A. & Sjöberg, L. 1997. Risk perception and the media: A review of research on media influence on public risk perception. *Journal of Risk Research* 3(1): 31–50.

Wynne, B. 1992. Public understanding of science research: New horizons or hall of mirrors? *Public Understanding of Science* 1: 37–43.

Yates, F. 1966. *The art of memory.* Oxford, UK: Clarendon Press.

8

COMMUNICATION ON RISK

Relations, power and rationality

Risk communication is a growing concern for government administrations, industry and research in the United States and Europe (Arvai & Rivers 2014; Löfstedt & 6 2008; Palenchar & Heath 2007; Wardman 2008) and is practised in many different communicative contexts (Bennett & Calman 1999; Kasperson & Stallen 1991). The variety of reasons to communicate about risk includes advocacy concerning risk assessment and management, so that consumers or patients can make informed decisions (Bostrom 2003: 560–561; Calman, Bennett & Coles 1999); creating readiness for action, for example, by issuing warnings or developing plans for emergencies (Argenti 2002); fostering social trust in authorities, promoting consent and conflict resolution, and legitimising decision processes or actual decisions (Peters, Covello & McCallum 1997; Renn & Levine 1991); and exercising power and control by means of rhetoric and argumentation, especially during public participation in contested environmental planning (Binde & Boholm 2004; Boholm 2005; Corvellec & Boholm 2008; Endres 2009; Stratman et al. 1995).

Risk communication can be structured as monologues, dialogues, group discussions and formal meetings, all of which may also be informal, spontaneous and narrative (Corvellec 2011; Finucane & Satterfield 2005; Mairal Buil 2003, 2008). As discussed in Chapter 4, the content of such communication can vary from 'experience-near', or knowledge of everyday matters in familiar situations, to 'experience-far', or abstract and formal knowledge, disseminated in technical and scientific terms (Geertz 1983; Wynne 1992). The social context may be consensual and cooperative, but, as seen in Chapter 6, this is not always the case. Risk communication in environmental and land-use planning and facility siting is often conflictive (Endres 2009; Stoffle & Arnold 2003; Stratman et al. 1995). Finally, risk communication can employ a range of media, including both verbal (spoken or written) and nonverbal (e.g., signs, symbols, images, gestures and sounds) communication.

The study of risk communication is a subfield of 'risk research' and mainly stems from American and European multidisciplinary research. In the late 1960s and early 1970s the field was new, and the research focus then fell upon public misperceptions and inadequate comprehension of risk information. In those early days, experts presented statistics without much thought about whether or how the numbers were understood by their audience. At the time, the rationale for risk communication research arose from the disconnect between public risk perception and expert risk assessment: the mission was pedagogical, to educate the public so that they apprehended the real risk as experts knew it (Fischhoff 1995; Leiss 1996; National Research Council 1989).

Today much has changed. Now communication on risk is noted to involve a melee of actors engaging variously as experts and laypeople, decision makers and stakeholders, regulators and politicians, citizens and nongovernment organizations (NGOs). What has come to the fore in the literature is the social dimension of conflict and cooperation in decision making on risk, together with the political and administrative processes and procedures for inclusion and exclusion in relation to policy making (Heath & Nathan 1990–1991; National Research Council 2001; Palenchar & Heath 2007; Renn 2008). Risk researchers argue that 'risk communication' processes must ensure that public values and priorities are included in risk assessment and management (Fischhoff 1987; Hance, Chess & Sandman 1988; Renn 2004; Zimmerman 1987), especially since risk issues are recognised to involve substantial scientific uncertainty (Funtowicz & Ravetz 1993). Scientific risk assessment and characterisation go hand in hand with uncertainty about outcomes and probabilities, contradictory or insufficient scientific knowledge and diverging perspectives and priorities of those concerned (van Asselt 2005). Instead of clear-cut, scientific statements about objectively identified and calculated risk, researchers and practitioners are confronted with issues muddled by uncertainty and an increasingly problematic role of science and expertise in policy making and regulation concerning risk issues (van Asselt & Vos 2008). No wonder then that the emphasis has shifted from education aimed at changing public attitudes and behaviours in favour of technocratic expertise to public participation and involvement in environmental decision making (Heath & Nathan 1990–1991), conflict resolution and fostering cooperation between the lay public on the one hand and policy makers, regulators and scientific experts on the other (Petts & Brooks 2006).

Influenced by Jürgen Habermas's (1985) theory of communicative rationality, a current trend recommends that communication about risk involve a dialogue rather than a one-way dissemination of scientific information on 'objective' risk to lay people. Addressing public values and priorities, accommodating divergent social interests and concerns, aiming for trust and transparency and, not least, acknowledging the inherent uncertainties in risk assessments are the major goals of contemporary risk communication. Proper dialogue allows a diversity of understandings, values and preferences to be voiced and heard (Petts 2001; Petts & Brooks 2006; Renn 2004). In this dialogic tradition, 'risk communication' often is used as a broad label for various government practices and programs that aim to enhance the legitimacy of the decision-making process, in which 'effective' risk communication is seen as a precondition for successful risk management (Arvai & Rivers 2014; Renn 2004, 2008). The Habermasian discourse on ethics proposes that differences can be resolved if all parties are included, have equal opportunity to participate and are willing to be empathetic to others by disregarding power differences and explaining their goals and intentions (Flyvbjerg 1998).

As laudable as these objectives are, empirical support for the theoretical assumptions is weak and there is meagre evidence of successful outcomes of participatory efforts to solve conflicts about risk (Chess & Purcell 1999; Innes & Booher 2004). Risk communication guidelines, such as the famous US Enivronmental Protection Agency 'seven cardinal rules of risk communication' that were built upon a combination of ideal norms and the view of communication as being the transmission of information, have proven to be problematic in achieving public participation in controversies related to risk (Endres 2009; Stratman et al. 1995).

As described above, the field of risk communication can be characterised as a hybrid of applied practice and science. As a practice, it is usually defined as the intentional transfer of information about the assessment, evaluation and management of risk, and often it is integral to regulation and policy work. Several normative objectives of risk communication are evident in the literature (ILGRA 1998; National Research Council 1989; Renn 2008: 206–208): communication must be informative, providing factual information based on scientific evidence; it must promote trust on the part of citizens and stakeholders towards managing agencies and bodies; it must be persuasive, shaping attitudes and behaviours; and it must be consensual, enhancing agreement and cooperation in decision making regarding risk (Renn 2008: 207). It is assumed that if it is to be effective, risk communication must be firmly based on scientific knowledge of both the factual dimension of risk *and* the modes of perception and cognition that influence the reception of risk information (see Renn 2008).

The amalgamation of practical goals and scientific approaches is typical planning, management or normative economics, all of which strive to improve social conditions. In such socio-technologies, the scientific, exploratory and descriptive objectives merge with normative goals of social engineering (Bunge 1998: 297). The discussions that now follow will make a distinction between 'risk communication' (RC) as a socio-technology and 'communication on risk' (CR) as social communication in which risk constitutes a theme or topic. This distinction is needed to examine CR as a social phenomenon in its own right and apart from the host of assumptions, normative recommendations and socio-technical aims inherent in RC as a design science (Plough & Krimsky 1987).

Current models and theoretical approaches in RC (Wardman 2008) share an idealised model in which communication is the transfer of information in coded messages from sender to receiver. The problem with this transmission model is that it treats context as simply one variable among others rather than as being constitutive of communication. The present discussion holds the position that context is fundamental to CR, just as it is to social communication in general. Accordingly, the following section presents a theoretical–methodological approach to the analysis of context, and the main points of argument will be illustrated by lessons from a case study of contested facility siting and land-use planning.

The transmission model of communication

The transmission (or code) model of communication (Shannon and Weaver 1949) presently is the dominant theory in the field of RC, and often it is assumed to be *the* universal model of communication in general (Leiss 1991; Fjeld, Eisenberg & Compton 2007; Renn 2008: 208–209).

> Risk communication is a form of communication that, like other forms, is represented by the traditional model of communication (Shannon 1948). That is, there is a source of communication that generates a message that goes through a channel to a receiver. For example, a regulatory agency (the source) may decide that a chemical poses an unacceptable risk to the public (the message) and issue a press release (the channel) published as a story by the news (another channel) that is read by members of the local community (the receivers) (Lundgren & McMakin 2004: 14).

The transmission model identifies two stages of communication: that of sending and that of receiving a signal. The sender translates a message into a signal using a code (language); the receiver interprets the message by decoding the signal according to the same code. This folk model of communication, also designated the 'conduit metaphor' (Lakoff & Johnsson 1980: 11–13; Reddy 1979), asserts that words and sentences have meanings in themselves, independent of context or speaker. According to this theory, a sender's thoughts are transformed into words that 'travel' by means of speech or writing to a receiver, who can 'understand' the thought 'behind' the linguistic expression (Sperber & Wilson 2003: 1–9).

Failures of communication have two causes, according to the transmission model, deriving either from coding errors (i.e., the sender and receiver do not use the same code or have inaccurate knowledge of it) or from 'noise' that destroys or distorts the signal during transmission (Shannon 1948; Shannon & Weaver 1949; for RC literature on this point, see Covello & Sandman 2001; Lundgren & McMakin 2004; National Research Council 1989). In terms relevant to this book, if the sender is a technical expert and uses formal and mathematical language to convey statistical information to a receiver who is a layperson, the message might not get through properly, since sender and receiver do not share the code of technical language (Zimmerman 1987). Examples of signal-distorting 'noise' include the receiver not trusting the sender and therefore being unwilling to listen and the receiver being upset emotionally and therefore unable to pay attention to the signal. In the RC field, it is assumed that such communication errors can be remedied by 'effective' risk communication by means of a skillfully designed pedagogical presentation of facts (Arvai & Rivers 2014; Chess *et al.* 1995; Fischhoff 1987; Hance, Chess & Sandman 1988; Lundgren & McMakin 2004).

Another approach to RC is known as the 'mental models' approach (Morgan *et al.* 2002). It has played an influential role in RC research and recommendations. Although the Shannon–Weaver paradigm of communication is not explicitly cited, a generic transmission model provides a basis for the mental models approach (Morgan *et al.* 2002: 3–6). The approach views the role of the RC practitioner as directing laypeople's (incorrect) mental models towards convergence with the scientific (correct) mental model by taking into account the communication needs of laypeople. Hence, the mental models approach has an explicit socio-technical goal, namely to create 'an adequate mental model of the risky process, allowing people to know what factors are relevant and how they fit together' (Morgan *et al.* 2002: 7).

The social amplification of risk framework (Kasperson *et al.* 1988; Renn 1991; Pidgeon, Kasperson & Slovic 2003) is a development and modification of the Shannon-Weaver transmission model. It focuses on the distortion of 'risk signals' in society due to various socially induced attenuations or amplifications; transmitters of information such as the mass media, institutions or organisations can amplify or attenuate risk by exaggerating or ignoring/underplaying information. The transmission of a 'risk signal' is understood to 'ripple' through society, giving rise to secondary effects on financial markets and triggering public opinion or consumer preferences (Kasperson *et al.* 1988). Criticism has been directed at this theoretical framework for not taking into account either the journalistic logic of the media that informs the production of news stories (Kitzinger 1999) or the complex social context of CR (Murdock, Petts & Horlick-Jones 2003).

The transmission model indeed has some, albeit limited, explanatory power in that it describes the basic, necessary conditions for communication: (a) there must be some kind of common 'language' by means of which meanings can be articulated and shared, and (b) the verbal or nonverbal expressions employed to communicate meaning must be perceivable by all participants. A severe criticism of the model is that it omits the social conditions and contexts of communication and ignores intrinsic uncertainties and power asymmetries (Beder & Shortland 1992; Heath & Nathan 1990–1991; Jardine & Hrudey 1997; Johnson 1987; Murdock, Petts & Horlick-Jones 2003; Plough & Krimsky 1987). It has been pointed out that political, economic, ideological, cultural and historical circumstances influence how risk messages are interpreted and understood (Chess, Burger & McDermott 2005; Johnson 1987; Mairal Buil 2003; Stoffle & Arnold 2003; Stoffle & Minnis 2008). One important contextual dimension for CR is 'social trust', referring to how an audience evaluates the communicator in terms of credibility, responsibility and competence (Löfstedt 2005; Renn & Levine 1991; Slovic 1993).

Understandings of risk, like other experiential phenomena, are informed by socially and culturally structured and historically conditioned conceptions and evaluations of the world – what it is like and what it should or should not be like. Perceptions of events and phenomena are conditioned by values that vary according to local bodies of assumptions, rules, conventions and practices (Rappaport 1996). The argument throughout this book is that risk is embedded in social institutions, local practices and experiences and is understood and judged in terms of emic, localized, collectively defined values and concerns. What the risks are 'in themselves', and how they are defined by the scientific community as the product of a calculus of probability and adverse effects, is not merely translated into 'situated risk' to be understood and contextualized in social settings (see Chapter 4).

The transmission model of communication is founded on a highly problematic idea about language, namely that thoughts or intentions are packed into words and delivered to a receiver independently of context (Sperber & Wilson 2003). Pragmatic philosophy and linguistics show that speech not only conveys factual information but also reveals a speaker's intention and attitude while performing conventional and institutionally defined speech acts (Austin 1976; Searle 1969). Congruence (or resonance) between intended meaning and interpreted meaning is an achievement that is socially and culturally conditioned by norms and conventions and the respective intentions of speaker and listener (Grice 1989). Therefore, a speaker's meaning and the listener's interpretation is a crucial analytical distinction (Sperber & Wilson 2003).

Utterances convey thought, reveal a speaker's attitude and perform conventional and institutionally defined speech acts (Austin 1976; Searle 1969). A sentence can convey many different thoughts depending on the context and can therefore have different meanings. For example, 'It is very hot in this room': One meaning of this utterance is a factual statement that the temperature is uncomfortably warm. Another meaning might be indirect and suggestive, prompting the listener to consider opening a window; in this case the sentence functions as a performative utterance, a 'speech act' (Austin 1976; Searle 1969). A mismatch between the speaker's and hearer's assumptions on context may result in misunderstanding, and this is not caused by some kind of 'noise' in the channelling of a signal (Sperber & Wilson 2003: 16–17). The study of meanings and utterances in context belongs to the multidisciplinary research field of pragmatism (comprising philosophy, linguistics, social anthropology and sociology; see McDermid 2006). In this research tradition, context is understood as premises and meanings shaped by the information, expectations, beliefs, memories and attributions held by participants (Grice 1989; Sperber & Wilson 2003: 15–16).

As outlined briefly above, the pragmatic perspective indicates that the notion of 'pure' information is fictive (Latour 2005), since information cannot be understood in any other way than in terms of the assumptions and expectations of speakers and listeners. The transmission model does not give sufficient consideration to communication as a temporally and spatially situated social activity (Allwood 2000) in which participants have social roles. In CR, these roles paradigmatically are those of experts or lay people, decision makers or stakeholders, producers or consumers and officials or citizens, and each role is associated with a concomitant mode of practical reasoning (Wallace 2003). These roles, as shown in Chapter 6 with regard to the Hallandsås rail tunnel case study, entail different institutional responsibilities and accountabilities, obligations and options, diverging intentions directed towards action and, occasionally, conflicting interests (Wynne 1992). The following section returns to the Hallandsås tunnel, to focus on how diverging ontological assumptions about risk shaped the communicative process in combination with asymmetrical power relationships and the diverse practical rationalities of the actors.

Lessons from a case study: speaking of tunnel risk

As shown in Chapter 6, the geological conditions of the Hallandsås were far from ideal for tunnel building and the problems encountered were many. The project gave rise to a multitude of risk issues of concern to local citizens, experts and regulators (Boholm 2005; Boholm & Löfstedt 1999; Ferreira, Boholm & Löfstedt 2001; Grimes 2008; Heiefort 2004; Löfstedt & Boholm 1999; Sjölander-Lindqvist 2004). Considering how many different actors were involved, many with different interests, goals and priorities, it is unsurprising that the identification and characterisation of events, objects and values in terms of risk often were intensely debated (cf. Boholm & Löfstedt 2004; Corvellec 2001; Healey & Shaw 1994). This section summarises results from research into this megaproject that relate to the contextual dimension of the communication of risk (Flyvbjerg, Bruzelius & Rothengatter 2003).

Beginning in 1998, the National Rail Administration, the government agency in charge of the project, arranged a number of consultation meetings to provide information and give local residents and stakeholders (owners of real estate such as land, buildings, dams and wells, who according to Swedish law have a right to be consulted and compensated for property damage) opportunities to ask questions, voice concerns and express viewpoints on the tunnel project. Details are provided in Chapter 6.

During the study period (2000 to mid-2004), the consultation meetings were persistently conflictive rather than constructive. The main adversaries were the Rail Administration officials and their technical and scientific experts and advisors on the one hand and the local stakeholders, including many farmers, who sometimes brought in evidence from 'counter-experts', on the other. Similarly to Endres's (2009) suggestion in her study of the role of science argumentation in public participation in the Yucca Mountain nuclear waste facility storage controversy, local stakeholders on the Hallandsås ridge mobilised scientific arguments to challenge the Rail Administration and the tunnel project. Despite this, it was clear that the two sides did not share the same mental model (Johnson-Laird & Goldvarg-Steingold 2007) of the hydrogeological conditions of the ridge and how these were understood to create risks with regard to the tunnelling. Despite a massive exposure to highly pedagogical scientific information on the hydrogeology and tunnel-building technology and opportunities to participate in dialogue, the stakeholder model did not converge with the expert model as the mental models approach to RC suggests it should (Bostrom 2003: 563–564). On the contrary, over time the models became increasingly polarized, a feature sustained by several conflictual contexts of communication. These contexts included the ontology of risk, that is, how the nature of risk was understood to be constituted in the real world; an asymmetric distribution of power, where some agents had a mandate to make decisions affecting others without having to heed their wishes; and the practical rationality of the actors, derived from their motives for communicating their intentions and plans as embedded in practical life.

Variable ontology

In the Hallandsås case, both Rail Administration officials and allied scientific experts and the local stakeholders superficially agreed that the lowered groundwater table caused by tunnel drilling constituted a matter of risk. Despite this, the two sides disagreed strongly as to what actually constituted the risk objects and the values at stake. The Rail Administration identified the ridge and its confounding geological characteristics as a risk object and the tunnel as the value at stake, framed as a complex, expensive and vulnerable technical artefact. In contrast, the local stakeholders tended to see the risk relationship as running in the opposite direction: by unleashing the groundwater leakage, the tunnel was understood as the risk object that threatened the ridge – framed as a complex natural object, a unique and endangered ecosystem – with drought. In their reasoning, the *ridge* constituted the value at stake. Ongoing CR at the meetings therefore evolved as a long set of exchanges between conflicting social constructions of the risk objects and the values at stake.

An associated point of disagreement concerned the nature of the groundwater and its origin and value (Sjölander-Lindqvist 2005). The Rail Administration officials argued that the groundwater was external to the ridge on the basis of scientific evidence provided by hydrogeology experts: water entered into the ridge as rain that penetrated the porous soil and gathered in underground cavities. From this perspective, it was entirely reasonable to suggest that should water continue to leak into the tunnels, groundwater losses could be compensated for by irrigating the land surface.

The local stakeholders, in contrast, argued that the ridge was a repository of age-old artesian water – sometimes even referred to as a subterranean lake – which had little correspondence to recent rainfall. This underground reservoir of water was understood to be pristine and unique; it moistened the soil and the vegetation from below and was regarded as a source of the natural fertility that made local farming so prosperous. Instances of practical, local knowledge and experience of farming and farm work were presented to validate this idea and to contest the opposing, scientific view on the origins of the groundwater. From the local stakeholder perspective it was entirely reasonable that the groundwater should be protected by all means and that it was irreplaceable by surface irrigation. Little wonder that the Rail Administration's proposal to surface irrigate parts of the countryside, if affected by dehydration, invoked such massive local hostility. However well-intentioned, the plan simply failed to address what local residents construed to be under threat.

Power asymmetry

An additional source of contention at the meetings derived from the distribution
of roles among the participants. The public officials represented decision-making
and regulatory authority, and the local residents/citizens were the stakeholders who
would be affected by the decisions made by the former (see Chapter 6). The Rail
Administration officials had the responsibility for decisions on issues pertaining
to the practical management and organisation of the building of the tunnel. They
argued that they had the capacity to make rational decisions and that they had the
competence required to implement the decisions of the national government in
the best possible way; such were the credentials necessary to be granted a sustained
'license to operate' (Corvellec 2007) as tunnel builders. The local stakeholders, on
the other hand, had neither a licence to operate nor any authority over how the
tunnel project would infringe on their land and property. In the meetings, local
stakeholders openly displayed their lack of trust in the Rail Administration and the
tunnel project and voiced their experiences of long-term suffering and disrespect
at the hands of the Rail Administration and tunnel contractors. Reflecting a real
asymmetric power relationship between decision maker and stakeholder, local residents identified themselves as victims of the operations, and victimisation by the
project constituted a long-term, almost ritualised, theme of communication.

Practical rationality

A Rail Administration official went to a consultation meeting to present a proposal
for continued tunnel drilling because overall project management was a requirement of their work; a local resident chose to go to the same meeting because they
lived close to a project that threatened to impact their lives. At the outset, the
participants had very different roles in the communication that unfolded at the
meetings. The Rail Administration officials and their experts had a specific practical
goal for their CR: their communicative intention was to achieve the legitimacy
and accountability for the project that was vital in maintaining a license to operate
(Stratman et al. 1995). The local stakeholders, on the other hand, were in a very different position. Their communicative reason was influenced by the location of their
homes and livelihoods on the ground above the tunnel and by their local identity
and sense of community, in turn shaped by collective memories, attachments to
place and local values (Sjölander-Lindqvist 2004). Many of the local stakeholders
were farmers, and they depended on favourable environmental conditions such as a
high groundwater table and drinkable water for their prosperity.

For a relational approach to risk

Given these kinds of contrasting perspectives on risk, there is a need for a closer
look at the phenomenon of risk in terms of ontological status and epistemological conditions. The concept of risk promotes a certain type of knowledge that

spells out and evaluates associations between objects in terms of uncertain (though sometimes statistically calculable) harm, value and benefits. Identifying something as 'a risk' involves a symbolic process of representation that uses categories, associations, distinctions, evaluations and arguments to establish the 'risky' character of an object (Boholm & Corvellec 2014; Corvellec & Boholm 2008; Binde & Boholm 2004; Murdock, Petts & Horlick-Jones 2003). The very process of identifying and assessing any specific risk, therefore, is a communication process between social agents that establishes semantic associations between objects (van Loon 2002). This means that what is referred to as 'risk communication' by the risk research community is not something 'added on' to a scientifically determined risk for the purpose of disseminating that scientific description to a (lay) public audience.

The case of RC in connection with the Hallandsås railway tunnel directs our attention towards risk being something with a concrete embodiment and materialisation in specific objectified instances, representations that stand, so to speak, as 'virtual' risk objects (van Loon 2002: 54–55). Objectification constitutes the fundamental mode according to which a risk becomes present to lay people; humans relate to and manage specific risk issues, such as a well drying up, a cow falling ill, or a contractor failing to fulfil a building contract, not 'risk' in general.

As noted in Chapter 1, a relational approach to risk focuses on the constituting of risk objects. The term 'risk object' as presented in Chapter 1 refers to an identified source of potential harm, and the term 'object at risk' points to an identified value at stake (Boholm & Corvellec 2011). The relationship (or association) between such objects derives from a hypothesised causal mechanism, according to which the risk object has a potential to inflict harm on the object at risk should the two come into contact (Hilgartner 1992). Assumptions about the relationship between the two objects and their manner of association can vary from one actor to another, whether a scientist, local resident, government official, journalist or whoever speaks out on a specific risk issue. Consequently, as Gregersen (2003) points out, it is an observer's knowledge and understanding of objects and their properties, not the properties of objects as such, that frame them as either risk objects or objects at risk. Risk is always a danger *of* something (sometimes natural, sometimes social) *for* somebody in a given social nexus. Gregersen (2003: 356) further notes that as a relational construct, the concept of risk therefore resembles the semiotic concept of 'meaning', which according to pragmatist philosopher Charles Sanders Peirce (Atkin 2010) can be construed as an outcome of a three-part relationship: 'meaning' means something (the content of meaning) for somebody (the interpreter of meaning) in a given situation (the context of meaning).

It follows, from a relational perspective, that the concept of risk is an epistemic construct that serves to categorise real-world objects in relation to other objects depending on what we believe regarding their potentially harmful causal relationships (Boholm & Corvellec 2011). Risk functions as a semantic frame for relationships, objects and categories (Fillmore & Atkins 1992) that creates the possibility of assessing foreseen future outcomes (Hilgartner 1992; Luhmann 1993). It is not an essential feature of phenomena as such to be either risk objects or objects at risk

(Ewald 1991), and a crucial implication of this is that any single phenomenon, such as a railway tunnel, can be regarded simultaneously as a risk object, as an object at risk or as an object devoid of risk by different observers operating under different assumptions.

Lessons for the study of communication on risk

Researchers must examine several analytical questions when investigating how communication on risk unfolds in social settings, so as to decontextualise the context(s) of communication (Corvellec & Risberg 2007; Hamilton & Wills-Tower 2006). As combined in traditional RC research, the transmission model of communication and the empiricist-positivist notion of risk do not offer a methodology to study RC empirically as an activity situated in time and space and framed by asymmetrical power relationships as well as legal, social, political and institutional conventions and rules. Based on the case study, three principal dimensions crucial to the communication of risk (Boholm & Corvellec 2014) are apparent: the variable ontology of risk; intentionality and the practical rationality of communication; and power asymmetry and the dimension of conflict.

The variable ontology of risk

The transmission model of communication goes hand-in-hand with a positivist-empiricist ontology and epistemology in RC research and practice. Despite linguistic and philosophical evidence that the concept of 'risk' in everyday use is multidimensional and polysemous and has sociological, political and administrative dimensions (see Chapters 1, 5 and 6), the RC paradigm is based on a crude distinction between objective (real) risk and subjective (perceived) risk. The notion of objective risk refers to phenomena and their causal conditions in the natural–material world, risk being defined in mathematical terms as the statistical probability of a measurable outcome (such as economic loss or occurrence of death, injury or ill health). The RC model assumes that risk is an inherent feature of the external world awaiting detection by science; it is viewed as an objective (mind-independent) product of the magnitude of an adverse effect and its probability (Bradbury 1989).

This empiricist conception is easily challenged. As shown in Chapter 1, risk depends on value, so to declare a risk requires that there must be something identifiable as a value that is being threatened (Hansson 2007, Hansson 2010; Rosa 1998; Shrader-Frechette 1991). If value sits at the heart of identifying risk, it follows that different actors might identify risk differently depending on what exactly they value and why (Rosa, Renn & McCright 2014). In most situations where risk is communicated, the actors will have different roles as affected parties or as government and project officials, and consequently they will have diverse practical rationalities and, inevitably, will identify risks differently (Luhmann 1993). CR inherently engages with and activates different social constructions of risk, deriving from particular practical rationalities (Bergmans 2008; Shaw 2000). In this context, untangling the collisions and collusions of such rationalities and their ontological and epistemological correlates is the challenge facing studies of the communication of risk as a situated social interaction.

Intentionality and the practical rationality of communication

The intent of the actors is central to the communication process in that it relates to agency and the planning of action. 'Intentions' and 'planning' refer to a practical mode of reasoning (Wallace 2003); actors strive to achieve goals they have set for themselves, whether individually or as a group. Actions undertaken to fulfil such goals are nested into coordinated collective programs (Bratman 1987). Communication with others is an integral part of intentionality and the planning of action, as well as of the execution of plans; communication has practical outcomes, and this is no less true for communication about matters relating to risk. This aspect is very much neglected in traditional RC and in Habermasian dialogical attempts to achieve an ideal method of communication.

Power asymmetry and the dimension of conflict

Successful communication has to be cooperative to some extent. Yet it does not follow that a conflict indicates some kind of lack or absence of communication. Indeed, it can be argued that greater communicative possibilities, means and opportunities increase the probability of conflict rather than the opposite (Luhmann 1995: 376), which is contrary to what communicative rationality and dialogue theory assume. Whether communication unfolds as a cooperative or a conflictive interaction depends on many factors, such as the purpose and overall characteristics of the activity being discussed and the participants' roles; their understandings of the activity; and their goals, motives, interests and social trust in one another (Allwood 2000). CR tends to be unstable and uncertain, open to interpretation and reinterpretation, precisely because risk is a 'thick concept' (Möller 2012), made up of both factual and normative dimensions. As a consequence, risk debates have a high susceptibility to new scientific findings and to the mediation of messages by means of symbolic meanings, values and norms (Jasanoff 1999). Consensualist approaches to RC on policy matters characterised by uncertainty and high-stakes decisions, therefore, will fail to address the underlying dimensions of power asymmetry and contradictory cultural meanings and perceptions. This argument resonates with Mouffe's (2005) criticism of understandings of democracy as consensual dialogue, as advocated by Giddens and Beck. For Mouffe, the antagonistic dimension is essential to political life, so a consensual framing of politics promotes civic disengagement, passivity and distrust in political matters, and therefore threatens to erode democracy.

Conclusion

As outlined here, a pragmatic perspective on the communication of risk has the strength of demanding that scholars consider communication as a complex social process of the creation and interpretation of meaning, situated in real life (Allwood 2000; McDermid 2006; Searle 1969; Sperber & Wilson 2003). Research into RC, therefore, must account systematically for the role and importance of context, both in the definition and communication of risk and in how this message is received. Assessments of the context of communication must take into account the participants' identities and roles as well as the conventions and structures that condition participation and expectations (Webler & Tuler 2002, 2006). Questions about the motivations and practical reasoning of participants, about how 'relevance' in communication is established – that is, what relationships are meaningful and to whom, and how interconnections between messages are forged (Allwood 2000) – are crucial for a better understanding of risk communication. Such questions are all demanding theoretically and analytically. They ask us to reflect critically on the role and function of the communication of risk in society, to look beyond its 'effectiveness' as a tool to govern, control and steer attitudes in relation to various 'risk problems' as defined in environmental and public policy (Boholm & Corvellec 2014).

References

Allwood, J. 2000. An activity-based approach to pragmatics. In *Abduction, belief and context: Studies in computational pragmatics*. Bunt, H. & Black, W. (eds.), pp. 47–78. Amsterdam, the Netherlands & Philadelphia, PA: John Benjamins Publishing Company.

Argenti, P. 2002. Crisis communication: Lessons from 9/11. *Harvard Business Review* 80(12): 103–109.

Arvai, J. & Rivers, L. (eds.). 2014. *Effective risk communication*. London, UK: Earthscan.

Atkin, A. 2010. Peirce's theory of signs. In *Stanford Encyclopedia of Philosophy (Summer 2013 Edition)*. Zalta, E.N. (ed.). Available online at http://plato.stanford.edu /archives/sum2013/entries/peirce-semiotics/ (accessed 29 September 2014).

Austin, J.L. 1976 [1962]. *How to do things with words*. Oxford, UK: Oxford University Press.

Beder, S. & Shortland, M. 1992. Siting a hazardous waste facility: The tangled web of risk communication. *Public Understanding of Science* 1(2): 39–160.

Bennett, P. & Calman, K. (eds.). 1999. *Risk communication and public health*. Oxford, UK: Oxford University Press.

Bergmans, A. 2008. Meaningful communication among experts and affected citizens on risk: Challenge or impossibility? *Journal of Risk Research* 11(1–2): 175–193.

Binde, P. & Boholm, Å. 2004. Schismogenesis in a Swedish case of railway planning. In *Facility siting: Risk, power and identity in land-use planning*. Boholm, Å. & Löfstedt, R. (eds.), pp. 160–176. London, UK: Earthscan.

Boholm, Å. 2005. 'Greater good' in transit: The unwieldy career of a Swedish rail tunnel project. *Focaal, European Journal of Anthropology* 46: 21–35.

Boholm, Å. & Löfstedt, R. 1999. Issues of risk, trust and knowledge: The Hallandsås tunnel case. *Ambio* 28(6): 556–561.

Boholm, Å. & Löfstedt, R. (eds.). 2004. *Facility siting: Risk, power and identity in land use planning.* London, UK: Earthscan.

Boholm, Å. & Corvellec H. 2011. A relational theory of risk. *Journal of Risk Research* 14(2): 175–190.

Boholm, Å. & Corvellec, H. 2014. A relational theory of risk: Lessons for risk communication. In *Effective risk communication.* Arvai, J. & Rivers, L. (eds.), pp. 6–22. London, UK: Earthscan.

Bostrom, A. 2003. Future risk communication. *Futures* 35: 553–573.

Bradbury, J. 1989. The policy implications of differing concepts of risk. *Science, Technology and Human Values* 14(4): 380–399.

Bratman, M. 1987. *Intention, plans, and practical reason.* Cambridge, MA: Harvard University Press.

Bunge, M. 1998. *Social science under debate: A philosophical perspective.* Toronto, ON: University of Toronto Press.

Calman, K.C., Bennett, P.G. & Coles, D.G. 1999. Risks to health: some key issues in management, regulation and communication. *Health, Risk and Society* 1(1): 107–116.

Chess, C. & Purcell, K. 1999. Public participation and the environment: Do we know what works? *Environmental Science and Technology* 33(16): 2685–2692.

Chess, C., Salomone, K.L., Hance, B.J. & Saville, A. 1995. Results of national symposium on risk communication: Next steps for government agencies. *Risk Analysis* 15(2): 115–125.

Chess, C., Burger, J. & McDermott, M.H. 2005. Speaking like a state: Environmental justice and fish consumption advisories. *Society and Natural Resources* 18: 267–278.

Corvellec, H. 2001. Talks on tracks – debating urban infrastructure projects. *Studies in Cultures, Organisations and Societies* 7: 25–53.

Corvellec, H. 2007. Arguing for a license to operate: The case of the Swedish wind power industry. *Corporate Communications: An International Journal* 12(2): 129–144.

Corvellec, H. 2011. The narrative structure of risk accounts. *Risk Management* 13: 101–121.

Corvellec, H. & Risberg A. 2007. Sensegiving as mise-en-sens: The case of wind power development. *Scandinavian Journal of Management* 23(3): 306–326.

Corvellec, H. & Boholm, Å. 2008. The risk/no-risk rhetoric of environmental impact assessments (EIA): The case of off-shore wind farms in Sweden. *Local Environment* 13 (7): 627–640.

Covello, V.T. & Sandman, P.M. 2001. Risk communication: Evolution and revolution. In *Solutions to an Environment in Peril.* Wolbarst, A. (ed.), pp. 164–178. Baltimore, MD: Johns Hopkins University Press.

Endres, D. 2009. Science and public participation: An analysis of public scientific argument in the Yucca Mountain controversy. *Environmental Communication* 3(1): 49–75.

Ewald, F. 1991. Insurance and risk. In *The Foucault effect: Studies in governmentality.* Burchell B., Gordon C. & Miller P. (eds.), pp. 197–210. Chicago, IL: University of Chicago Press.

Ferreira, C., Boholm, Å. & Löfstedt, R. 2001. From vision to catastrophe: A risk event in search of images. In *Risk, media and stigma*. Flynn J., Slovic, P. & Kunreuther, H. (eds.), pp. 283–299. London, UK: Earthscan.

Fillmore, C. & Atkins, B. T. 1992. Toward a frame-based lexicon: the semantics of RISK and its neighbors In *Frames, fields, and cognition: new essays in semantics and lexical organization*. Lehrer, A. & Feder Kittay, E. (eds.), pp. 75–102. Hillsdale, NJ, Hove & London, UK: Lawrence Erlbaum Associates, Inc.

Finucane, M. L. & Satterfield, T.A. 2005. Risk as narrative: A theoretical framework for facilitating the biotechnology debate. *International Journal of Biotechnology* 7 (1-3): 128–146.

Fischhoff, B. 1987. Treating the public with risk communication: A public health perspective. *Science, Technology & Human Values*, 12(3): 13–19.

Fischhoff, B. 1995. Risk perception and communication unplugged: Twenty years of process. *Risk Analysis* 15(2): 137–145.

Fjeld, R.A., Eisenberg, N.A. & Compton, K.L. 2007. *Quantitative environmental risk analysis for human health*. Hoboken, NJ: John Wiley & Sons.

Flyvbjerg, B. 1998. *Rationality and power: Democracy in practice*. Chicago, IL & London, UK: University of Chicago Press.

Flyvbjerg, B., Bruzelius, N. & Rothengatter, W. 2003. *Megaprojects and risk: an anatomy of ambition*. Cambridge, UK: Cambridge University Press.

Funtowicz, S. & Ravetz, J. 1993. Science for the post-normal age. *Futures* 25(7): 735–755.

Geertz, C. 1983. *Local knowledge*. New York, NY: Basic Books.

Gregersen, N.H. 2003. Risk and religion: Toward a theology of risk taking. *Zygon* 38(2): 355–376.

Grice, P. 1989. *Studies in the way of words*. Cambridge, MA: Harvard University Press.

Grimes, M. 2008. The civic benefits of imperfect deliberation. *Journal of Public Deliberation* 4(1): 1–29.

Habermas, J. 1985. *The theory of communicative action*. Uckfield, UK: Beacon Press.

Hamilton, D.D. & Wills-Toker, C. 2006. Reconceptualizing dialogue in environmental public participation. *The Policy Studies Journal* 34(4): 755–775.

Hance, B.J., Chess, C. & Sandman, P.M. 1988. *Improving dialogue with communities: A risk communication manual for government*. New Brunswick, NJ: Environmental Communication Research Program, Rutgers University.

Hansson, S.O. 2007. Risk. In *Stanford Encyclopedia of Philosophy (Winter 2003 Edition)*. Zalta, E.N. (ed.). Available online at http://plato.stanford.edu/entries /risk (accessed 1 November 2008).

Hansson, S.O. 2010. Risk: Objective or subjective, facts or values. *Journal of Risk Research* 13(2): 231–238.

Healey, P. & Shaw, T. 1994. Changing meaning of 'environment' in the British planning system. *Transactions of the Institute of British Geographers* 19(4): 425–438.

Heath, R.L. & Nathan, K. 1990–1991. Public relations' role in risk communication: Information, rhetoric and power. *Public Relations Quarterly* 35(4): 15–22.

Heiefort, R. 2004. When complexity becomes a problem: 'Law' and 'fairness' on separate tracks in Sweden. In *Facility siting: Risk, power and identity in land use planning*. Boholm, Å. & Löfstedt, R. (eds.), pp. 177–188. London, UK: Earthscan.

Hilgartner, S. 1992. The social construction of risk objects: Or, how to pry open networks of risk. In *Organizations, uncertainties and risk*. Short, J.F. & Clarke, L. (eds.), pp. 39–53. Boulder, CO: Westview Press.

Innes, J.E. & Booher, D. 2004. Reframing public participation: Strategies for the 21st century. *Planning Theory and Practice* 5(4): 419–436.

Inter-Departmental Liaison Group on Risk Assessment (ILGRA). 1998. *Risk communication: A guide to regulatory practice*. London: Health and Safety Executive, Risk Assessment Policy Unit. Available online at www.hse.gov.uk/aboutus/meetings/committees/ilgra/risk.pdf (accessed 1 October 2014).

Jardine, C. & Hrudey, S.E. 1997. Mixed messages in risk communication. *Risk Analysis* 17(4): 489–498.

Jasanoff, S. 1999. The songlines of risk. *Environmental Values* 8: 135–152.

Johnson, B.B. 1987. Accounting for the social context of risk communication. *Science and Technology Studies* 5(3): 103–111.

Johnson-Laird, P.N. & Goldvarg-Steingold, E. 2007. Models of cause and effect. In *The mental models theory of reasoning: Refinements and extensions*. Schaenken, W., Vandeirendonck, A., Schroyens, W. & d'Ydewalle, G. (eds.), pp. 167–189. London, UK: Lawrence Erlbaum Associates, Inc.

Kasperson, R.E. & Stallen, P.M. (eds.). 1991. *Communicating risks to the public: International perspectives*. Dordrecht, the Netherlands: Kluwer.

Kasperson, R.E., Renn, O., Slovic P., Brown, H.S., Emel, J., Goble, R., Kasperson, J.X. & Ratick S. 1988. The social amplification of risk: A conceptual framework. *Risk Analysis* 8: 177–188.

Kitzinger, J. 1999. Researching risk and the media. *Health, Risk & Society* 1(1): 55–69.

Lakoff, G. & Johnson, M. 1980. *Metaphors we live by*. Chicago, IL & London, UK: University of Chicago Press.

Latour, B. 2005. From realpolitik to dingpolitik – or how to make things public. In *Making things public: Atmospheres of democracy*. Latour, B. & Weibel, P. (eds.), pp. 14–41. Cambridge, MA: MIT Press.

Leiss, W. 1991. On the vitality of our discipline – new applications of communications theory: The 1990 Southam Lecture. *Canadian Journal of Communication* 16(2): 291–305.

Leiss, W. 1996. Three phases in the evolution of risk communication practice. *Annals of the American Academy of Political and Social Science* 545: 85–94.

Löfstedt, R. 2005. *Risk management in post-trust societies*. New York, NY: Palgrave Macmillan.

Löfstedt, R. & Boholm, Å. 1999. Off track in Sweden. *Environment* 41(4): 16–20, 40–44.

Löfstedt, R.E. & 6, P. 2008. What environmental and technological risk communication research and health risk research can learn from each other. *Journal of Risk Research* 11(1–2): 141–167.

Luhmann, N. 1993. *Risk: A sociological theory.* New York, NY: Aldine de Gruyter.

Lundgren, R. & McMakin, A. 2004. *Risk communication: A handbook for communicating environmental, safety, and health risks.* Columbus, OH: Battelle Press.

McDermid, D. 2006. Pragmatism. In *The Internet Encyclopaedia of Philosophy.* Fieser, J. & Dowden, B. (eds.). Available online at www.iep.utm.edu/pragmati .htm (accessed 5 May 2007).

Mairal Buil, G. 2003. A risk shadow in Spain. *Ethnos* 68(3): 179–191.

Mairal Buil, G. 2008. Narratives or risk. *Journal of Risk Research* 11(1–2): 41–54.

Möller, N. 2012. The concepts of risk and safety. In *Handbook of risk theory.* Roeser, S., Hillerbrand, R., Sandin, P. & Peterson, M. (eds.), pp. 56–85. Berlin & Heidelberg, Germany: Springer.

Morgan, M.G., Fischhoff, B., Bostrom, A. & Altman, C.J. 2002. Risk communication: A mental models approach. Cambridge, UK: Cambridge University Press.

Mouffe, C. 2005. *On the political.* London, UK & New York, NY: Routledge.

Murdock, G., Petts, J. & Horlick-Jones, T. 2003. After amplification: rethinking the role of the media in risk communication. In *The social amplification of risk.* Pidgeon N., Kasperson, R.E. & Slovic, P. (eds.), pp. 156–178. Cambridge, UK & New York, NY: Cambridge University Press.

National Research Council. 1989. *Improving risk communication.* Washington, DC: The National Academies Press.

National Research Council. 2001. *Understanding risk: Informing decisions in a democratic society.* Washington, DC: The National Academies Press.

Palenchar, M.J. & Heath, R.L. 2007. Strategic risk communication: Adding value to society. *Public Relations Review* 33: 120–129.

Peters, R.G., Covello, V.T. & McCallum, D.B. 1997. The determinants of trust and the credibility in environmental risk communication: An empirical study. *Risk Analysis,* 17(1): 43–54.

Petts, J. 2001. Evaluating the effectiveness of deliberative processes: Waste management case-studies. *Journal of Environmental Planning and Management* 44(2): 207–226.

Petts, J. & Brooks, C. 2006. Expert conceptualisations of the role of lay knowledge in environmental decision making: Challenges for deliberative democracy. *Environment and Planning A: Environment and Planning* 38: 1045–1059.

Pidgeon, N., Kasperson, R.E. & Slovic, P. (eds.). 2003. *The social amplification of risk.* Cambridge, UK: Cambridge University Press.

Plough, A. & Krimsky, S. 1987. The emergence of risk communication studies. *Science, Technology & Human Values* 12(3): 4–10.

Power, M. 2007. *Organized uncertainty: Designing a world of risk management.* Oxford, UK: Oxford University Press.

Rappaport, R.A. 1996. Risk and the human environment. *Annals of the American Academy of Political and Social Science* 545(May): 64–74.

Reddy, M. 1979. The conduit metaphor – a case of frame conflict in our language about language. In *Metaphor and thought*. Ortony, A. (ed.), pp. 284–324. Cambridge, UK: Cambridge University Press.

Renn, O. 1991. Risk communication and the social amplification of risk. In *Communicating risks to the public: International perspectives*. Kasperson, R.E. & Stallen, P.M. (eds.), pp. 287–324. Dordrecht, the Netherlands: Kluwer.

Renn, O. 2004. Participatory processes for designing environmental policies. *Land Use Policy* 23: 34–43.

Renn, O. 2008. *Risk governance. Coping with uncertainty in a complex world*. London, UK: Earthscan.

Renn, O. & Levine, D. 1991. Credibility and trust in risk communication. In *Communicating risks to the public: International perspectives*. Kasperson, R.E. & Stallen, P.M. (eds.), pp. 175–217. Dordrecht, the Netherlands: Kluwer.

Rosa, E.A. 1998. Metatheoretical foundations for post-normal risk. *Journal of Risk Research* 1(1): 14–44.

Rosa, E., Renn, O. & McCright, A.M. 2014. *The risk society revisited: Social theory and governance*. Philadelphia, PA: Temple University Press.

Searle, J. 1969. *Speech acts: An essay in the philosophy of language*. Cambridge, UK: Cambridge University Press.

Shannon, C.E. 1948. A mathematical theory of communication. *Bell System Technical Journal* 27: 379–423, 623–656.

Shannon, C.E. & Weaver, W. 1949. *The mathematical theory of communication*. Urbana, IL: University of Illinois Press.

Shaw, A. 2000. Conflicting models of risk: Clinical genetics and British Pakistanis. In *Risk revisited*. Caplan, P. (ed.), pp. 85–107. London, UK: Pluto Press.

Shrader-Frechette, K.S. 1991. *Risk and rationality: Philosophical foundations for populist reforms*. Berkeley, CA: University of California Press.

Sjölander-Lindqvist, A. 2004. Local environment at stake: The Hallandsås railway tunnel in a social and cultural context. Lund Dissertations in Human Ecology, 2. Lund, Sweden: Lund University.

Sjölander-Lindqvist, A. 2005. Conflicting perspectives on water in a Swedish railway tunnel project. *Environmental Values* 14: 221–239.

Slovic, P. 1993. Perceived risk, trust and democracy. *Risk Analysis* 13(6): 675–682.

Sperber, D. & Wilson D. 2003 [1986]. *Relevance: Communication and cognition*. Malden, MA, Oxford, UK, Melbourne, Australia & Berlin, Germany: Blackwell Publishing.

Stoffle, R.W. & Arnold, R. 2003. Confronting the angry rock: American Indians' situated risk from radioactivity. *Ethnos* 68(3): 230–248.

Stoffle, R.W. & Minnis, J. 2008. Resilience at risk: Epistemological and social construction barriers to risk communication. *Journal of Risk Research* 11(1–2): 55–68.

Stratman, J.F., Boykin, C., Holmes, M.C., Laufer, M.J. & Breen, M. 1995. Risk communication, metacommunication, and rhetorical stases in the Aspen-EPA Superfund controversy. *Journal of Business and Technical Communication* 9(5): 5–40.

van Asselt, M. 2005. The complex significance of uncertainty in a risk era: logics, manners and strategies in use. *International Journal of Risk Assessment and Management* 5(2/3/4): 125–158.

van Asselt, M. & Vos, E. 2008. Wrestling with uncertain risks: EU regulation of GMOs and the uncertainty paradox. *Journal of Risk Research* 11(1–2): 281–300.

van Loon, J. 2002. *Risk and technological culture*. London, UK: Routledge.

Wallace, R.J. 2003. Practical reason. In *Stanford Encyclopedia of Philosophy (Winter 2003 Edition)*, Zalta, N. (ed.). Available online at http.//plato.stanford.edu /archives/win2003/entries/practical-reason (accessed 8 May 2008).

Wardman, J. 2008. The constitution of risk communication in advanced liberal societies. *Risk Analysis* 28(6): 1619–1637.

Webler, T. & Tuler, S. 2002. Unlocking the puzzle of public participation. *Bulletin of Science, Technology & Society* 22(3): 179–189.

Webler, T. & Tuler, S. 2006. Four perspectives on public participation process in environmental assessment and decision making: Combined results from 10 case studies. *The Policy Studies Journal* 34(4): 699–722.

Wynne, B. 1992. Misunderstood misunderstanding: Social identities and public uptake of science. *Public Understanding of Science* 1: 281–304.

Zimmerman, R. 1987. A process framework for risk communication. *Science, Technology and Human Values* 12(3): 131–137.

INDEX

Made in the USA
Monee, IL
31 August 2021